COMMANDOS
IN EXILE

Also by Nick van der Bijl:

Argentine Forces in the Falklands (Osprey)
Royal Marines 1939–1993 (Osprey)
Nine Battles to Stanley (Leo Cooper)
Brean Down Fort and the Defence of the Bristol Channel (HawkEditions)
5th Infantry Brigade in the Falklands (Leo Cooper)
No. 10 (Inter-Allied) Commando 1942–1945 (Osprey)
Victory in the Falklands (Pen & Sword Military)
Confrontation (Pen & Sword Military)

COMMANDOS IN EXILE

No. 10 (Inter-Allied) Commando
1942–1945

Nick van der Bijl BEM

Pen & Sword
MILITARY

First published in Great Britain in 2008 by
PEN & SWORD MILITARY
An imprint of
Pen & Sword Books Ltd
47 Church Street
Barnsley
South Yorkshire
S70 2AS

ISBN 978-1-84415-790-7

A CIP catalogue record for this book is
available from the British Library

Typeset by Concept, Huddersfield, West Yorkshire
Printed and bound in England by Biddles Ltd

Pen & Sword Books Ltd incorporates the Imprints of Pen & Sword Aviation, Pen & Sword Maritime, Pen & Sword Military, Wharncliffe Local History, Pen & Sword Select, Pen & Sword Military Classics, Leo Cooper, Remember When, Seaforth Publishing and Frontline Publishing

For a complete list of
PEN & SWORD BOOKS LIMITED
47 Church Street, Barnsley, South Yorkshire, S70 2AS, England
E-mail: enquiries@pen-and-sword.co.uk
Website: www.pen-and-sword.co.uk

Contents

List of Maps

Acknowledgements

No. 10 (Inter-Allied) Commando was a unique unit of exiles brought to-gether to form a Commando at a time when the Army was looking every-where to replace its casualties and those locked up in prison camps. The national contingents each had their own characteristics and yet when they were committed to battle, they each had a single cause – liberate their countries, although the Poles wanted to defeat Nazism so they could get at the Russians. The Commando was part of the British Army in every way and was represented at Dieppe, in Italy and the Far East, on D-Day, at Arnhem, Walcheren and the advance through Germany, quite apart from raiding Norway and France. Most were parachute-trained. No other Com-mando was so widely deployed and yet it functioned as a unit just twice. Its existence spawned Allied commandos in Belgium, France and the Netherlands post-1945.

It is a pleasure to thank those who have helped with this project. The first must be Ian Dear, who wrote the first book on these exiles – *10 Commando*. He allowed me unrestricted access to his mass of information held in the Imperial War Museum, which then allowed me to add flesh to the story. Mrs Wiet Harpur-Rymakers translated accounts from the Dutch. Mr Wybo Boersma helped me with the Dutch in the Far East and at Arnhem. Colin Anson, Brian Grant and the later Peter Masters gave me steerage with 3 Troop, as did the Jewish Museum, and Pierre-Louis Marichal told me of the relationship between the Belgian Troop and the Belgian SAS. Ivar Kraglund helped with the Norwegians, in particular the provision of photos, as did the Sikorsky Institute in London with the Poles. As always, the Internet provided a massive source of information.

I must also complement the staff of Burnham-on-Sea's Library, who managed to obtain some obscure books that I suspect had not seen the light of day for decades.

I am most grateful to Brigadier Henry Wilson, the Commissioning Editor, for giving me the opportunity to complete another ambition that first emerged when I was serving with the Intelligence Corps in West Germany. I am indebted to Bobby Gainher for editing this project. John Noble, once again, was meticulous in indexing. I must also thank Noel Sadler for typesetting this book in a meticulous manner.

My wife, Penny, has once again been a mountain of patience in not only supporting me but also proofreading and asking all the right questions.

Nick van der Bijl
Somerset

Glossary

Abwehr – *Amt Ausland/Abwehr im Oberkommando der Wehrmacht* (Overseas Department/Office in Defence of the Armed Forces High Command). Military Intelligence organization concentrating on human intelligence.

BBO – Bureau Bijzondere Opdrachten (Bureau of Special Operations).

Bren Gun – Standard infantry .303-inch light machine gun with a distinctive curved thirty-round magazine. Development of the Czech ZB33 and could fire out to 2,000 yards.

CIGS – Chief of the Imperial General Staff.

CO – Commanding Officer.

DD – Duplex Drive. Fitted with equipment that enabled tanks to be amphibious.

DSO – Distinguished Service Order.

DUKW – **D** (designed in 1942) **U** (utility) **K** (all-wheel drive) **W** (two powered rear axles). Six-wheel-drive amphibious truck.

FNFL – *Forces Navales Francaises Libre* (Free French Naval Forces).

GHQ – General Headquarters.

Goatley – Lightweight collapsible assault boat with a wooden bottom and canvas sides carrying seven men, with six paddling. Could be assembled by two men in about ninety seconds, most suited to river crossings.

GS(R) – General Staff (Research). War Office department studying irregular warfare.

LCA – 13-ton Landing Craft Assault that could land thirty-five troops over a ramp and lift an additional 800lb of equipment up to 80 miles at 7 knots. Usually crewed by four Royal Navy or Royal Marines, its wooden sides were protected by armour.

LCI(S) – Landing Craft Infantry (Small). A 110-ton wooden landing craft based on a MGB and fitted with silenced petrol engines, they were designed for long-distance voyages and could carry 102 fully equipped troops and their equipment, such as PIAT anti-tank weapons and eighteen bicycles, and had a naval crew of seventeen. In addition to Embarked Force weapons, it was armed with two 20mm cannon and two Lewis guns.

LCP(L) – 9-ton Landing Craft Personnel (Large). Could carry twenty-five troops about 120 miles at 8 knots. Crewed by three and armed with up to medium machine-guns; disembarkation was the troops jumping from the bow.

LSI – Landing Ships Infantry.

MC – Gallantry award issued to officers.

MFC – Marine Fusilier Commando Battalion.

MGB – 95-ton Motor Gun Boat with a maximum speed of 28 knots. Equipped with two power-mounted, turreted 6-pdrs fore and aft, an aft twin 20mm Oerlikon, a single 20mm forward of the bridge and two twin .303-inch Vickers on the bridge wings.

MI5 – Military Intelligence 5 – Security Services.

MI(R) – Military Intelligence (Research). War Office department studying use of small raiding forces.

MM – Military Medal. Gallantry award for non-commissioned ranks.

'Mouseholing' – Using explosives on a portable frame to blow holes in walls of buildings.

NAAFI – Navy, Army and Air Force Institute.

NBS – Netherlands Binnenelandsche Strijdrachten (Netherlands Forces of the Interior).

NCO – Non-Commissioned Officer. From Lance Corporal to Staff/Colour Sergeant and equivalent.

NSO – Netherlands Special Operations.

OBE – Order of the British Empire.

OCTU – Officer Cadet Training Unit.

PIAT – Projectile Infantry Anti-Tank. Portable anti-tank weapon weighing a cumbersome 34lb and firing a 2lb bomb out to 100 yards. Effective out to 350 yards when mounted on its bipod against buildings.

PT – Physical training.

RAF – Royal Air Force.

RAOC – Royal Army Ordnance Corps.

RAP – Regimental Air Post.

SAS – Special Air Service.

SBS – Special Boat Section.

SEAC – South East Asia Command.

SFHQ – Special Forces Headquarters.

SHAEF – Supreme Headquarters Allied Expeditionary Force.

SOE – Special Operations Executive.

Spandau – German MG-42. 9.92mm belt-fed light machine gun.

TLC – Tank Landing Craft.

VC – Victoria Cross.

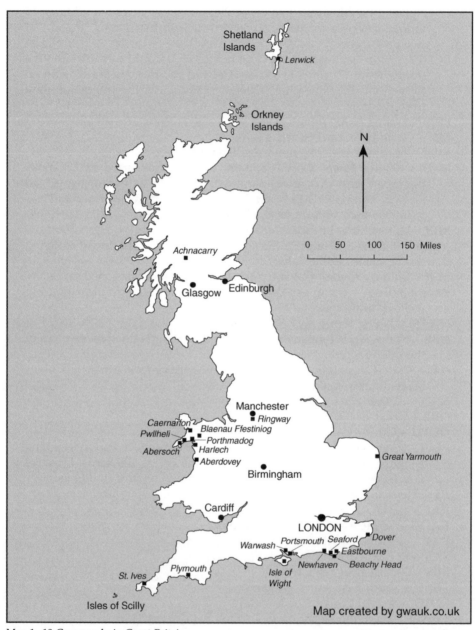

Map 1. 10 Commando in Great Britain

Map 2. Raiding Operations

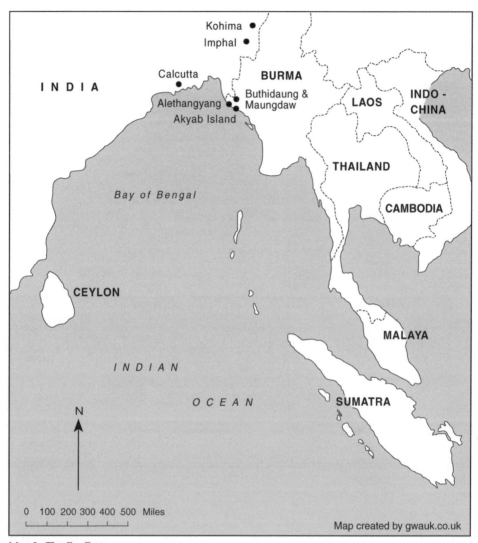

Map 3. The Far East

xiv

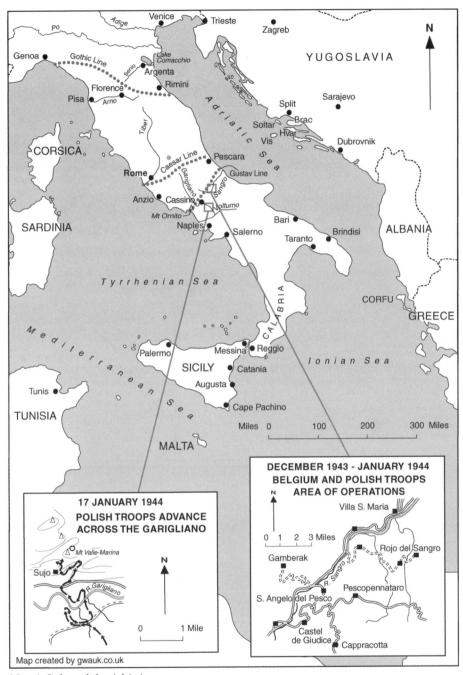

Map 4. Italy and the Adriatic

XV

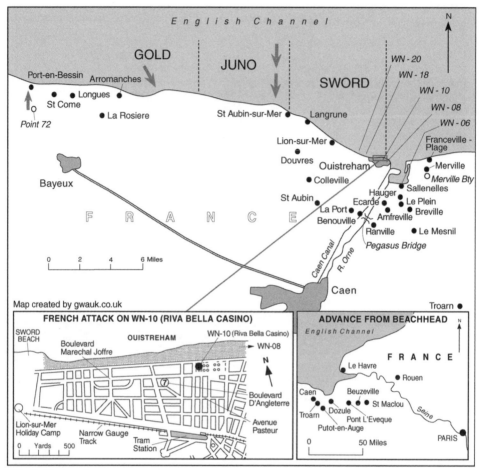

Map 5. Normandy

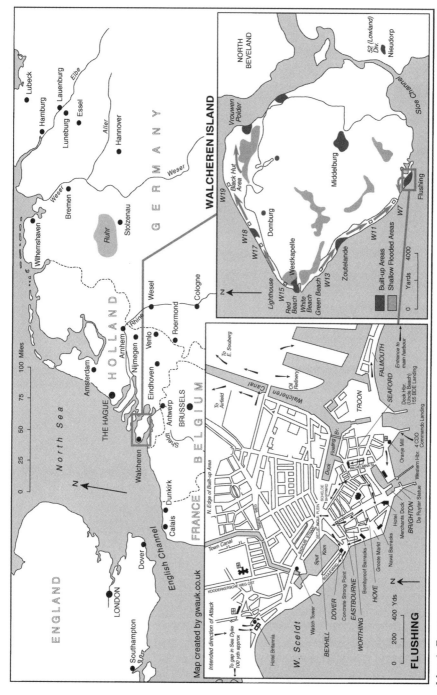

Map 6. Europe

xvii

Chapter 1

The Commandos

By the beginning of 1942, the war for Great Britain was not going well and we were under economic pressure as U-boat wolf packs tore into fragile convoys crossing the Atlantic. The appearance of General Rommel and the Afrika Korps brought depressing news from North Africa, while in the Far East, Hong Kong had fallen to the Japanese after a gallant defence, but in Malaya, the defence of Singapore wilted. The Battle of Britain was followed by the Blitz, and the retaliation by bombers trundling across Europe at night was seeing significant losses in aircraft and men. There was, however, hope. The entry of the United States after the Japanese attack on Pearl Harbour on 7 December 1941 promised almost endless support and commitment in terms of men and supplies, although their battle experience was limited. Chancellor Adolf Hitler's volte-face and his attack on the Soviet Union had produced advances deep into the communist republics but the seasons were showing that 'General Winter' was the Soviets' best ally.

The well-publicized exploits of the Commandos as the only ground forces taking the war to Occupied Europe reinforced public morale from 1940 to 1942 in a period of hardship, uncertainty and danger. The name 'commando' became a byword for stealthy raiding and it soon seemed all the Armed Forces wanted a slice of the action. By 1945, the Royal Navy had formed Beach Commandos to land in the first assault waves and control beach operations, while RAF Servicing Commandos serviced aircraft on airfields still under enemy artillery fire and threatened by attack. At least one Home Guard battalion, the 47th (24th General Post Office Birmingham) Warwickshire Battalion, created an unofficial commando company for guerrilla training. The 24th South Staffordshire (Tettenhall) Battalion created an assault course which included a river crossing and cliff climbing.

The origins of the Commandos can be traced to March 1938 when Admiral 'Quex' Sinclair, then head of Military Intelligence 6 (MI6), otherwise known as the Security Intelligence Services, was lent Major Lawrence

1

Grand, Royal Engineers, from the War Office to establish Section D and develop plans to degrade the performance of an enemy through clandestine and covert operations. At the same time, but unknown to Sinclair, Major Joseph Holland was working with General Staff (Research) (GS(R)) at the War Office developing irregular warfare. Also a Royal Engineer, he had studied British internal security operations in Ireland and Palestine, and was an acknowledged expert in unconventional warfare. When his ideas were studied by Military Intelligence, GS(R) was absorbed into MI (Research) where Holland developed the concept of tying down large numbers of troops by small forces. With war imminent, the Chief of the Imperial General Staff (CIGS) noticed the work of Section D and MI(R) and from it created, on 23 March 1939, the Special Operations Executive (SOE). However, the two majors were chalk and cheese and when Holland returned to the War Office, he took with him a like-minded Royal Artillery officer, Major Sir Colin McV. Gubbins. Every army has challengers to military conventions and, by spring 1940, Gubbins and Holland had persuaded the War Office to establish ten Guerrilla Companies. However, in a Regular Army imbued with conservatism, the units were retitled first to Special Infantry Companies and then to Independent Companies in accordance with their self-sufficient role of operating from their own ships, usually former ferries equipped with landing craft. On 20 April, No. 1 Independent Company was formed from Territorial Army volunteers supported by a few Regular Army from the 52nd (Lowland) Division. This was followed by nine more companies raised from infantry divisions, such as No. 10 Independent Company from 66th (Lancashire and Border) Division. The establishment of each company was twenty-one officers and 270 ORs.

When the Germans invaded Norway, Brigadier Gubbins commanded four Independent Companies in northern Norway from HMS *Royal Ulsterman* on 13 May 1940 and a fifth with a strategic role to cut the supply of Swedish iron ore to Norway. The Independent Companies had proved their worth, although Gubbins did commit the career-limiting sin of sacking a Guards officer close to the Crown for incompetence. While the Dunkirk evacuation was underway, MI(R) demonstrated the value of raiding when three officers blew up 200,000 tons of fuel at Harfleur on 2/3 June and then, collecting an Army straggler, rowed 13 miles out to sea to be collected.

On 4 June, when Prime Minister Winston Churchill asked the CIGS if there was there any reason why Great Britain should not retaliate, that evening Lieutenant Colonel Dudley Clarke (Royal Artillery), who was the Military Assistant to General Sir John Dill, the CIGS, proposed establishing a raiding force. When submitted next day, Churchill was enthusiastic:

Specially trained troops of the hunter class who can develop a reign of terror down the enemy coast ... I look to the Chiefs of Staff to propose measures for a ceaseless offensive against the whole German-occupied coastline leaving a trail of German corpses behind.

Mindful of the dire straits that the Nation was in after Dunkirk, he stipulated that no units should be diverted from opposing invasion and the force would have to do with the minimum of weapons.

Two days later, after a meeting between Dill and Churchill, Clarke's proposals were accepted and a raid was to be mounted as soon as possible under the operational co-ordination of Military Operations 9 (MO9), which had been established the same day to organize raids. When Clarke proposed the new force be known as 'Commandos', it appealed to Churchill's fertile imagination from the long British military tradition of raiding, and his experiences during the Second Boer War when columns of mounted Boers hit hard and ran. The word 'commando' is thought to have been introduced into Africa by the Portuguese and was used by the Boers to describe mounted conscripts serving with the armed forces of the republics of Transvaal and Orange Free State. On 12 June, Lieutenant General Sir Alan Bourne (Royal Marines) was placed in charge of raiding operations from the Admiralty. When Churchill then instructed Lord Hankey, who was Secretary to the Cabinet, to co-ordinate unconventional and irregular warfare, next day, Majors Holland and Grand were told that raiding and subversive operations would be co-ordinated by a single Minister, Dr Hugh Dalton, Minister of Economic Warfare, independent of War Office control.

Ten Commandos were raised from the five Independent Companies that had been in Norway and the Territorial Divisions in Great Britain – for instance No. 2 Commando, originally formed in July 1940, became No. 11 Special Air Service Battalion, forerunner to the Parachute Regiment, however lack of aircraft led to the Commando being reformed. No. 3 Commando, raised in Plymouth in July 1940 from a high proportion of Dunkirk veterans who had fought against the Waffen-SS, refused to acknowledge the Special Service nomenclature. No. 8 Commando was raised by Lieutenant Colonel Robert Laycock (The Blues) in July 1940 from the Household Cavalry, the Guards, Somerset Light Infantry, Royal Artillery, Royal Engineers and some Royal Marines. No. 10 Commando was disbanded after Northern Command failed to find sufficient volunteers. Orders were then despatched from MO9 on 20 June seeking volunteers for hazardous duties:

Able to swim, were immune from air and sea sickness, able to drive motor vehicles ... with courage, physical endurance, active, marksmanship, self-reliance and an aggressive spirit towards war ... and must become experts in the military use of scouting ... to stalk ... to report everything taking place ... to move across any type of country, day or night, silently and unseen ... and to live off the land for considerable periods.

The response from the Army, defeated at Dunkirk, was overwhelming and the commanding officers appointed by the War Office to form Commandos chose their officers, who in turn selected the about 530 all ranks that made up the Commando establishment. Brigadier Peter Young (Bedfordshires and Hertfordshires), who commanded No. 3 Commando, later said, 'We only wanted maniacs in the Commandos ... friends.' Lieutenant Colonel John Durnford-Slater (Royal Artillery) raising No. 7 Commando selected Dunkirk veterans, former Independent Company men and Spanish Civil War veterans, although the latter were screened for their loyalties, just in case they took 'guerrilo' concept too seriously. Retaining their cap badges, they were administered by their corps or regiments and were billeted with local families. Within three weeks of Dunkirk, Major Ronnie Tod and 115 men from Nos 6 and 8 Independent Companies formed into the fictitious 'No. 11 Commando' and raided France in Operation Collar. Fortuitously, Captain S.G. Garnons-Williams DSC RN had gathered launches and RAF rescue boats in the Hamble and manned them with a mixed bunch of Regular and Reserve sailors. Of the four raids that comprised Operation Collar, one party encountered nothing of interest, the second failed to land, and the third went ashore near Tocquet and killed two Germans guarding a dance hall. The fourth ran into a German cyclist patrol and in the ensuing fight, the only British casualty was Lieutenant Colonel Dudley Clarke whose ear was clipped by a bullet. When one group returned to Folkestone, they were arrested by the Military Police for being dirty and dishevelled first thing in the morning. During Operation Ambassador on occupied Guernsey during the night of 14 July, a lesson learnt was the value of swimming in amphibious operations. Somewhat unrealistically, Churchill envisaged tanks landing and although he called the raids fiascos, they had considerable propaganda value for a country bracing itself for invasion.

In July, Admiral of the Fleet Sir Roger Keyes was appointed as Director Combined Operations and retained Lieutenant General Bourne as his deputy. When MI(R) was reformed as Combined Operations HQ and placed under command of GHQ Home Forces, it envisaged 200-strong units remaining ashore for a day and examined operations in support of conventional forces. On 19 July, Churchill ordered SOE to 'set Europe ablaze' by mobilizing the Resistance from its Baker Street offices, however internecine rivalry blighted co-ordinated intelligence activities, quite apart from the Abwehr and Gestapo working hard to undermine Allied planning.

On 11 November, after the immediate threat of invasion was reduced by the Battle of Britain, as an anti-invasion measure, Brigadier John Haydon assembled the Commandos and surviving Independent Companies into the Special Service Brigade. Although some senior officers preferred the term 'Special Service', in spite of the link with the Schutz Staffel (SS), 'Commando' did not and both terms coexisted until late 1944. Nos 7, 8 and 11 Commandos were formed into LAYFORCE under the command of Lieutenant Colonel Laycock and sent to the Middle East to join Nos 50 and 52 Commando, which had been raised from British troops serving in the Middle East. In deteriorating situations, the Commandos were frequently used as infantry, particularly when Crete was overrun, a decision that infuriated Churchill. The survivors were formed into the Middle East Commando until it was disbanded in early 1942 with most men transferring to the 1st Special Air Service Regiment.

The year 1941 saw a gradual increase in raids against Europe, in particular Occupied Norway. In April 1940, the Royal Norwegian Legation in London had laid the foundations for an army-in-exile by registering English-speaking Norwegians willing to serve as liaison officers with the British in Norway. Exiled sailors and whalers were being assembled at Shoeburyness coastal artillery camp until a Norwegian military mission finally established a reception camp at Dumfries. On 10 June, King Haakon arrived in Great Britain and ten days later established the Norwegian Army Command in London. On 21 June, in the last broadcast to Norway, General Carl Gustav Fleischer recommended the conscription of Norwegians aged between twenty and thirty-five years in Great Britain and, at a meeting at the War Office, confirmed that Norway would fight. By the New Year, Norwegian Brigade was operational under GHQ Home Forces and trained with the Cameronian Highlanders and 126th Field Regiment, Royal Artillery. On 1 January 1941, conscription of Norwegian men in Great Britain began. Many who had left Norway did so under dangerous conditions, with some crossing the North Sea with inadequate navigation equipment for open-water voyages in small boats, but making landfall among the Scottish islands. A few were caught in gales that took them far out to sea. All were at risk from German aircraft patrolling the coast.

Nevertheless, simmering disagreements between the Norwegian and British Government over the use of the Norwegian Armed Forces persisted until the isolationist Foreign Minister, Koht, who was blamed for the neutrality that led to occupation, was replaced by Trygve Lie, later appointed the first Chairman of the United Nations. A firm believer in alliances, he signed the Armed Forces Agreement in May 1941 and the St James's Palace Inter-Allied Declaration in June, which resulted in the Norwegians being accepted into the Allied order of battle for 'the defence of the United Kingdom or for the purpose of regaining Norway'. Norway also provided several units, including No. 1 Norwegian Detachment of gunners on South Georgia and winter warfare instructors in Iceland. When, in mid-1940, Lieutenant General Bourne had suggested that the Norwegians should form two Independent Companies, the 47-year-old former actor Captain Martin Linge raised Norwegian Independent Company 1, which operated under the auspices of SOE. Colloquially known as Linge Company (Lingekompannie), it trained at Inverailort House, not far from Glenfinnan, near where Bonnie Prince Charlie had raised his nationalist standard in 1745. Recruits were first treated to the alarming spectacle of the former Shanghai police officers, Major Bill Fairbairn and Captain Eric Sykes, rolling down a staircase in a display of hand-to-hand fighting. These two designed the double-edged dagger that is synonymous with British commandos and which is commemorated today by the insignia for Army personnel serving as commandos.

The distance to Norway precluded parachute operations in the summer. Although the long winter nights offered long-distance flying, the weather was unpredictable and so it was by small ships, such as the 'Shetland Bus' trawlers, that the Norwegian Resistance was supplied with arms, ammunition and equipment, and agents were collected and dropped. The head of the SOE Norwegian Section, Mr J.S. Wilson, brought his scoutmaster's patience and accuracy to planning raids with Norwegian commanders, the principle targets being economic, but also to remind outlying German garrisons that they were at risk. Linge Company accompanied Nos 2, 3, 4 and 6 Commandos as interrogators and liaison on Operation Archery on 27 December 1941 at Vaagso to attack shipping, warehouses, dockyards and fish-oil processing plants of use to the Germans. Among the nineteen British killed in fierce fighting was Captain Linge, attacking a hotel in Måløy. The raid had far-reaching consequences when the Germans strengthened their defence of Norway with formations that they could have deployed elsewhere. At the same time, the diversionary Operation Anklet took place between 26 and 28 December when No. 12 Commando and elements of Linge Company landed on the Lofoten Islands to destroy installations. Operation Claymore on 4 March was an economic raid on the two towns on Lofoten by Nos 3 and 4 Commandos, supported by a small party from Linge Company, to destroy fish oil being processed by the Germans to produce nitro-glycerine explosive. Lieutenant Richard Willis, of No. 3 Commando, sent a telegram from Stamsund addressed to A. Hitler, Berlin: 'You said in your last speech German troops would meet the British wherever they landed. Where are your troops? Prisoners from Operation Claymore.' On all the raids, the commandos returned with prisoners, Quisling collaborators and several hundred Norwegian volunteers, including a few women. Parts of an Enigma cipher machine that helped the Bletchley Park code-breakers were brought back from Lofoten.

Meanwhile, commandos were the amphibious recovery force during the Bruneval raid on 27/8 February by C Company, 2nd Parachute Battalion, tasked to capture key parts of the Wurzburg radar. On 27/8 March, commandos destroyed the St Nazaire dry dock in the 'greatest raid of all'.

By 1942, several divisions had been sent to North Africa and the Far East. Those left behind in the UK trained for the invasion of Europe. Also in the country were Frenchmen and Poles plucked from Dunkirk and Czechs, Norwegians, Belgians, Dutchmen and others who had escaped from Occupied Europe, all under the overall command of their respective governments-in-exile and fretting at their inability to liberate their countries. Some had lived in Great Britain all or most of their lives but, without British passports, were aliens and could not enlist.

Chapter 2

Formation of No. 10 (Inter-Allied) Commando

In Great Britain, the few opportunities for exiled armies to take the war to the Germans were leading to dissatisfaction, demoralization and distrust of the political and military aims of the governments-in-exile. Apart from the Linge Company, exiles were condemned to waiting either for deployment to an overseas theatre of war or for the opening of the Second Front, and the endless training, uncertainty and boredom boiled over into frustration. New arrivals from Occupied Europe had the psychological problem of arriving with a will to fight but then faced the tough job of being forced to settle down to the hurry-up-and-wait routine. Some had experienced incredible hardship. The only contact with families was the occasional letters through the Red Cross or a neutral power, but this contact risked reprisal. Private Chris Helleman who later joined 2 (Dutch) Troop, was a former merchant sailor who had escaped from Holland via Sweden in 1943. He managed to send a letter to his family via the Swedish Consulate and was ticked off for lambasting the Dutch Nazi Party in it.

When the evacuation of Allied servicemen from France was over, those who escaped from Occupied Europe were initially screened by Scotland Yard, however, as the flow continued, it became clear to British counter-intelligence that while the Germans could not prevent escapes, they could use escape lines to insert spies. To counter the threat, under the auspices of MI5, a Dutch Military Intelligence officer, Lieutenant Colonel Oreste Pinto, established the London Reception Centre at the Royal Victoria Patriotic School in Wandsworth where new arrivals were given a vetting interview and intelligence was gathered on their experiences. Pinto had gained his counter-intelligence experience with the French Deuxieme Bureau, and trained his interrogators to dissect minutely each account and examine possessions – a forgotten bus ticket, an old-fashioned watch, clothing, cigarettes – for clues of German penetration. Throughout the war, they successfully achieved the fine balance of trapping spies and ensuring that bona fide exiles did not feel that they escaped from the Gestapo only to fall into the hands of an equally unpleasant security organization.

Among the 139,000 French who were either evacuated from Dunkirk and other ports, or who sailed their ships to England, were 20,000 sailors and marines. When France surrendered on 22 June 1940, most took repatriation. The 1,160 who remained had the choice of joining the Royal Navy or forming the Free French Naval Forces (FNFL – *Forces Navales Francaises Libre*) under the command of Admiral Muselier, the senior French naval officer in UK. Among them was Sub-Lieutenant Philippe Kieffer, who had joined the French Navy on the lower deck when war broke out. Born to French parents in Haiti, he had learnt English in the USA, had escaped from France with a few soldiers that made up the garrison at Saint Vaast la Hougue on the Cotentin Peninsula and had responded to the appeal to join Colonel Charles de Gaulle's fight against Hitler. The Royal Navy's bombarding of the French fleet at Mers el-Kebir led to some people questioning their decision. The French battleship, *L'Amiral Courbet*, berthed at Portsmouth, was the naval training establishment for officers and NCOs, and basic courses included a fortnight with the newly-raised 1st Marine Rifle Battalion, which had been formed on 17 July. Training was sometimes interrupted by air raids and instructors and students manned the ship's anti-aircraft guns to defend Portsmouth Naval Base.

The 1st Marine Rifle Battalion later took part in the Dakar operation and was then sent to the French colony of Gabon. In April 1941, it arrived in Palestine and took part in the fighting in Syria against the Vichy French before joining the Free French forces in Libya, where it joined the Fighting French Brigade in the defence of Bir-Hacheim, and eventually joined the pursuit of the Afrika Korps to Tunisia. The 2nd Battalion was formed in October and later joined the 1st French Marine Brigade in the defence of French Equatorial Africa until, in November 1941, it took over the defence of Beirut.

Among the staff officers on board the *Courbet* was Kieffer. Inspired by the raids on the Lofoten Islands, he proposed to the French Naval Headquarters on Clapham Common that there was potential to raise a French Commando specifically to raid the French coast. Although it was received with some indifference, Kieffer was interviewed by Admiral Muselier, who, while sympathetic, emphasized that most of his resources were needed to keep French warships at sea. If Kieffer wanted to form a Commando, the British must be persuaded to supply arms, equipment and training, but this, he suggested, might be difficult since they were also under-resourced; nevertheless, he undertook to arrange an interview for Kieffer with the British. At the end of March 1941, Kieffer met Brigadier Haydon and although he emphasized the advantages of a French unit raiding France, he felt that, in spite of long and complicated negotiations, his idea was rejected

When Captain Lord Louis Mountbatten took command of Combined Operations on 27 October 1941 and recognized that the demands on the various Commandos was beginning to exceed supply and affect their ability to undertake the necessary training, he suggested that the Royal Marines should form Commandos, as befitted their tradition of amphibious warfare. He also suggested that suitable exiled men be given the opportunity to take the war back to their homelands as commandos. It was an eminently sensible suggestion – after all. Polish and Czech pilots had shown during the Battle of Britain that they hated the Germans with a vengeance, while at sea, exiled men were contributing to the war effort in merchant ships, on escorts and in submarines. In Europe, Resistance movements were active. To some extent Mountbatten was influenced by several left-wingers using their experiences of the Spanish Civil War to develop irregular warfare, particularly in the Home Guard, but he saw several advantages of raising a Commando of exiled servicemen – linguistic skills, translation of documents, mobilizing of indigenous forces and civilians, and their knowledge of their countries, quite apart from having a score to settle with the Axis.

When Brigadier Haydon referred his discussions with the French to Mountbatten, to his delight Kieffer was authorized to form a Commando as part of the FNFL. Establishing his HQ at Old Dean Camp, Camberley, Kieffer recruited Lieutenant Charles Trepel, Warrant Officer Francis Vourc'h and sixteen Marines, including the ex-legionnaire De Wandaleur, who had been in Norway. Master-at-Arms Frederic Klopfenstein brought six men released from military detention. Chief Petty Officer Jean Pinelli had been with the 1st Marine Rifle Brigade at Dakar and had been a physical training teacher as a civilian. Among the units at the camp was the embryonic French Parachute Regiment.

Naming his unit the 1er Compagnie Fusilier Marin (1st Marine Rifle Company), the men wore British battledress topped by the characteristic French blue beret and red pompom. In July 1941, the Royal Navy allocated part of the shore establishment HMS *Royal Arthur* at Skegness to Kieffer, where the French trained on British machine guns and mortars, and learnt English. By the end of 1941, the previously pale and tired young Frenchmen were fit and healthy. The company then moved to the French Bir-Hacheim Barracks, Portsmouth to train with the Royal Marines.

On 26 June 1942, Lieutenant Colonel Dudley Lister (The Buffs) attended the Establishment Committee at the War Office and was instructed by Western Command to raise No. 10 (Inter-Allied) Commando, the nomenclature formerly allocated to Northern Command to raise a Commando in 1940. It was to consist of a Commando HQ and four Troops, each of a headquarters and two sub-sections with the potential of increasing the establishment to eight Troops. The new Commando was to assemble in Troon and the men were to be billeted locally. Lister had won the Military Cross during the First World War and had commanded No. 4 Commando during the Lofoten raid. During his tenure, the officers had developed a Death's Head cap badge. A competent amateur boxer, Lister was a hard trainer and when No. 4 Commando was based in Scotland, he is reputed to have sometimes exchanged his bed, bath and meals in the Officers' Mess for a sleeping bag, a cold morning swim in the Firth of Clyde and rations cooked on a Primus stove by his long-suffering, well-educated batman, Private Smith.

On 3 July, Lister arrived at Troon with his Second-in-Command, Major Peter Laycock (Nottinghamshire Yeomanry), the younger brother of Robert Laycock. Another set of brothers who achieved fame in the Commandos were the Churchills. The Adjutant was Lieutenant Jocelyn Clark (Gordon Highlanders) and Second Lieutenant/Acting Captain John Coates (Intelligence Corps) had the dual role of Intelligence Officer and Security Officer. Nine days later, everyone travelled by train to Harlech in Wales where Commando Headquarters was established. Lieutenant Bruce Beattie (Royal Signals) joined as Signals Officer on 21 July and was followed by Captain Lutyens (Coldstream Guards) as the Commando Liaison Officer three days later. On 20 August, Major Hodges (Royal Army Medical Corps) arrived as the senior Commando Medical Officer, although each Troop had its own doctor, as it did with chaplains.

After the Dutch surrendered in May 1940, the several hundred soldiers and about 250 marines who had escaped to England were formed into the Royal Dutch Legion, among them Private Hubertus Gubbels, who had served with 4th Regiment, Field Artillery (Foot). Initially, the Dutch Government-in-exile was chaotic and without firm command, the Legion was shuffled from one camp to another and, by the end of 1940, was languishing in tents in an abandoned factory in Congleton, south-east of Liverpool. The fact that Holland was surrounded to the west by water, to the east by Germany and to the south by Belgium meant escape was very difficult. Of the 100 who attempted to sail across the North Sea, only about a dozen are thought to have been successful. It took significant planning to find a boat, gather rations and fuel, and then navigate to Great Britain. The former Medical Corps private, Wilhem de Waard, and two friends prepared a rowing boat in the furnace where de Waard used to work before the war. In mid-March 1941, having found an outboard engine, and after instruction on basic navigation by a retired trawler skipper, they slipped past German military and naval patrols, and motored out to the grey expanse of the North Sea until they were picked up by a British destroyer and landed at Harwich.

11

The Dutch appealed to her citizens living overseas to enlist to 'liberate The Netherlands', and, opening up camps in Canada, first in Guelph and then Princess Juliana Barracks in Stratford, Ontario, inducted volunteers to come from twenty-six countries, including Dutch living in the US and Canada, South Africa and the Dutch colonies. Many had never lived in The Netherlands. Martin Knottenbelt, for instance, had been raised in England and was at Oxford University when he joined the Legion. On 27 August 1941, the Royal Dutch Legion was reformed as Royal Princess Irene Brigade (Koninklijke Nederlandse Brigade Prinses Irene) and named after Irene, the second child of Princess Juliana and Prince Bernhard, then living in Canada. The Brigade never reached its 3,500 establishment, levelling at about 2,000 all ranks. When the Dutch Government agreed to raise a Commando and Captain P.J. Mulders was appointed to command it, by 22 March, he had selected two officers and forty men, who were then divided between Nos 3, 4, 9 and 12 Commandos at Largs, Troon, Island of Bute and Dunoon for training.

During the two world wars of the twentieth century, Jews had played their part by forming the Zion Mule Corps and enlisting in the 38/42nd Battalion, Royal Fusiliers during the First World War, and with the Jewish Brigade and the unfortunate Special Identification Group in the Second World War. Also to be added to the list must be 3 Troop, No. 10 (Inter-Allied) Commando, which had several European Jews in its ranks.

In the mid-1930s, large numbers of Jewish refugees had made their way to Great Britain from Germany, Austria and Eastern Europe, some deported and others forced by circumstances to leave their homes. Sometimes families were split. The combination of the brief seizure of power by Vidkun Quisling in Norway, the spectre of the Fifth Column deposing the British Government and a breach of security over the theft of telegrams between Churchill and President Roosevelt led to the enactment of Defence Regulation 18B on 23 May 1940. In early 1939, as the threat of war escalated, the Government had enacted the draft Defence Regulations under the 1939 Emergency Powers (Defence) Act and split them into three Codes ranging from immediate action to no risk.

After the fall of France, Prime Minister Churchill wanted to form a 'Foreign Legion' of 5,000 foreign soldiers serving in the British Army, however, many potential veterans and recruits were classed as undesirable for various reasons, including being stateless, socialists, intellectuals and Spanish Civil War veterans. Defence Regulation 18 initially restricted aircraft movement but on 23 May it evolved into widespread internment of several thousand 'enemy aliens', mainly Jewish Austrian and German refugees. The round-up was largely confined to Southern England and enforced without warning on the pretext of prevention of 'acts prejudicial to the public safety' and 'hostile origins or associations'. It was generally chaotic and it was not unknown for men serving in the Forces to be detained while on parade. The internees were held in holding centres and camps, some on the Isle of Man. In June 1940, with invasion seemingly imminent, the Government asked Canada and Australia to take about 3,000 medium-risk internees each, along with several thousand prisoners of war captured in Norway and France, and German members of the French Foreign Legion. Those shipped on board the SS *Dunera* for the six-week voyage to Australia experienced conditions a Conservative Member of Parliament, Major Victor Cazalet, later described as 'a bespatted page in our history'. The internees were kept in the same barbed-wire enclosures as the prisoners of war, sanitary conditions were appalling and the poor food was limited to one meal a day. Property was often thrown overboard by the guards. On arrival, armed escorts with fixed bayonets escorted the internees to camps. Those sent to Canada on board the SS *Ettrick* experienced similar conditions.

Meanwhile, 112 Alien Tribunals reviewed 74,000 potential internees, of which 600 aliens considered to be an immediate threat to the security of the country were graded Category A; this figure was whittled down to fourteen known Nazi sympathizers. About 6,800 were grouped into Category B and allowed restricted freedom, with the remainder being placed in the unrestricted Category C and allowed to enlist. When the immediate invasion scare decreased in 1941, and with it the spectre of the Fifth Column, Defence Regulations 18B came under political and pressure-group attack, and the internees began to be released. Many of those who enlisted in the Army were posted into one of nineteen Pioneer Corps 'Loyal Alien' Companies to undertake manual tasks, such as forestry, unloading coal for power stations, building railways and repairing bomb damage, and styled themselves the 'King's Own Loyal Enemy Aliens'. For most who wanted to fight, it was a humiliating experience. Many of those who volunteered for 3 Troop came from 77 and 87 (Loyal Alien) Companies with one objective – to get the Nazis.

Otto Wasserman was a Jewish tailor of Czech extraction who married a Pole, Inge. After the Night of the Long Knives, he and his brother, Bruno, tried to leave Germany but, after being handed over to the Nazi authorities by the Dutch frontier police, were sent to Dachau concentration camp and broke rocks during the winter of 1938/39. Bruno died in the freezing conditions. In March 1939, after Inge had purchased tickets to leave for China, Otto was released and arranged for an uncle to sponsor residence in the United States. As was the practice, Wasserman left Germany to arrange travel for his family and, on arriving in Great Britain, ended up in Kitchener Transit Camp in Sandwich. There, he found employment for Inge and sent the work permit and affidavit to her in Berlin, however, she and their two children were trapped a week later when war broke. Otto enlisted in 69 Company, Auxiliary Military Pioneer Corps and, while serving with the Royal Engineers digging trenches and repairing railways near Rennes, heard, in January 1940, that Inge was expecting their third child. When the Germans overran France, Wasserman's unit was evacuated through St Malo. He never heard any more from his family.

The German Eric Nathan was a Jew, whose lawyer father had been sent to Dachau as a political prisoner in 1938. The family reached England where Nathan learnt English and attended King's College, Canterbury. Before the outbreak of war, his father had also reached England. On Whit Sunday 1940, Nathan was arrested and, after a short internment on the Isle of Man, was shipped to Canada on the *Ettrick*. When Prison Commissioner Alec Paterson was sent to Canada in 1941 to sort out the internment problem, he was impressed with Nathan's commitment and arranged for him to return to Great Britain to join the Pioneer Corps. The Viennese Jewish socialist Paul Hornig was a member of the banned Roten Falken and, although pursued by the Gestapo, reached Great Britain where he continued his political activities until 1939 when he volunteered for the Royal Air Force. Several days after his enlistment papers arrived, he found himself on board the *Ettrick*. At his Canadian internment camp, Honig was one of several intellectuals and academics who began a university until he too was selected by Paterson to enlist in the Pioneer Corps.

On the night of the *Anschluss* on 12 March 1937, when the father of Peter Tischler received a phone call from the Duke of Windsor asking if he could help, he turned the offer down in the belief that the situation would calm down. But Dr Tischler and his son were arrested by the Gestapo, although powerful connections again proved valuable when Dr Arthur Seyss-Inquart, a patient of Dr Tischler, was appointed Chancellor of Austria. Dr Tischler contacted the Duke who not only organized for the British Embassy to place a car at his disposal, but also sponsored their emigration to England where they were met by his secretary at Victoria Station. The Tischlers escaped internment, probably because of their connections.

In 1942, as a potential manpower source, European Jews were invited to serve in the Armed Forces, SOE seeing the provision of German speakers accompanying raiding forces as interrogators, and shouting conflicting orders in German, as an advantage. The Special Service Brigade assembled those who wanted to join the Commandos in 3 Troop, 10 (Inter-Allied) Commando. Churchill's fertile imagination preferred that the Troop be known as 3 (X) Troop.

A week before the Belgian surrender on 28 May, Lieutenant General Baron V. van Strydonck de Burkel and several 1st Military District staff officers placed themselves at the disposal of the War Office. Three days later, when he was appointed Defence Minister, he instructed Lieutenant General Denis to command the Army Fighting Unit at the Belgian Military

14

Regrouping Camp at Penally Barracks in Tenby. Three days later, Marcel-Henri Jaspar, the only Minister to have reached England, announced that Belgium would continue the fight with men who had escaped occupation, and Belgians resident in Great Britain. By December, the 1st Rifle Battalion had been formed, followed by an armoured car squadron and an artillery battery in January 1942. When a parachute company was formed in May 1942, this led to the establishment of the Belgian SAS. On 4 June, the Belgium Armed Forces were officially placed at the disposal of the Allies and by 1944 consisted of the 1st Belgian Independent Brigade commanded by the charismatic Brigadier Jean-Baptiste Piron, who arrived from Gibraltar in 1941 after being captured in 1940 while serving HQ 5th Armed Force. The formation was often referred to as Brigade 'Piron'.

At the beginning of July 1942, when the Belgian Government agreed to form a Commando Troop, Reserve Artillery Captain Baron George Danloy, met Lieutenant Colonel Lister in London on 17 July. He then circulated notices calling for volunteers for 4 (Belgian) Troop and among those who responded was Sergeant Noel Dedeken who had been wounded while defending Dunkirk. In March 1941, he escaped from Bruges Hospital and after spending several weeks in hiding, he and a friend cycled to Paris where they bluffed their way through German checkpoints to reach Vichy France, only to be arrested. Escaping from detention, they reached Portugal and contacted the Belgian Embassy in Lisbon, which arranged for them to be taken to a ship bound for Gibraltar. He landed at Greenock a year after he had escaped from Bruges.

After discussions between the War Office and Norwegian High Command on 28 August 1942 about forming a Norwegian commando Troop, two platoons from the newly formed 4th Mountain Company (Captain Rolf Hauge) were selected for training, because they had recently completed the 'Shock Assault Course' at Fort William. When Norway fell in 1940, Hauge had crossed into Sweden and, making his way across the Soviet Union, reached the Bosporus. He then travelled by ship and train to Egypt where he secured a berth on a ship filled with refugees and Italian prisoners of war from North Africa and, arriving at Greenock on 9 September 1941, joined the Norwegian Brigade. Four of the volunteers were three seamen and a passenger from among ten Norwegian merchant ships with cargos of ball bearings and special steel destined for Great Britain, but held by the Swedes in Gothenburg. On 1 April 1942, British pressure on the Swedes saw the ships being released, however the German Navy was waiting, five were sunk and their crews captured; three returned to Gothenburg and two sailed for Great Britain. En route, the MS *Rigmor* beat off a U-boat attack but was then sunk by enemy aircraft, while the MS *Lind* escaped a submarine and made port.

Among the soldiers evacuated from France were two divisions of Poles who had escaped Poland in September 1939 and were now training hard in Scotland. On 13 March 1942, Mountbatten thanked General Sikorsky for agreeing to form a Commando Troop under the command of a British officer, and ordered that it should remain in the Polish order of battle and be subject to Polish military law. Captain Andrzej Bohomolec, who had been badly wounded serving with the 1st Carpathian Brigade in North Africa, was appointed as the Polish liaison officer. When orders were sent to the 2nd Rifle Battalion, which was based in Cupar in Scotland, to form a Commando Troop, volunteers, some already parachute trained, took part in exercises as part of the selection process. By the time Lieutenant Colonel Lister had final discussions with Colonel Merecki, the Polish Chief of Operations, and it had been agreed the men would retain their national rank insignia, on 28 September, Sikorski signed the order for the 1st Independent Commando Company establishment of seven officers and eighty-four other ranks, with Captain Wladsylow Smrokowski, a professional soldier, as its commander. Aged thirty-one, he had fought against the Germans in Poland in 1939 and had then escaped to Hungary. Making his way to France, he joined the 1st Grenadier Division and was wounded in the fighting. By the time he recovered, the French had signed the armistice and so he made his way across the Pyrenees through Spain to Gibraltar without being arrested. Smrokowski arrived in Harlech on 8 September 1942 to form 6 (Polish) Troop.

On 7 December 1942, although Eighth Army were pursuing the Afrika Korps towards Tunisia – the fighting still had months to go before the Axis forces surrendered on 11 May 1943 – Lieutenant Colonel Lister and his officers discussed raising a Troop for the Mediterranaen theatre. On 15 February 1943, Lister was authorized by the War Office to raise 7 (Mediterranean) Troop. Three days later, Lieutenant James Monahan joined the Commando as the 3 (British) Troop Intelligence Officer. Born in 1913, he was the Political Editor of the *Manchester Guardian* and had a poetic air about him. At the outbreak of war, he enlisted in the Royal Fusiliers and, as a fluent French speaker, was transferred to the Political Warfare Unit. Captain Coates enlisted Monahan to help him raise the new Troop from Italians, however the British Army proved a poor source and an alternative emerged among Italian-speaking Slovenes serving with the Royal Yugoslavian Army in Egypt. Major Peter Boughey, a SOE liaison officer, helped identify potential recruits and on 24 May, several Yugoslavians, responding to a call for 'parachute packers', were selected by Coates and Monahan to attend the commando course. On 20 August, the two officers met General M.N. Radovitch, the Yugoslavian Military Attaché in London, and told him that Lieutenant Lodich, Second Lieutenant Tripovic and five other ranks had passed the course and were the nucleus of 7 (Yugoslavian)

Troop to be commanded by Monahan. Lieutenant Kerovin and ten other ranks completed the commando course on 21 October. Returning to Eastbourne four days later, they joined a contingent, including the first batch of Yugoslavians to complete the course, under orders to move to the Middle East with twelve men from 3 (British) Troop. A proposal to raise a Japanese Troop for the Far East foundered.

Chapter 3

Training the Commando

When the Commandos were formed, commanding officers had responsibility for training and consequently standards varied. The Irregular Warfare School, which had been established in May 1940 to train soldiers to resist the German invasion, produced several unconventional soldiers, whose legacy is evident today – David Stirling who formed the SAS, Mike Calvert, who helped prove, as a Chindit, that the British could survive and fight in the jungle, and several commando leaders. As the threat of invasion receded, the style and purpose of training changed from defence to offence.

Achnacarry House was the spiritual centre of the Cameron clan and, in June 1940, was the home of the hereditary chief, Sir Donald Cameron of Lochiel. When he had donated it to the War Office, the house was used by No. 1 Independent Company until December 1940 when it became the Holding Unit, Special Warfare Training Centre. Achnacarry was then identified as suitable for the Commando Depot and was taken over, in January 1942, for the duration of the war, by the formidable Lieutenant Colonel Charles Vaughan (The Buffs). Vaughan, who had enlisted as a private in 1914, was briefed by Brigadier Haydon to design a course to select men for the Special Service Brigade with the will to win. Sooner or later, the commandos were expected to play a leading role during the assault on Occupied Europe. Selecting his instructors from commandos with at least one raid under their belt, Vaughan developed the training programme ready for the first intake on 17 March.

With newsreels and photographs showing scruffy raiding parties returning from a night's work with confused German prisoners helping to perpetuate the myth of irregular warfare, Vaughan's priority was to undermine the perception that the commando was an individualistic cut-throat with little regard for the rigours of military discipline. He developed the Commando Spirit, which expected determination and enthusiasm under all conditions, a keen sense of personal responsibility, self-reliance, physical and mental fitness, and an ability to fight in a large body in conventional warfare, and as a member of a small team in raids. Courses were originally three months long, however, with the need to train full Commandos, including the nine from the Royal Marines, it was reduced to a month. Between 1942 and 1945, 25,000 men, including US Rangers, underwent basic and instructor training. In late 1942, officers in No. 1 Commando decided that the seventy-nine different cap badges and a variety of headgear, ranging from Royal Tank Regiment black berets to Glengarries, failed to enhance the Regimental spirit and they persuaded a local Tam O'Shanter firm to design a beret using Lovat Green – the Green Beret. This then became the goal for a commando undergoing training, and was a symbol not only of military prowess, but of self-discipline and elitism.

Training began as soon as the men arrived at Spean Bridge railway station with a 7-mile march past the Spean Bridge Hotel, through the village, over the river, onto the bleak moors, over the Caledonian Canal, and up and down back-breaking hills until arriving at the main gates at Achncarry House. The march is now commemorated annually by the Dutch No. 10 (Inter-Allied) Re-enactment Society. The French 1st Marine Rifle Company arrived in March 1942 after training with the Royal Marines and was the first foreign unit to train at Achnacarry. Lieutenant Kieffer:

> Then commenced a period of enough physical life to cripple a horse. Experienced commandos who been on raids were the instructors and they taught us to control the fear from the third day when live ammunition was used. Each squad of forty men. Approximately forty men lost their lives at Achnacarry, that is two out of every thousand in the drive to win the Green Beret. Each time a candidate commando was killed, a fictitious grave was dug at the entrance of the camp with a sign briefly explaining the circumstances of his death and how it could have been avoided. The French were proud to be the only foreigners in this hell. A march of 11 km with a small pack and individual weapon was expected to be completed in less than sixty minutes, the section complete and ready to fight. Two other marches, 19 km and the other of 32 km were to be completed two hours, twenty minutes and five hours respectively ... The course lasted ten weeks without rest, except for half-day of rest per week, which was generally put to writing letters, wash clothes, taking a shower and sleeping. Sometimes in the evening after a day, there was a film documentary on a raid or a lecture. The lecturer, officer or warrant officer, were perhaps an instructor of the school who had returned from action with new ideas. The commando often left these evenings, his morale raised and desire to fight fanatical.

A Highland piper sounded Reveille at 6.00am by marching through the huts and thirty minutes was then allowed to wash and prepare for a hut inspection before an hour of physical training (PT), with long lines of commandos in shorts and singlets following the example of the instructor at the front. Breakfast at 8.00am was followed by Troop parade an hour later followed by morning's training and an hour's break for lunch at 1.00pm. Training continued until 4.30pm when there was an hour for the evening meal and then sedentary training until 6.00pm. Most classroom periods were an average of fifty-five minutes with a five-minute break. The rest of the evening was taken up with personal chores and, if time permitted, a visit to the NAAFI until Lights Out at 10.30pm. Throughout the training hung the dreaded 'Returned to Unit' for not keeping to the standard required. Training was divided into the four general headings of tactics, skill at arms, demolition and close-quarter battle.

Tactical phases included day and night map appreciation and sketching, and understanding field cooking and nutrition. Live ammunition and explosives used to miss – but not by much – helped inoculate the commandos against the shock of battle. Obstacle-crossing skills were improved using scrambling nets, balancing planks, tunnels and barbed wire. In addition to river crossing by toggle-rope bridges, the 'Death Ride' designed by Lieutenant Alick Cowieson (Cameron Highlanders) – a long length of wire attached to a fixing point on a tree on the near bank, across the River Arkraig, to a fixing point at the base of a tree – enhanced confidence as the commandos slid down using their toggle ropes. Sergeant Frickleton, the chief PT instructor in 1942, designed the Tarzan Course of ropes stretched high in a glade of beech trees.

Basic watermanship took place at the Commando Boat Training quay at Bunarkaig on Loch Ailort, where the sergeant instructors had a range of boats, including the Landing Craft Assault (LCA), Goatley assault boats, whalers, dories, cutters, canoes and dinghies. The night landing was a spectacular event as close to battle as Vaughan could devise with the instructors firing a range of mortars, machine guns and rifles, dispersed with explosives blowing columns of cold water. Skill at arms included unarmed combat, using knives and bayonets, and fighting in woods and built up areas. Weapon training included the use of the standard bolt-action .303 SMLE rifle, the .45 Thompson and Sten sub-machine guns, the .38 Smith and Wesson revolver, the Canadian 9mm Browning pistol and the very accurate .303-inch Bren light machine gun. For anti-tank work, Troop HQ usually had a PIAT section of a corporal and a private. There was also familiarization with enemy weapons.

Exercises tested the commandos. The pleasure of the final 36-hours scheme depended on the weather and involved an approach along roads, across the moors, wading the River Arkraig, an overnight tactical harbour and the finale of attacking Arkraig Bridge. The final day before Pass Out was not dissimilar to now long-forgotten school sports days of inter-Troop tests – drill, barrack room inspection, assault course, short-distance speed marches, a regatta and 'milling' in which the contestants wore boxing gloves, except that the Marquis of Queensbury Rules were ignored. On completion of the course, men were posted to the Commando Holding Unit where they learnt additional skills before being posted to a Commando, except that No. 10 (Inter-Allied) Commando men returned direct to their Troops.

After attending the commando course, the 1st Marine Rifle Commando Company was attached to No. 2 Commando at Ayr for further training, and as an immediate battle casualty replacement after the commando raid on St Nazaire. On 29 June, seven officers and forty-five Dutch under the command of Captain Mulders, thirty-seven direct from Achnacarry, went to form 2 (Dutch) Troop; and a French detachment commanded by Lieutenant Charles Trepel, who had completed the course, arrived at Troon to wait for Lieutenant Colonel Lister and his party. They were accommodated in Portland and Auction Halls. Born in Odessa to Czech parents who moved to Germany about 1917, and then to Paris in the mid-1930s, Trepel had been commissioned into the artillery. Escaping from internment in Spain, he signed up as a ship's stoker in Barcelona and reached England via Gibraltar in September 1941.

On 14 July, Bastille Day, the French, still wearing their FNFL naval caps, paraded at Wellington Barracks, London. Then, three days later, wearing their Green Berets sporting a red and white hexagonal badge incorporating the Cross of Lorraine and retaining their naval ranks, they arrived as 1 (French) Troop and styled themselves the 'Fighting French Troop'. On being told that the Troop was to be based at Criccieth in North Wales, close to the rugged mountains around Snowdon, Kieffer took over the George Hotel next day as a temporary HQ until the requisitioned house, 'Llety', was ready. The Dutch moved to Porthmadoc where Troop HQ was established in the Blaenau Ffestiniog Railway Station. Twelve days later 4 (Belgian) Troop raised their flag in Abersoch Yacht Club.

On 24 July, Captain Bryan Hilton-Jones (Royal Artillery), a Welsh Cambridge languages graduate, arrived with eight Czechs previously attached to No. 1 Commando for training to form 3 (British) Troop, and established his HQ at Aberdovey. The only person in the town who officially knew of the make-up of the Troop was the police officer, PC Davies. Hilton-Jones was an expert climber who had honed his hobby while serving with C Troop, No. 4 Commando, which had set the standard for climbing and winter warfare. On 15 August, four days before the Czechs took part in the Dieppe raid, as we shall see, Acting Captain Coates met with Lieutenant Colonel Williams, the Combined Operations Security Officer and Captain Lee (Intelligence Corps) at the War Office to discuss expanding the Troop to Eastern Europeans, in particular Jews, and methods of interviews. When the summons for alien volunteers was circulated, Captains Coates and Hilton-Jones began the first of a series of three rounds of interviews on 20 August at the Grand Central Hotel, Marylebone in London and by 10 September, they had assembled forty-four volunteers at No. 10 Pioneer Corps Training Centre in Bradford to undergo training until 12 November, before being sent to Achnacarry. The selection included veterans of the Spanish Civil War and former French Foreign Legion. Since a large number of Pioneer Corps in a single front line unit could betray its origins in the Alien Companies, the men were badged in one of several Home County infantry regiments, including the Queen's Own Royal West Kent's, East Kents (Buffs), Royal Sussex and Hampshires. If they served with another Commando, they sometimes wore the insignia of that unit. Later, pre-Achnacarry training was shifted to Aberdovey. On 12 January 1943, Captain Coates held a fourth round of interviews. By now, the nomenclature X favoured by Churchill had quietly been dropped. In spite of the suggestions of the Jewish chronicler Martin Sugarman in his research that the Troop was 3 (Jewish) Troop, this firstly misrepresents its structure as a British Army sub-unit, unlike the other Troops in 10 Commando which reported to their national headquarters, and secondly those who served in it included British officers and their batmen, a Dane, a Russian, a Swiss and several stateless men. While it is accepted that a high percentage of the Troop originated from Germany, Austria and Eastern Europe, as Staff Sergeant 'Colin Anson' wrote to the author in 2007: 'We volunteered for ideological reasons to oppose a detestable and intolerant, brutal dictatorship, and not for any narrow religious or racist reasons. Assimilated Jews in Germany and Austria were not Jews who happened to live there, but Germans and Austrians who happened to be Jewish – good citizens and pillars of their communities.'

Since German security officials were assumed to know the personal details of Jews who had left Europe before the war, and therefore reprisals were a possibility, in order to protect their identities and background, the men adopted British names, and created false personal histories and military careers so that if they were captured, they had a chance of surviving interrogation. On 25 November 1941, the Nazis had introduced the Reich Citizenship Law in which German Jews and those in the occupied territories were denied their citizenship, and those serving with enemy armed forces were categorized as traitors. The problem for 3 Troop was that the 1929 Third Geneva Convention demanded prisoners of war must give their correct name. In a Parliamentary question in the House of Lords on 16 March 1943 on the naturalization of foreigners serving in the Armed Forces, Lord Cranbourne emphasized that it was unfair that stateless foreign servicemen and women had no one to represent them in the event of capture, while Britons had the full weight of the British Empire behind them. It was therefore felt the aliens should be given as much protection as possible.

In this account, adopted names in quotation marks will be used. Otto Wasserman took the name 'William Watson' from Sherlock Holmes's assistant. Nathan became 'Eric Howarth' and Paul Honig became 'Paul Streeten'. Peter Tischler adopted the name 'Paul Terry'. Claus Ascher became 'Colin Anson' because an Anson aircraft flew overhead during his interview. For those changing their names, while there was pleasure that they would be receiving new paybooks, there was some concern when it was noted that those whose regimental numbers begun with '1380' betrayed their origins in the Pioneer Corps. The issue was resolved with the men allocated new numbers. Mr Dawkins, the War Office Casualty Department civil servant looking after No. 10 (Inter-Allied) Commando administration, was one of very few people who knew their real identities.

On 14 August, the seventy-one Belgians, five more French and twenty-seven more Dutch went to Achnacarry. On 30 October, six Norwegian officers and eighty-four men commanded by Captain Hauge arrived at Nevin near Pwllheli, as 5 (Norwegian) Troop, and were followed five days later by the five officers and eighty-six Poles, forming 6 Troop at Fairbourne where Captain Smrokowski placed Troop HQ in the school.

The exiled commandos were amazed not to be accommodated in barracks but in billets and it was not long before friendly relationships were being forged. Some landladies complained to Captain Smrokowski that 'our Polish boys' were going home tired, and not eating and sleeping enough. Some billeting families took their responsibilities seriously. Otto Hess had joined No. 3 AMPC Training Unit at Richborough and went to France with 165 Pioneer Company. In 1942, he joined 3 (British) Troop with Private 'Robert Kent' but, beset by ill-health, was forced to leave. By 1944, he was a lieutenant in the General Service Corps and when he was reported missing on a SOE mission to Yugoslavia, his next of kin, the Giles family of Mary Tovey, Devon sent several letters asking what happened to him, but with no result.

The assembly of 10 (Inter-Allied) Commando was celebrated on 20 October with the opening of the Melting Pot Club in Harlech by Lieutenant General E.C.A. Schruber CB DSO, who commanded Western District. The Troops also had their favourite pubs and formed Troop clubs. The Poles were noted for their raucous parties. On 5 December, Vice Admiral Auboyneau, Commander-in-Chief FNFL inspected 1 (French) Troop and presented French awards for the Dieppe raid. Petty Officer Balloche had already been presented with the Military Medal by Lord Mountbatten. Sport was a vital element of promoting team spirit with inter-Troop football matches helping the Commando to select a team that defeated the Dutch Brigade in January 1943 three goals to two at soccer – a notable scalp.

On 12 November, Captain Hilton-Jones and forty-three members of 3 (British) Troop left for Achnacarry, to be followed on 5 December by the Norwegians, with five officers and 74 Poles. When Lieutenant Colonel Lister visited the Poles, he shouted, 'As your commanding officer, I greet you!' As was the custom in the Polish Army, the Poles replied, 'We greet you, Colonel!' When Lieutenant Colonel Vaughan bid them a good morning, they would reply, 'Good morning, teacher!' On 13 February, the Poles moved from Fairbourne to Caernarvon. By now, they had a Troop newspaper.

On 16 November 1942, the Norwegians were the third Troop in action when Lieutenant Harald Risnes, Sergeant Rostoen and ten soldiers joined 12 Commando and Motor Torpedo Boat (MTB) flotillas raiding Norway from bases at Lerwick. 12 Commando had been formed from Irish units on 5 August 1940 and generally remained outside the Special Service Brigade by providing small teams to support large commando operations. After its involvement in the St Nazaire raid, it divided in two with 'Northforce' raiding the Norwegian coast and the other raiding France in Operation Forfar. On 4 December 1942, Corporal 'Bentley' and Private 'Miles', of 3 (British) Troop, joined the Small Scale Raiding Force (SSRF) as linguists. The SSRF was a raiding force under the direct command of Lord Mountbatten and operated from the SOE's *Maid of Honour* Force as Station 62. Never more than fifty strong, raiding parties landed in small groups from the ship, as it was believed small groups were difficult to detect. It was the SSRF raid on 3 October 1942 on Sark, and the shooting of a German prisoner in crossfire, that led to Hitler's notorious Commando Order that all 'commandos operating in uniform or not, whether escaping from the battle or not, will be destroyed to the last man'. Both men returned to Aberdovey on 30 March 1943 shortly before SSRF was disbanded the following month. On 14 April 1943, seven Frenchmen and seven 3 (British) Troop were detached to No. 12 Commando for training for raids across the Channel.

No. 10 (Inter-Allied) Commando also trained with other units. On 24 October 1942, the Dutch provided 'enemy' for a local Home Guard unit defending a pillbox covering a beach near Harlech, while a week later on Exercise Vin Rouge, 1 (French) Troop carried out an opposed landing and attacked 2 (Dutch) Troop defending a wood. On 12 January 1943, on Exercise Spitfire, 3 (British) and 6 (Polish) Troops tested their speed to a 'crash out' that an enemy force had landed. On 19/20 February, the Commando, less 3 (British) and 5 (Norwegian) Troops, attacked the Guards Armoured Division Administration Area near Oxford on Exercise Longford.

Captain Coates ran the first intelligence course on 7 December 1942 at (Llanwilli) Harlech, in which Troops each sent an officer, a sergeant and three junior ranks to establish their Troop Intelligence Sections, except for 3 (British) Troop, which sent a lance corporal and three privates because they lacked officers and senior ranks. This was followed on 8 February when Coates ran an intensive course concentrating on German Army training and tactics, and was concluded with a test on enemy uniform recognition, rank nomenclature and weapons. A week later, Major R. Hartley and Captain Williams, from the School of Military Intelligence, instructed 3 (British) Troop as part their Advanced Intelligence training. Lieutenant Colonel Lister was still not sure how the Troop should be deployed – individually or in small detachments, but was veering towards offering them to the Special Service Brigade as detachments of interrogators, interpreters and translators backed up by a good knowledge of the enemy. When the Commando moved to Eastbourne in April 1943, training continued with the third intelligence course at Brighton Library on 21 June, and then a week later, the Intelligence Training Centre, Cambridge ran a course for Troop Intelligence Sections.

Building on the basic demolition at Achnacarry, the first commando demolition course was held at Harlech on 28 September 1942 and a second course followed on 13 July 1943 at Eastbourne. Curriculum included the technical and practical application of destroying railways, machinery, boilers, lock gates and fuel storage tanks, as well as gaining skills driving trains and boring holes. Explosives included Guncotton, Plastic Explosive, which could be moulded, and Cordtex, which could be wrapped around trees and railway lines. Pole charges of four Hawkins No. 75 grenades fixed to a frame were useful for 'mouseholing' between houses. Tubes, 10 to 12 foot long, packed with explosive known as Bangalore torpedoes were used to breach beach and field defences. On 14 January 1943, Troop Mortar Sections of a sergeant, a corporal and two privates attended a 3-inch mortar course. In action, two bombs were usually carried by each man in the Troop and deposited in a dump. Sections also had 2-inch mortars. Snipers, usually one to each Sub-section HQ, were trained with the No. 4 Lee Enfield rifle fitted with a Mark III No. 32 Telescope and learnt to stalk and identify enemy uniforms. On 20 January 1943, Troop signallers attended a Commando Signals course at Blaenau Ffestiniog, the 2 (Dutch) Troop HQ. By 1942, Commandos had been issued with the No. 46 Wireless Sets for Troop communications. The No. 46 offered speech and Morse transmissions, was supposedly waterproof for up to a minute's immersion and had a range of up to 50 miles, providing the signallers sited the antenna to its best advantage. One commando officer claimed it was unsuitable for use behind or close to enemy lines because it gave a 'most dreadful squealing noise'. It was heavy, weighing between 24lb and 33lb, and the storage life of the batteries was short. No. 68 Wireless Sets provided Troop rear links to Commando HQ.

Others learnt to drive jeeps, 15cwt trucks and water bowsers. Part of Troop HQs included two despatch riders using War Department Birmingham Small Arms Company (BSA) M20 motor cycles. Lance Corporal Pierre Boulet of 4 (Belgian) Troop was killed when his motorcycle crashed near Swindon. Troops also formed up their Medical Sections and sent men on courses with the Royal Army Medical Corps. This included Private 'Griffith'. Born Glaser, he accompanied his German doctor father to the Spanish Civil War on the Republican side and had picked up sufficient medical knowledge from his father to be appointed a 3 Troop medical orderly.

In preparation for raiding operations, in mid-April, Captain Coates was sent to find a suitable base along the South Coast between Bexhill and Bournemouth, and recommended Eastbourne. Commando HQ moved into the requisitioned 'Engedi' in Upper Avenue while the Troop HQs took over Roborough School. The men, as usual, were billeted, mostly around Woodgate and Ringwood Roads. A Mrs Wade initially accommodated some Norwegians and discovered that they were fond of fish, but was able only to give them tins of sardines. When they left for Lerwick in the autumn of 1943 most of their billets were taken up by 3 (British) Troop. It seems that the naturally inquisitive landladies, wondering about their Germanic-speaking tenants with English names, found tantalizing clues as to their identities – a name in a book, conversation in their first language. One English boy noted that they sometimes disappeared for 'exercises', only to appear a few days later, quiet, very tired, dirty and got undressed from their soaking wet clothes in the garden. Several exiled commandos married British women, for instance Private Gubbels of the Dutch Troop married Sybil in Cardiff in January 1943.

The assembly of the Commando at Eastbourne allowed Lieutenant Colonel Lister to mould his unit. Underneath the Union flag at the top of the flagpole outside Commando HQ flew the ensign of the duty Troop. International rivalry soon led to competition among the Troops to be the best turned out. On one occasion when the French were the Duty Troop at Harlech, the guard commander, a corporal, paraded his Guard outside Commando HQ and waited for Lieutenant Colonel Lister to inspect it. When Lister did not appear at the appointed time, the corporal dismissed the Guard declaring that he was sure that his watch was right and that if the Colonel did not believe that he had carried out his duties correctly, then he would march the Guard to Criccieth, there and then. Inter-Troop competitions in camp, on the ranges, on training and in weekly football and other sports fostered a fierce regimental spirit. The Poles were noted for the quality of their military etiquette, turnout and discipline, and the

Norwegians, Dutch and Belgians for their relaxed approach. Fortunately, there were sufficient enlightened officers at Combined Operations who did not insist on conformity to British military culture and philosophy. Commando HQ issued instructions in English and Troops were expected to adhere to them. How it was achieved was inconsequential.

On 2 June, No. 10 (Inter-Allied) Commando paraded as a complete unit for the only time, a complicated affair with the orders given being translated into six languages and then each Troop carrying out its national drill movements, the most flamboyant being the French. Lister then gathered the entire Commando in the Winter Gardens cinema and gave a rousing speech on the need for his disparate unit to adopt a 'togetherness' approach. This was no easy task, with several languages and cultures, French aloofness and unfamiliarity with British cultures causing the worst problems. The French then became involved in a fight with French-Canadians in a pub, not for the only time, and next day several Frenchmen were noted on parade swathed in bandages applied by Major Hodges and his medics. Two days after the parade, the school was machine-gunned by a Focke Wulf 190 and a lorry hit, no doubt a welcome card, but too much of a coincidence to be coincidental to their arrival.

Soon after No. 10 (Inter-Allied) Commando had moved to Eastbourne, 70 Frenchmen, mostly from the 2nd Marine Rifle Battalion, which had been disbanded in Lebanon, and others who had escaped from Occupied France, formed into 8 (French) Troop under command of Lieutenant Trepel. With two Troops, Lieutenant Kieffer formed a small Battalion HQ and appointed Sub Lieutenant Alex Lofi to take command of 1 (French) Troop.

A member of the Troop was Seaman Maurice Chauvet. Formerly a gun-layer on a French cruiser, he was in Algiers when the French surrendered and refused to fire when the fleet was attacked by the British at Mers-el-Kebir. Demobilized and sent back to Paris in January with a large group of French sailors, a German Army band welcomed them as heroes. Chauvet decided to escape to England and reached Marseille where he signed up as a deckhand. En route to Dahomey and with the ship close to Gibraltar, Chauvet and two Norwegians threw a dinghy over the side and started rowing, but they were 'rescued' by a Spanish patrol boat and sent to Seville military prison. At the end of November, the Norwegian consul secured the release of the Norwegians but Chauvet was transferred to the infamous Miranda de Ebro prison camp, which was full of prisoners from the International Brigade, anti-Fascist detainees and others picked up trying to reach Gibraltar. In spite of the appalling conditions, Chauvet formed a Rover Scout troop and over the next two years, its members survived incarceration. By early 1943, the Spanish realized the Allies would win the war and released most of its detainees, including Chauvet. Boarding a steamer bound for Casablanca, he was again arrested, this time by the Allies. On release, he volunteered to join the Free French forces and arrived in Greenock on 6 June 1943, 883 days after he had left his parents in Paris.

Lieutenant Lofi, Troop Sergeant Major Pinelli and twenty-four men arrived at Spean Bridge station on a bleak day in mid-1943. Huddled in their greatcoats and aghast at the bleak Scottish moors, Lofi drew a chuckle when he demanded a return ticket to London, however their sense of humour disappeared when told that they would be marching the 7 miles to Achnacarry House. Most were relatively recent arrivals in Great Britain and some were still suffering from the effects of malnourishment. Captain Donald Gilchrist, the Commando Depot Adjutant, accompanied the Frenchmen on their 14 miles in two hours speed march. Soon after half-way, he noted that the stronger men were carrying the rifles of those in distress, but at least the Troop was marching as a squad. Gilchrist noticed that Seaman Chauvet was limping badly, oblivious to his surroundings, and watched, as the Troop reached the final flat ground, Chauvet miss the corner and plunge over a grass bank into a ditch. Two Frenchmen grabbed him, shook him out of his zombie state and coaxed his rubbery legs to the rifles ranges where he saw Chauvet gingerly remove his boots to reveal a mass of congealed blood. The Depot Medical Officer concluded that Chauvet had completed the march suffering from a carbuncle.

In April, Sergeant 'Lane' was selected to attend a 148 Training Brigade Pre-OCTU course, the first soldier from the Commando to be considered for commissioning. Returning on 25 July as a second lieutenant, he was appointed the 3 (British) Troop Second-in-Command.

On 31 July, the Commando again divided into three forces for amphibious training at Plymouth. The first course had been in February when the Commando divided into three groups for watermanship training at the Combined Operations base HMS *Tormentor* at Hoe Moor, near Warsash on the River Hamble. Although many of the Poles were parachute-trained before joining the Commando, the other Troops sent men to the Central Parachute School at Ringway. On 2 August, the Commando suffered its second non-battle fatality when Private Duffy (East Lancs), who was batman to Captain Coates, was killed when his parachute failed to open. Coates suggested that at thirty-six years, Duffy should not have been jumping. On 14 October, Coates handed over to Lieutenant Maidment and joined 30 Commando. A conscientious objector when the war broke out, he later joined SOE and was parachuted in to Hungary with a small group of officers when its government proposed to surrender if the Allies reached Budapest before the Germans. However, he was captured and after enduring a brutal interrogation, surrendered to a Soviet patrol during the siege of the city. He later became a diplomat and a lecturer at the University of East Anglia. He died in 2007.

Training continued with exercises at Thetford training area for fighting in woods at Grimes Graves camp. The charismatic Belgian, Viscount Captain de Jonghe, joined No. 10 (Inter-Allied) Commando as a liaison and signals officer, and doubled up as the public relations officer.

Daily Orders No. 244 for Friday, 26 November 1943 signed by WO ERF Langley for 'Commanding No 3 Troop, 10 Commando Det' show a relatively typical training programme:

- 09.00 Muster parade - dress denims, berets and personal weapons
- 09.10 Beach range - firing and grenade throwing
- 10.30 Lecture - hasty demolition
- 11.15 Signalling
- 12.00 Issue of NAAFI supplies
- 13.40 Outside (Littlehampton) Railway Station – dress denims, high-necked sweaters, berets, SV boots, battle jerkin, Field Service Marching Order, map, torches, compasses, ropes, line and pitons will be drawn. Haversack rations for tea and supper to be taken. Abseiling at Seaford, infiltration, demolition, map reading scheme – Seaford to Littlehampton. Approx time of return 02.00 on Saturday. First parade on Saturday for men taking part on the scheme is 10.30.

By mid-1943, No. 10 (Inter-Allied) Commando had been in existence for a year and consisted of eight Troops, each one, unlike British Commandos, displaying individual national characteristics. On 7 January 1943, the *News Chronicle* suggested that No. 10 (Inter-Allied) Commando was an 'experiment embarked on with some trepidation, for it involved the creation of an unknown quantity, bringing together men of all nationalities with, in some cases, conflicting points of view'. This was accurate.

While British Commando officers had to deal with regimental rivalries, Lister and his officers had moulded these foreign soldiers into a Commando fraught with problems – the spectre of occupation and distance from home for the exiles; various national customs and traditions, politics, military philosophy, rank structures and insignia; and language difficulties including different dialects within the Troops. The French, humiliated and angry at their 1940 defeat, did not take kindly to orders from anyone but their own officers, and certainly not their hereditary enemies. The main problem for some Troops was that there was no battle casualty replacement programme, as there was with the other Commandos, and it was only when the French, Belgians and Dutch liberated their countries could they replace casualties.

Chapter 4

Dieppe

By the spring of 1942, the German offensive on the Eastern Front had weathered the winter and with a Soviet military collapse apparently imminent, Chairman Josef Stalin pleaded for an offensive in the West to reduce the pressure. Although supported by the Americans, some senior US officers believed that unless an offensive was executed quickly, they should concentrate on fighting Japan in the Pacific. Public agitation resulted in mass rallies in Trafalgar Square, London and New York supporting Stalin during April. The pressure on Prime Minister Churchill to present a threat to force the existing German divisions to remain in France was considerable.

Originally conceived in April 1942 by Combined Operations as Operation Rutter, a division would seize a German-held port on the Atlantic coast and hold it for a day during which intelligence would be gathered and enemy facilities destroyed. Dieppe was chosen because the town had a long beach positioned between two dominating chalk headlands with beaches at Puys and Pourville that could be used to develop a beachhead and, being just 69 miles from Newhaven, was within fighter cover. Although air recce had shown considerable artillery assets, the town was thought to be weakly held.

The Dieppe sector was defended by the 302nd Infantry Division (Lieutenant General Konrad Haase). Largely horse drawn and equipped with captured Belgian, Czech and French weapons, the Division was understrength and had a large number of conscripts from Occupied Europe replacing Germans sent to the Russian Front. Dieppe was converted into a strongpoint surrounded by barbed wire entanglements that ran from Puys around to Pourville. The defence was entrusted to the 571st Infantry Regiment supported by field and anti-aircraft artillery, and engineers with reserves available from the LXXXI Corps reserve, 676th Infantry Regiment from the 332nd Infantry Division, and Army Group D of the 10th Panzer Division and SS Leibstandarte Adolf Hitler Infantry Brigade. On the flanks were:

- 216th 'Goebbels' Coast Battery of three 17cm and four 105mm guns, about 450 yards inland near the village of Berneval-le-Grand.
- 813th 'Hess' Coast Battery consisting of six 5.9-inch guns about 1,000 yards inland, spread over about 10 acres in a built-up area behind Varengeville. Behind the position were two light anti-aircraft guns on flak towers. The battery observation post was near a lighthouse.
- 2/770 'Hitler' Coastal Battery of four 5.8-inch guns inland near Arques-la-Bataille.

The Outline Plan developed by HQ South-East Command (Lieutenant General Bernard Montgomery), after he had been delegated the task by GHQ, Home Forces, ran as follows:

Object
1. Intelligence reports indicate that Dieppe is not heavily defended and that the beaches in the vicinity are suitable for landing Infantry and Armoured Fighting Vehicles at some. It is also reported that there are forty invasion barges in the harbour.
2. It is therefore proposed to carry out a raid with the following objectives: (a) Destroying enemy defences in the vicinity of Dieppe. (b) Destroying the aerodrome facilities at St Aubin. (c) Destroying the (Luftwaffe) Radio Direction Finding (i.e radar) stations, dock and rail facilities and petrol dumps in the vicinity. (d) Removing invasion barges for our own use. (e) Removing secret documents from the Divisional Headquarters at Arques-la-Bataille. (f) To capture prisoners.

Intention
3. A force of Infantry, Airborne troops and Armoured Fighting Vehicles will land in the area of Dieppe to seize the town and vicinity. This area will be held during daylight while the tasks are carried out. The force will then re-embark.
4. The operation will be supported by fighter aircraft and bomber action.

The troops were to be drawn from South East Command and when Montgomery was pressed for British and Canadian units, he felt that for unity of command, a Canadian formation would be preferable, and accepted the suggestion of Lieutenant General Henry Crerar, who commanded the 2nd Canadian Corps, that the 2nd Canadian Infantry Division (Major General John Roberts) should be selected. The Parachute Regiment was to seize the 'Hess' and 'Goebbels' batteries. Operation Rutter was approved by the CIGS on 13 May and training began near Bridport on the Isle of Wight.

Included in the order of battle were five Czechs from 3 (British) Troop. Privates 'Bate', 'Rice' and 'Smith' were attached to Royal Marine Commando A with orders to break into Dieppe town hall and remove files and anything of intelligence value. Privates 'Platt' and 'Latimer' were attached to a detachment from 2 Field Security Section, Canadian Intelligence Corps, which was part of HQ 4 Canadian Infantry Brigade and consisted of two sergeants, a Canadian sapper section and three Churchill tanks, with orders to search the German HQ and look for items of intelligence interest, in particular, a newly issued German respirator. To what extent the Czechs were connected to a SOE major who landed at Dieppe is not known.

Lieutenant Goronwy Rees had recently been commissioned into the Welsh Guards from the Royal Artillery and was posted to GS (Intelligence) at GHQ, Home Forces when he was instructed to collect a sealed parcel from a sergeant underneath the clock at Victoria Station and then give it to the Czechs. He neither received nor asked for a receipt. Travelling to Bridport, he met up with 3 Troop but was unable to distribute all the contents, which turned out to be thousands of francs for the Resistance, because not every Czech was available. He assumed they were on some sort of suicide mission. Rees was later unearthed as one of the Cambridge Apostles communist spies along with Donald McLean, Kim Philby and Anthony Blunt.

Operation Rutter was scheduled for 4 July, however poor weather persisted until the 6th. Orders were then issued that the landings would take place on 8 July, the last day for a suitable tide and moon. But the concentration of shipping around the Solent had not gone unnoticed and, at 6.15am on the 7th, four German bombers raided the anchorage and damaged two Landing Ships Infantry, the *Princess Astrid* and *Princess Josephine Charlotte*. This necessitated the transfer of the Royal Regiment of Canada on board to other ships. Much to the disappointment of the keyed-up assault force, Royal Navy commanders then assessed that the weather was still not suitable and Operation Rutter was cancelled.

Increasing Soviet and American political pressure on Churchill forced Combined Operations to re-examine Operation Rutter on 14 July and a planning committee approved an option that it would be less weather dependant if the parachute drop was replaced by commandos. The option was approved by the CIGS on 20 July and so Captain John Hughes-Hallet, who was the Combined Operations Naval Adviser, ordered the naval force to disperse to harbours along the south-east coast, to make it less easy to be detected, and that the first assault waves should cross the Channel in landing craft, as opposed to transferring from LSIs. Five days later, on 12 August, when the Allies decided not to open a Second Front, Churchill met Stalin in Moscow to tell him so.

The plan was renamed Operation Jubilee. From north to south:

- No. 3 Commando was to land on Yellow Beach One 8 miles from Dieppe at Point Berneval and Yellow Beach Two at Belleville, and silence the 'Goebbels' coastal battery.
- The 2nd Canadian Infantry Division was to land in four separate locations:
  - 4th (Ontario) Canadian Infantry Brigade on Blue Beach at Puys.
  - 4th Canadian Infantry Brigade on Red Beach and White Beach in a frontal assault on Dieppe. In support were Churchill tanks of 14th (The Calgary Regiment) Armoured Regiment.
  - 6th (Prairie Provinces) Canadian Infantry Brigade to land on Green Beach at Pourville.
- Royal Marine A Commando was to attack German assault shipping in Dieppe harbour.
- No. 4 Commando, including fifty US Rangers, was to land on Orange One and Two 6 miles from Dieppe and neutralize the 'Hess' coastal battery.
- In addition to the Czechs, No. 10 (Inter-Allied) Commando provided fifteen men from Sub Lieutenant Vourc'h's Section in 1 (French) Troop:
  - No. 1 Group of Vourc'h and six men attached split between the Canadian brigades.
  - No. 2 Group of six men commanded by the former French Foreign Legion Petty Officer de Wandaleur attached to No. 3 Commando (Lieutenant Colonel Dunford-Slater).
  - No. 3 Group of three men commanded by Petty Officer Balloche attached to No. 4 Commando (Lieutenant Colonel Lord Lovat (Lovat Scouts)).

The French mission was to act as interpreters and liaison officers with the civil population, gather information on German activities and encourage suitable Frenchmen to return to England. All were instructed to remove the 'Commando' and 'France' shoulder titles from their battledress jackets and not to wear their French naval caps.

The assault force of about 4,960 Canadians, 1,075 British and fifty men from the 1st US Ranger Battalion were to be landed by the Royal Navy and evacuated once the operation was complete. Motor launches were to escort the assault landings ships. Landing Craft Support (LCS) provided direct-fire support to the beaches while a force of destroyers provided naval gunfire support. Unfortunately, ship-to-shore communication was poor and so they resorted to shelling opportunity targets. The forty-six fighter, fighter-bomber and bomber squadrons were opposed by an understrength Luftflotte 3, which covered northern France, The Netherlands and Belgium. RAF support during the landings was disappointing, particularly as the Luftwaffe had been prevented from taking off by a mist over northern France.

On 15 August, German interception of Allied communications in southern England suggested that transmissions were more secure. They also noted that recce flights over the Dieppe area had increased. Everything seemed to indicate a major operation and after analysing moon, weather and tidal forecasts, HQ Fifteenth Army issued instructions for special alerts during the periods, 27 July to 3 August, 10 to 19 August and 25 August to 1 September. The understrength reserve 302nd Infantry Division was brought up to full strength with 2,503 reinforcements, most straight from basic training.

The 225 ships set sail after dark on 18 August. At 1.27am on 19 August, a signal sent by Commander-in-Chief, Portsmouth from radar supporting the Coast Regiment, Royal Artillery, warned of a small German convoy sailing south from Boulogne. A second warning was signalled at 2.44am but it seems that not every ship received it. The twenty-three Eureka landing craft carrying No. 3 Commando left Newhaven escorted by Steam Gunboat (SGB) 5 (Commander D.B. Wyburd) in the van with Flak Landing Craft 1 (Flak LC) and Motor Launch (ML) 346 astern, all grouped into Group 5. The former was armed with twin 4-inch guns. On the left flank were two destroyers, the Polish *Slazak* and HMS *Brocklesby*. The French detachment was divided with de Wandaleur on Eureka 3 containing twenty commandos commanded by Major Young, the Commando Second-in-Command. Chief Petty Officer Montailleur and Leading Seaman Cesar were on Eureka 14 and Ropert and Errard on Eureka 15. Cesar had also served in the French Foreign Legion. At 3.47am, about 15 miles off the French coast, the German convoy of five small coasters and three escorts clashed with Group 5 and in a frantic battle illuminated by star shells bursting over the landing craft, Flak LC 1 set one ship on fire and sank another. But four landing craft were damaged and four sunk. The surviving boats, included Eureka 15, turned for England. Four had already returned to England during the night with engine trouble. The two destroyers thought that the gunfire was German coast artillery. When Lieutenant Colonel Durnford-Slater then agreed with Commander Wyburd that the No. 3 Commando landings should be abandoned, they were unaware that seven landing craft were heading for the coast determined to press on with the attack. Six, including Eureka 14, escorted by ML 346, contained 120 men from 2, 5 and 6 Troops, including the French No. 2 Group, and several US Rangers, commanded by Captain Richard Wills (Duke of Cornwall's Light Infantry). Major General Haase was not expecting an attack and his first assessment was that the clash was another MTB raid on Channel shipping.

When the single Eureka beached on Yellow Two at Belleville-sur-Mere at 4.10am, on time, the commandos breached a barbed-wire obstacle in the gully of the Ciseaux cliff and reached a road where a teenager told them where they were. 'Goebbels' Battery opened fire, the commandos marched inland and met several French near Berneval church, who directed them to the guns. Approaching it through an orchard, Major Young spread his men into two long lines 200 yards short of the guns and, with magnificent impertinence, they hindered the gunners by sniping at them from 5.10am until 7.45am in the expectation that the remainder of No. 3 Commando would arrive. By 8.00am, with ammunition low and under fire from mortars, the commandos withdrew to Yellow Two where they embarked in landing craft.

At 5.10am, the six landing craft beached on Yellow One in broad daylight, the commandos breaching the beach defences and a minefield until they were pinned down by a machine gun which Corporal Halls silenced with a bayonet charge. Still under fire from machine guns, Captain Willis advanced up a gully along a road from the beach, with mounting casualties. Chief Petty Officer Montailleur was much in evidence. When they tried to fan out from the road as it topped the gully, they clashed with a counter-attack organized by Major von Blücher, commander of the 302nd Anti-Tank Battalion, who had assembled cyclists from 3/570th Infantry Regiment and a company of divisional engineers. As the Germans drove the commandos back down the gully, Willis and Montailleur were badly wounded and Lieutenant Edward Loustalot, of the 1st (US) Rangers, was the first American to be killed in Europe during the Second World War. Reaching the beach, the commandos found that the tide had ebbed and the landing craft were either stranded on rocks or badly damaged. When they finally ran out of ammunition, the eighty-two surviving commandos were forced to surrender.

The approach to the Orange Beaches by No. 4 Commando, which had embarked on the LSI *Prince Albert* at Southampton, was helped by the flashing lighthouse. The plan was for the eighty-eight men of Group 1 (Major Derek Mills-Roberts (Irish Guards), the Second-in-Command, to provide fire support while the 164 men of Group 2 (Lord Lovat) assaulted the Hess Battery after a flanking march. The three French commandos joined C Troop, along with four Americans.

Since Mills-Roberts was expected to land below two 8-foot gaps in the cliffs, precision navigation was provided by Lieutenant Commander Mullinueux. About 3 miles from the coast, the escorting MTB left and purred into the darkness. A mile short of the beaches, a flight of Brewster Buffalos roared overhead and the lighthouse lantern was doused as anti-aircraft flak opened up. Fearing that the Buffalos might have compromised the operation, the landing craft closed inshore below the high chalk cliffs and motored about half a mile north until, at 4.30am, Mullinueux identified Orange Beach One. Crunching onto a small pebbly beach, No. 1 Section (Captain David Styles (Lancashire Fusiliers)), from C Troop (Captain Robert Dawson (The Loyal (North Lancashire) Regiment), which was specially trained for cliff assault, reported that the eastern gully was a tangle of barbed wire while the western one was suitable. Two Bangalore torpedoes dislodged the entanglements and, with C Troop leading, Group 1 emerged near some villas that formed Vasterival-sur-Mer. The sun was rising. Part of the Troop formed the defensive perimeter, while the remainder, accompanied by Leading Seamen Rabouhans and Taverne, searched several houses for Germans between the beach and 'Hess' Battery. Encountering an elderly Frenchman in his nightshirt, Mills-Roberts was explaining, with Petty Officer Balloche translating, that they were British soldiers when a girl appeared and asked if they were going to shoot her father. When the guns opened fire at targets out to sea, Mills-Roberts dispensed with the search and advanced on the battery. Pushing through waist-high undergrowth of a wood, when a Frenchman appeared with a basketful of eggs, Balloche refused his kind offer, at least for the moment. As the Group emerged into fields and topped a small rise, they were about 100 yards from the battery perimeter fence and quickly came under fire from a 20mm flak gun on a tower, and from machine-gun and mortar fire. Occupying several houses and a barn about 250 yards from the battery, and with others in a strip of wood, C Troop paralysed the flak gun by killing three successive gun crews. Bren gunners and snipers effectively dominated three machine-gun positions. US Ranger Corporal Franklin Coons is credited as the first American to kill a German soldier in the Second World War. When Troop Sergeant Major Jimmy Dunning brought his two 2-inch mortars into action, his second bomb detonated a pile of cordite near No. 1 Gun. It was 6.07am. Meanwhile, part of A Troop had cut the telephone line from the lighthouse and protected the right flank of Group 1 by seizing the crossroads east of St Marguerite from a German infantry company known to be in the village.

The five LCAs and one LCS carrying part of Group 2, also guided by the lighthouse, landed at Orange Beach Two across the River Senne north of Quiberville. A Troop breached the heavy wire by laying coconut matting and chicken netting over the wire and reached the seawall under fire. Using tubular ladders, Lieutenant Vesey and his section climbed the cliff and assaulted two pillboxes, one of which turned out to be empty. The remainder of Group 2 backed off the beach and, landing about 150 yards to the north, were led by B Troop around a marked minefield and doubled along the flooded banks and high grass surrounding the Senne. Disappointed when 'Hess' Battery opened fire, they were encouraged by Group 1 opening fire. On reaching Blancmenil Woods, B Troop fanned right and reached a position overlooking the battery after filtering through an orchard. F Troop, on the left, advancing down the road toward the corner of the perimeter, shot up thirty Germans preparing to attack Group 1 from a farmhouse. Alerted to the threat from their rear, the Germans reacted vigorously and Captain R.G. Pettiwood, the F Troop officer, was killed. When a sergeant who took command was also killed, Captain Pat Porteous (Royal Artillery), who was the liaison officer between the two groups and had just been wounded in the hand by a German he had killed, rallied the Troop and reached a ditch behind the gun emplacements. He was awarded the VC for his gallantry and leadership. When Mills-Roberts learned that Group 2 was forming up in the woods behind the battery, at 6.25am he tightened fire control onto specific targets. Three minutes later, a flight of 129 Squadron Hurricanes raked the battery but were chased away by Focke Wulf 190s. At 6.30am, a Very light soared into the morning sky from Lovat and B Troop rushed the buildings, while F Troop attacked the guns.

When Group 2 advanced, Petty Officer Balloche accompanied Major Mills-Roberts and his batman, Corporal Smith, along the road to the battery, which was still firing. German snipers were picking off commandos. The diminutive Balloche hauled himself up the parapet of the battery but fell off the top and was confronted by a German who he shot. While demolition teams set about destroying the six guns, he searched Le Haut, a hamlet close to the battery, for documents. A large Union Jack was raised to indicate to the RAF that the battery had been captured.

Shortly after, a flight of Messerschmitts had flown over the battery and A Troop reported they had ambushed a patrol probing from St Marguerite; Lovat ordered No. 4 Commando to withdraw. As A Troop were withdrawing, an elderly Frenchwomen, who had watched the ambush, gave each man eggs, which were scarce in England. Lovat then summoned his medical officer to triage the twenty casualties assembled in Hotel de la Terrace. Thirteen commandos were missing, of whom nine were known to be wounded. The first to be evacuated were the two dead officers and ten other ranks, and those seriously wounded commandos who could withstand a rigorous journey to England. Several needing urgent hospital treatment were left behind. With several prisoners acting as stretcher-bearers, the Commando was guided to Orange Beach One by C Troop. When the commandos reached Vasterival-sur-Mer, Balloche bid farewell to the elderly Frenchman and his daughter, both clearly delighted by the destruction of the battery but anxious about reprisals. The wounded were slowly manoeuvred to the beach, which was under inaccurate mortar and rifle fire from the lighthouse. This was returned by the Mortar Section, the Bren group and the LCA naval gunners. Smoke generators previously placed at the top of the cliff helped to screen the re-embarkation. The three French helped take the wounded 200 yards across rocks to a boat ferrying them to the LCS. By 8.15am the evacuation was complete and the landing craft arrived at Newhaven at 5.45pm. Twelve of the wounded were back on duty within two months.

Meanwhile, the 2nd Canadian Infantry Division was in trouble. The approach by the Royal Regiment of Canada to Blue Beach was delayed by navigational difficulties and surprise was lost when the landings were made in daylight. Confined to the narrow beach by two German platoons, attempts to blow holes in the wire and move into shelter in buildings beyond the seawall or under the cliff were defeated. The landings by the Essex Scottish on Red Beach and the Royal Hamilton Light Infantry on White Beach momentarily stunned the defenders until the hail of fire from pillboxes, machine-gun and support weapon positions and caves so dominated the beach that the Canadian engineers were unable to destroy beach obstacles. At 5.30am, LCTs landed twenty-eight of the thirty Churchills of the 14th (Calgary) Army Tank Regiment; however their steel tracks were unable to grip the shingle. Large stones entering the suspension led to broken track pins and thrown tracks. Some progress was made in the area of the semi-demolished casino, however exploitation was hampered by large concrete anti-tank walls across the streets. Most tanks resorted to immobile pillboxes.

Privates 'Platt' and 'Latimer' both arrived on the beach in Tank Landing Craft 124 carrying HQ 4 Infantry Brigade. 'Platt' was about to follow a Churchill down a ramp at about 6.05am when someone shouted that it was too dangerous to land and the landing craft backed off. Returning to the beach three hours later, when 'Platt' again followed a tank down the ramp, German anti-tank and machine-gun fire was directed at the ramp, he was badly wounded in the leg and dragged into the relative shelter of the landing craft. 'Latimer' joined the Canadian Intelligence Corps sergeants and engineers swimming from the galley aft and, then sheltering in a hollow of pebbles, watch the chaos of burning tanks and infantrymen suffering from intense frontal and crossfire. One sapper tasked with cutting barbed wire returned to the landing craft wounded. Only 120 yards inland were rocks and sand, but the small group was pinned down and so they edged back to the water, and, swimming to a tank landing craft, found that its steering gear was wrecked. Its naval crew managed to rig a line to a motor launch and the landing craft was towed back to Newhaven, arriving at about 9.30pm. Three Canadian Intelligence Corps were killed and five captured. At Green Beach, 6 Infantry Brigade landed in good order but astride the River Scie, nevertheless the Canadian advance stalled when a determined German counter-attack led to the German seizure of the bridge at Petit Appeville and prevented further advances inland.

When Haase reported that Dieppe itself was under attack, he had every reason to be confident. The landing at Puys had been contained and by 6.00am, the situation in Dieppe had improved with the Canadians stalled on the beach. At 7.15am, LXXXI Corps informed Fifteenth Army that the operation could be handled locally, nevertheless, Commander-in-Chief West, Field Marshal von Rundstedt, alerted army and air force commands in case the landings were a diversion.

Offshore, Major General Roberts had received conflicting and sketchy reports on the situation at Dieppe and committed his floating reserve, Les Fusiliers Mont-Royal from 6 Infantry Brigade, to break the deadlock. However when their landing on Red Beach at 7.04am was shattered, he instructed Lieutenant Colonel Phillips and his Royal Marine Commando to reinforce White Beach. Transferring from the French fast launches known as *chasseurs*, that had brought the Royal Marines from England, as Phillips emerged from a smoke screen and saw the chaotic situation ashore, he signalled the landing craft to go about into the shelter of the smoke screen, but he was killed. The majority of the landing craft swerved away, nevertheless it does seem that several beached, including, it appears, those with three 3 (British) Troop Czechs and the SOE major.

By 9am, Captain Hughes-Hallet and Major General Roberts agreed to evacuate the troops at 10.30am, however this was slipped to 11.00am so that the Cameron Highlanders of Canada, who had made reasonable advances, could withdraw and that air support could be arranged. Under intense fire, the landing craft, covered by naval gunfire support, embarked several hundred Canadian troops before the beaches became impossible to defend. At 12.20pm, orders were given to stop the evacuation as the beaches were virtually in enemy hands. By 2.02pm, the Germans ceased firing.

Of the 2nd (Canadian) Division, the 4 and 6 Canadian Infantry Brigades were virtually destroyed. Of the seven major units, only Les Fusiliers Mont-Royal returned with its commanding officer. During the nine-hour battle, their losses as prisoners were more than the Canadians captured during the eleven months of fighting in North-West Europe and in the twenty months in Italy from 1943 to 1945.

So far as No. 10 (Inter-Allied) Commando is concerned, of the Czechs, when Lieutenant Rees later wrote that he 'imagined that they disappeared on the beaches of Dieppe and that their names ... never appeared in an official record', he was correct. Although 3 Troop killed in action are listed in Commonwealth War Graves Commission records by their noms de guerre and their regiments, there is no record of 'Bate', 'Rice' and 'Smith'. According to a former Troop member, Peter Masters, 'Bate' was killed while 'Rice' and 'Smith' were captured and never heard of again. The SOE major was killed. They were probably executed when German interrogators established their true identities. Badly wounded, 'Platt' became the Troop storeman. No. 3 Commando lost 120 men, killed, wounded and taken prisoner. Petty Officer Montailleur and Leading Seaman Cesar were posted missing, believed killed. Montailleur is thought to have been executed when the Germans found out he was Free French.

In its attack on the 'Hess' Battery, that No. 4 Commando carried out a near perfect attack was reflected in February 1943 when the War Office published *Notes from Theatres No. 11 – Destruction of a German Battery by No. 4 Commando during the Dieppe Raid*. This outlined the planning, training and execution of the raid and includes the list of sixty-two cap badges represented in the attack. Interestingly, No. 10 (Inter-Allied) Commando is not mentioned, although the US Rangers are.

Great effort was made by the principal proponents of Operation Jubilee, including Mountbatten and Churchill, to justify the failure and high losses as necessary for the development of the Second Front. Mountbatten, who had lost his ship off Crete, was inexperienced in amphibious operations, however, valuable lessons were learnt, in particular that attacking a defended port is less favourable than landing on wide beaches. The raid showed that Allied naval forces were approaching the point from which major landings could be managed, but there was a need for dedicated command ship and also specialist engineer equipment to clear beach obstacles. This led to the establishment of the 79th Armoured Division and its range of 'Funnies' engineer armour. Air superiority was vital. If combined operations were to succeed, unity of command and political goals and objectives welded into a coherent plan were critical.

Chapter 5

Raiding Norway

On 16 November 1942, Lieutenant Harald Risnes and eleven Norwegians travelled by train and ferry to Lerwick in the Shetland Islands and were attached to 'Northforce' for Norwegian MTB operations against Occupied Norway. The commandos had been specially selected because they were familiar with the target area around Bergen. Raiding Norway stemmed from Lord Mountbatten's opinion that operating in the sub-zero temperatures was crucial in keeping the Germans off balance. Part of 12 Commando, 'Northforce', was using the pretence of being Royal Marines engaged in acclimatization training to cover its role. (See Appendix 4 for a summary of 10 Commando raiding operations.)

MTBs 5 and 6 were the first two Norwegian warships commissioned into the Free Royal Norwegian Navy and operated from Felixstowe with Coastal Forces 11th MTB Flotilla protecting convoys, and on search and rescue. In late 1940, MTB 6 was abandoned in heavy weather and when, in July 1941, MTB 5 was destroyed by an explosion in Dover Harbour, five MTBs were issued to form the Norwegian MTB Flotilla, Portsmouth. In 1943, the Norwegians were issued with six 105-ton Fairmile Class D MTBs – the Dog Boats. Manufactured from plywood, carrying 5,000 gallons of fuel and stable in rough weather, their top speed was 34 knots. They were formidable boats with four power-mounted, twin .50-inch Vickers machine guns, four .30 Vickers machine guns mounted on the bridge wings, two 20mm Oerlikons and four 18-inch torpedo tubes. They could also lay mines and drop two depth charges. Ship's companies usually numbered about thirty-one buccaneering young men suited to unconventional sea warfare divided into two watches, and could accommodate about fifteen commandos. Deployed to the Coastal Forces Base, HMS *Fox*, at Lerwick in November 1942, the between six and eleven Fairmiles that formed the 30th MTB Flotilla was later renamed 54th (Norwegian) MTB Flotilla. Winter storms and long nights gave the Dog Boats the best opportunity to slip unnoticed into fjords, hide in caves or lay in wait draped with camouflage nets in inner leads. From the start of operations in November 1942 until the end of the war, Norwegian MTBs sank twenty merchant ships and seven warships in 161 sorties.

Within the week, on 22 November, a commando patrol on board a MTB in a hide south of Bergen scampered back to Lerwick chased by a German patrol boat. Five evenings later, another MTB anchored in a small fjord north of Bergen was guarded by two commandos in a house overlooking the fjord to prevent locals from warning about its presence. Next day, several fishing boat and rowing boat crews were taken on board to be debriefed on German activities. The commandos then used a fishing boat to meet a loyal Norwegian and recced the fjord. Bad weather prevented a quick return to Lerwick for a further day. In December, Second Lieutenant Kaspar Gudmundseth and eight men were transferred to 14 Commando to support long-distance raids against Luftwaffe bases and German installations above the Arctic Circle. The Commando consisted mainly of Canadians and American Indians who specialized in using canoes and kayaks to enter harbours and plant limpet mines – a risky venture in winter weather and North Atlantic storms.

Storms prevented any sorties from Lerwick for a month, and then during the night of 22/23 January 1943, in Operation Cartoon, Captain Risnes and ten men joined 52 'Northforce' commandos to attack the Lillebo mine on the island of Stord, near Leirvik, which was providing the Germans with 160,000 tons of pyrite annually. Although he knew it would raise morale in Norway, the Norwegian General Staff refused to give Risnes and his men permission to wear Norwegian insignia on their uniforms on the grounds that British insignia should be worn to prevent the Germans assuming that the Norwegian authorities had sanctioned operations and thereby avoid retaliation. The signatory of the letter, Captain Tronstadt, also ordered that no Norwegians were to be brought back because for every one that left, forty could be shot. Unlike the French at Dieppe, the ruling was strictly enforced and the Norwegians were given false identification papers – if captured or separated, they were instructed to return to England by Sweden.

Embarked on seven 54th (Norwegian) Flotilla Dog Boats, the force left Lerwick about 8.00am in good weather visibility, however three hours later, Senior Naval Officer, Scapa Flow signalled the MTBs that their sighting by German aircraft had been confirmed by signal intercepts. The flotilla commander attempted to confuse the shadowing aircraft by altering course several times and arrived off Lillebo about ninety minutes behind schedule. Although the coastal defences had been alerted, when the MTBs were spotted entering Selbjorn Fjord by an observation post, the message sent to the Stord garrison was misunderstood and the alert state relaxed sufficiently that most soldiers went to bed. At 10.45pm, three MTBs entered Leirvik but found no shipping to attack until they were returning and sank a 2,000-ton ship. The German shore defences were shelled.

The commandos on the four remaining MTBs were divided into two Forces lettered A to D of eleven men each, sub-divided into Groups 1 and 2.

At about 12.15am, Group 3 of Forces A and B landed at the Boat House jetty at Leirvick on the northern side of the tip of the fjord, about 2 miles from the mine. With each man each carrying 50lb of explosives and his own equipment, the commandos reached it within about thirty minutes and put it out of action for a year. Corporal Trygve Sigvaldsen was the B Group demolition leader. He also advised several watching civilians to go to bed immediately. When the German commander heard the explosions, he demanded that the local doctor use his car to drive him and two German soldiers to the mine. The car was ambushed by a cut-off group at 2.05am and a tree was blown up across the road. When the Bren gunner opened fire at the car, the doctor ran toward the commandos shouting that he had been forced to drive. The German officer and a soldier disappeared into the dark woods and sniped at the road block. The second soldier was killed near the car. Under increasingly accurate sniping, a commando crawled to the car and recovered a briefcase and two Norwegian weapons.

At 1.00am on 24 January, the MTB carrying Group 2 approached Sagvåg quay and, as a diversion, fired two torpedoes at ships, one of which was hit with a massive explosion. However, the Germans opened fire, Corporal Ivar Haga was killed and two commandos, waiting on the foredeck to land, were wounded, as were several sailors. Nevertheless, the MTBs came alongside the jetty and although it was about 25 feet above the deck, Group 2 clambered ashore. Force C destroyed communication equipment while Force D prepared the pyrite silo near the jetty for demolition. By 3.00am, the entire raiding force had assembled at the jetty where the commandos and three prisoners dropped 30 feet onto the MTB decks. Twenty minutes later, the two Groups met outside the fjord at 3.40am, and en route to Lerwick the navy gunners on two MTBs shot down an attacking Ju-88 light bomber.

On Operation Crackers, a small force from Nos 12 and 30 Commando, supported by three Norwegians led by Sergeant Bjornstad, landed at Stokkevaag on 24 February and established an observation post at Gjeteroy to watch the Tungodden and Sognsjoen anchorages. An attack on two German observation posts was cancelled because of bad weather and so the commandos remained in the area for a week observing the German defences, identifying future landing sites, investigating the activities of Quislings and collecting copies of German-controlled newspapers. This was the last raid by Lieutenant Risnes and his detachment, and he handed over to Acting Captain Daniel Rommetvedt and sixteen men before returning to Wales on 12 March.

At 1.50am next day in Operation Brandy, Rommetvedt and six men in a Norwegian-led 'Northforce' operation were ferried to a hide on the north-west coast of Skorpa Island near Floro where MTBs 619 and 631 were draped with camouflage nets. During the day, two commandos established an observation post overlooking Floro and questioned several fishermen. When they reported that three ships escorted by an armed trawler had entered the harbour, at 11.00pm, the MTBs dropped mines in the main channel, torpedoed two ships and watched the third hit a mine. MTB 631, with Norwegian commandos on board, was then hit, nevertheless, even with the trawler bearing down on them, its crew and commandos were transferred to MTB 619, which reached Lerwick in a gale late on 16 March. Three days later, one of two Norwegians on a 'Northforce' raid near Stadt that clashed with a German patrol on a bridge between two islands, shot one of two Germans killed. In the raid planned for 10 April, seventy men from 'Northforce', Captain Rommetvedt and nine Norwegians were to attack the Rugsundoy convoy anchorage in Nordfjord, south of Stadt, however it was protected by a coastal battery, which the commandos were tasked to attack. During the crossing, a MTB developed engine trouble and when the flotilla arrived at Skorpa, locals mentioned that the Germans had placed an observation post on the lee of an island off which the MTBs intended to lurk before attacking. When this was reported to Lerwick, permission was refused for an alternative target.

By spring, the evenings were lengthening and when reports from Norway suggesting that the raids were resulting in an increase in German reprisals, they were postponed. The Norwegians had impressed the British commandos and Captain Fynn recommended Corporal Trygve Sigvaldsen for the MM for his coolness in Operation Cartoon and on two other raids. The Norwegians then rejoined No. 10 (Inter-Allied) Commando at Eastbourne.

In preparation for more winter operations, in September, Lieutenant Olav Gausland and twenty-three commandos joined the Norwegian MTBs in 'Timberforce' in which MTBs ambushed shipping from hides while the commandos went ashore and protected them from landward attack. On occasion, agents were delivered and collected. On 9 February 1944, Captain Hauge took the balance of his Troop of seven officers and fifty-nine men to Lerwick. February was a busy month. On the 10th, while returning from an operation, MTB 625 was abandoned in a gale at the

Skerries with the commandos losing equipment. From the 11th to the 14th, seven commandos embarked on MTBs 653 and 627, while the patrol boat *Molde* raided the Kristiansand area and torpedoed the mail steamer *Irma* and the steamer *Henry*. The Germans were fully alert to these MTB sorties and by April 1944 the raids had ceased, however there were no immediate plans for the Norwegian Troop to return to Eastbourne.

Chapter 6

2 (Dutch) Troop in the Far East

By the beginning of 1942, the Japanese had overwhelmed the British and Dutch colonies in the Far East and were tolerating a Vichy French Government in precarious control of Indo-China. In 1943, Brigadier Wingate's first Chindit campaign penetrated into Burma but an attack down the Arakan coast stalled in front of vigorous Japanese defences. In Europe, the tide was slowly turning in favour of the Allies, however apart from a few French, Norwegians and 3 (British) Troop, the exiled commandos were restless, as were their military missions in Great Britain, because unlike the British Commandos, the units were not being presented with opportunities to get to grips with the enemy. In mid-1943, Lister began to receive demands for his Commando. With the Norwegians committed to raiding their homeland, both French Troops were warned for an invasion of Corsica in Operation Crossbow and a raid on U-Boat pens in Lorient in Operation Coughdrop, neither of which happened, and then for raiding Occupied France and Belgium. In August, Lister warned 2 (Dutch), 6 (Polish) and 7 (Yugoslavian) Troops for deployment to the Mediterranean. There was also delight when Leading Seaman Cesar reappeared.

When his No. 3 Commando group were captured on Blue Beach at Dieppe, Cesar joined some Royal Regiment of Canada sheltering at the base of a cliff at Puys until at midday when they surrendered. Cesar then overheard British officers being asked by German interrogators if there were any Free French, and discarded his battledress jacket, pompom and wedding ring. During the afternoon, the prisoners were marched to Enverneu and herded into a building before being loaded onto a train bound for Germany next day. Cesar and some French-Canadians levered the slat from a window, he climbed onto the buffers of the wagon and jumped as the train passed through a wood. Picking himself up, he heard three rifle shots and began running just as a machine gun opened up. Sheltering with a family near Aufar, Cesar walked south to Spain, but became exhausted and was taken in by another family who nursed him back to health. He then went to the family home at St Quentin where his brother provided him with false papers. Eventually, Cesar joined a group of shot-down Allied airmen on an escape line and was picked up by a SOE-operated boat flying a Portuguese ensign from a beach at St Pierre-sur-Mer, and was taken first to Gibraltar and then England.

After Lord Mountbatten departed for India to command HQ South East Asia Command (SEAC), an early consideration was to invade the occupied Dutch colony of Sumatra as a springboard to attack Malaya and Singapore from Ceylon. 2 (Dutch) Troop joined 3rd Special Service Brigade (Brigadier D. Nonweiler), which consisted of Nos 1, 5, 44 and 45 (Royal Marines) Commandos, and were earmarked to join Fourteenth Army. In March, 2 (Dutch) Troop consisted of five officers, twelve SNCOs and sixty-seven JNCOs and privates, commanded by Reserve Captain Jan Linzel. Captain Mulders, who had suffered a serious broken arm, had returned to Princess Irene Brigade after three officers had told Lieutenant Colonel Lister that they had lost confidence in his leadership but not his administrative ability. Several commandos were disinclined to serve in the Far East and thus when the Troop embarked on the troopship SS *Strathaird*, the detachment numbered three officers, ten SNCOs and forty-five other ranks.

During the voyage through the Mediterranean, the first by an Allied convoy en route to the Far East, the Dutch helped man the air defence machine guns, nevertheless German aircraft bombed the ship carrying Nos 1 and 42 (Royal Marines) Commandos and was so badly damaged that she put in to Alexandria for lengthy repairs. On 15 January 1944, the Troop disembarked at Bombay and was taken by train 110 miles south to Poona, and then 40 miles by road to the transit camp outside the village of Ked Goan. While the Dutch were acclimatizing in Spartan conditions and training in jungle warfare, they provided close protection when Mountbatten visited the camp. He dismayed them by reporting that at the Teheran Conference on 20 November, the principal Allied strategy was the invasion of Europe and therefore the Sumatra option was cancelled. During an interview with Mountbatten, Linzel was authorized by him to visit the Dutch Korps Insulinde in Ceylon to examine a role for the Troop in operations against Occupied Dutch East Indies.

The Korps Insulinde, like 2 (Dutch) Troop, was an offspring of the Princess Irene Brigade. In January 1942, Lieutenant Colonel L. van der Berge, of the Royal Dutch East Indies Army, assembled 150 volunteers from the Brigade as an advance guard for operations in the Dutch East Indies. The Japanese conquest of Java meant the detachment got no further than Ceylon where the Dutch Government decided the men should undergo commando training to support Netherlands Special Organisation (NSO) guerrilla operations against Occupied Dutch East Indies. The NSO was the equivalent of SOE and was commanded by Major Mollinger. By 16 May, forty soldiers were deemed capable for irregular warfare. On

1 August, the NSO was renamed the Korps Insulinde and moved into a camp at Laksapatiya, south of Colombo, where it trained in an area of marshes, hillocks and lakes not dissimilar to Achnacarry, except that it was tropical jungle. On 16 December, the Korps carried out its first operation when the Dutch submarine O-24 landed eleven commandos, led by Mollinger, on the west coast of North Sumatra to collect information from the loyalist village headman at Troemon, only to find that he had been replaced by a collaborator. Linzel arranged for a sergeant and four soldiers to train the Korps in commando techniques.

By the spring of 1944, the fighting in Burma was reaching a climax as the Fourteenth Army clashed with the Japanese Twenty-Ninth Army on the borders of India around Imphal and Kohima. By the end of March, XV Corps (Lieutenant General Phillip Christison), in a brutal encounter with 55th Division on the right flank, held a line along the road from Maungdaw to Buthidaung. Christison's strategic objective was to seize Akyab Island and use its airfields to gain air superiority over central and southern Burma. However, the 'wet' monsoon was approaching and although he captured the port of Maungdaw, the Japanese vigorously defended the two tunnels with roads to Buthidaung. He decided to threaten the Japanese lines of communication south by landing 3rd Special Service Brigade at the kampong of Alethangyaw, well to the south of XV Corps, and harass Japanese rear areas. The small kampong was separated from the beach 500 yards to the west by dunes and scrub. The surrounding paddy fields and tracks were relatively hard and the watercourses marshy. Two shallow rivers flowed into the sea north and east of the village and 5 miles to the east were the Mayu Hills.

When Reserve Lieutenant Martin Knottenbelt, who was commanding the Troop in Linzel's absence, heard about the operation, although he was told by Brigade HQ there was no role for them, nevertheless he secured places for five volunteers. Competition was keen and the lots resulted in Knottenbelt and Sergeant van der Veer joining No. 44 (Royal Marines) Commando, while Corporal Ubels and Privates Blatt and Nick de Koenig joined No. 5 Commando. The volunteers travelled to Cox's Bazaar at the end of February where Ubels was then hospitalized with malaria.

At about 11.30pm on the night of 10 March, No. 44 (Royal Marines) Commando landed north of Alethangyaw in three waves from leaky old landing craft and fought a confusing battle in and around the thin-walled thatched huts, and although harassed by snipers in the mangrove, had ejected the Japanese by morning and established two bridgeheads across the waist-deep River Tong. A patrol recceing a Japanese logistic route of a road and tracks inland clashed with an enemy patrol, and the Japanese, hoping that a patrol would rescue him, dragged a captured wounded Royal Marine into a paddy field where he lay all day in considerable pain.

Commando discipline held firm and the casualty was recovered by villagers during the night. When English-speaking Japanese signallers interfered with radio messages from Brigade HQ, Knottenbelt was used to transmit important messages, in Dutch, to van der Veer with the Commando, however, the Japanese were wily enough to plot where the two Dutchmen were and mortared their positions. After dusk next day, the Commando advanced toward the Mayu Ranges to attack Japanese logistic routes, but the jungle was thick and the men so heavily laden that the only practical route was to wade along the Tong. By dawn, the Commando was in the standard defensive box in the jungle and patrols fought several sharp actions until late in the afternoon of 12 March. By then the danger of being isolated and the difficulties in evacuating casualties to Alethangyaw were making life extremely difficult for a small unsupported force and the Commando withdrew, leaving banzai-yelling Japanese to attack an empty position.

No. 5 Commando, earlier than originally planned, landed south of Alethangyaw in terrain from which it would be easier to attack the logistic routes, receive supplies and evacuate casualties. The ground to the south was paddy and reached by a small bridge over a stream. When the Japanese realized that they were confronted by another landing, they shelled and mortared the kampong and launched several attacks from three hills to the south, causing several casualties. Nevertheless, with a Troop left in Alethangyaw, another Troop ambushed the coast road and attacked tracks in the Mayu Range. Privates Blatt and de Koenig were also used to transit messages in Dutch.

After an attack on the mortar pits in the kampong, a 100-strong fighting patrol, which included Lieutenant Colonel Shaw's Tactical Commando HQ, was crossing the bridge en route to reinforce the Troop in the mountains at night, when the scouts saw three columns of Japanese crossing the paddy, apparently intending to cross the bridge and attack the kampong. 'Lie down' was whispered along the line. De Koenig was at the rear while Blatt was with Commando HQ in the centre. De Koenig saw the Japanese slip into the stream bed and creep towards them. Although the order had not been given to fire, he quietly drew the pin from a grenade, and watched the Japanese approach the bridge and the centre of the column. Suddenly, a shot rang out and a confusing short-range battle developed. De Koenig threw his grenade into the stream bed and, while trying to find Commando HQ, joined up with a commando shooting from behind a low mud wall bordering a paddy dyke. All around were Japanese soldiers, including one carrying a sword, however they did not make much effort to search the area, possibly concerned about being attacked from Alethangyaw. Meanwhile, the Japanese, hindered by casualties, were driven back across the paddy fields. The two commandos crept back to

Alethangyaw and were on its outskirts until daybreak, when they found several seriously wounded needing treatment.

During the fighting, Private Blatt was badly wounded by grenade fragments. Regaining consciousness and alone in the darkness with a large hole in his chest, he injected himself with morphine, and in the darkness stumbled along a sandy track toward Alethangyaw. He was resting against a mud wall when he saw two Japanese, supporting a third, approach him and sit the wounded man next to Blatt. After the two soldiers had disappeared into the night, Blatt heaved himself over the wall, walked towards the sound of breaking surf, reached the beach and staggered along it until he fell into a stream bed, which he followed until he met two commandos in the darkness. One turned out to be de Koenig who then carried the semi-conscious Blatt to safety. De Koenig left Blatt with the British Commando and returned to his Troop in the kampong where he briefed a Troop Commander about the wounded. By now contact had been lost with Lieutenant Colonel Shaw's column. As there were Japanese still lurking in the area, and most of the Commando were outside the perimeter, orders were issued that the wounded were not to be collected until daybreak. However de Koenig, who strongly believed that there were no Japanese in the area, led a small patrol to recover the wounded he had found.

After being relieved by the Royal Marines, No. 5 Commando moved to Maungdaw where, on 23 March, it fought several actions and attacked a Japanese position overlooking an artillery position at bayonet point. Two days later, de Koenig accompanied a boat patrol near Codsusa. Meanwhile, Private Blatt was evacuated to hospital in Calcutta and rehabilitated in Secunderabad, near Hyderabad, where he was joined by Sergeant van der Veer, who had contracted malaria. By April, Fourteenth Army had forced the Japanese back across the River Chindwin. To plugs gaps in the defences, 3rd Special Service Brigade was moved to protect Silchar, an important communication junction to the west of the vital logistic centre at Imphal, just as the monsoon broke. In May 1944, Knottenbelt and Ubels took part in several recces in Assam.

By now, when it was obvious in the Troop that there was no role for the Dutch in the Far East, morale slumped, particularly as the invasion of Europe seemed imminent. After an interview with Captain Linzel, on 16 May, Mountbatten signalled Major General Laycock, who was now Chief of Combined Operations, that after two years of training and with little prospects in the Far East, the Dutch were disillusioned. He emphasized that the Troop had been guaranteed discharge six months after the liberation of Holland and, if they saw no action, then undoubtedly most, if not all, would take the option. He nevertheless still believed there was a role for the Troop in the liberation of the Dutch East Indies, particularly as Linzel believed the Princess Irene Brigade could bring the Troop to full strength. In the meantime, Mountbatten gained agreement with the Dutch Minister for the Colonies to authorize the Troop to return to Europe, which was agreed. Knottenbelt and de Koenig were both awarded the Dutch Bronze Cross for their gallantry.

It was not until 15 August that 2 (Dutch) Troop was back in Eastbourne. Apart from the five in Burma, the Troop had not seen any action and several men wondered if their applications to join the Commandos were worthwhile, particularly as the Princess Irene Brigade was taking part in operations in Europe.

Chapter 7

The Mediterranean
Nos 3 (British), 4 (Belgian) and 6 (Polish) Troops

By 1943, when British and American forces met at Protville, in Tunisia, on 8 May and trapped the Axis forces into surrender, Allied planners finalized the invasion of Sicily in Operation Husky. XXX (British) Corps was to land on the Pachino peninsula, south of Syracuse, with 5th and 51st Highland Divisions, fresh from the fighting in North Africa, sailing from Suez to rendezvous with 1st (Canadian) Infantry Division en route from Great Britain. II (US) Corps would land to the left of the British.

Protecting the flanks by knocking out coastal batteries were Nos 40 and 41 (Royal Marines) Commandos. Attached to the Commandos were members of 3 (British) Troop with the Germans, Lance Sergeant 'Patrick Miles' and Private 'Colin Anson', joining No. 40 (Royal Marines) Commando at Troon. When 'Anson', a Berliner, was posted to Liverpool, he was billeted with the Clelands, who had shown such kindness that he gave their daughter, Pat, as his next-of-kin. When he went overseas, Mr Dawkins, the War Office civil servant looking after No. 10 (Inter-Allied) Commando, rented a room from the Clelands. 'Anson's' father had died in Dachau in 1937 after being handed over to the Gestapo by the police for making anti-Nazi remarks. Sergeant 'Paul Streeten' and Private 'George Franklyn', also both Germans, joined No. 41 (Royal Marines) Commando at Irvine in Scotland.

After a vigorous Combined Operations training programme, on 28 June, No. 40 (Royal Marines) Commando embarked on the MV *Derbyshire* with orders to secure the western flank of the beachhead. No. 41 (Royal Marines) Commando filed on to MV *Durban Castle* with a role to attack a coastal battery at Punta Castallazzo covering the beaches. Both ships had been converted into LSIs fitted with twenty-two LCAs. Controlling Commando operations was a Special Service Group Tactical HQ commanded by Brigadier Laycock, the brother of Peter, the Second-in-Command of No. 10 (Inter-Allied) Commando.

Early on 8 July, a few miles north of Malta, the convoys met in fine weather, but this freshened during the afternoon into a fierce onshore wind. By the evening, deteriorating sea conditions threatened the landings, however, after dark, the wind abated and the seas calmed to a strong swell; the LCAs were lowered from their davits and swung inboard for the troops to board direct from the top deck. Fully manned, they were electrically lowered and cast off as soon as they hit the water. With the moon full and H-Hour timed for 2.30am, as a naval launch guided the landing craft toward the dark shores split by bombing and fluttering flares, the blunt bows of the LCAs dug into the dark swell and threw sea water over the troops crouching in the well deck, where it slopped about with the vomit of seasickness. Overhead aircraft of 1st Airborne Division rumbled to their targets. After three weeks cooped up in a ship and most not used to bouncing around in landing craft, the commandos had just one wish – to land; however some coxswains lost site of the launch and it was not until 3.00am, after a two-hour approach, that No. 41 (Royal Marines) Commando approached the beaches. Inexperienced coxswains failed to form line abreast for the assault and others seemed reluctant to beach their boats. One waterlogged LCA sank and some Royal Marines swam ashore. Eventually 'Prepare to land!' and then the crouching commandos, their legs stiff and in soaking uniforms, stumbled down the ramp and waded ashore to rocky shelving beaches west of Punta Castallazzo. Some of the wireless sets and mortar bomb fuses were damaged by the soaking. Opposition was limited to a few shots from lacklustre Italians.

Sergeant 'Streeten' savoured the spicy aroma of the Mediterranean as he waded ashore with P Troop. When the order was given to get off the beach quickly, the lack of determined opposition and an inability to recognize expected features, because the Commando were in the wrong place, confused many Royal Marines. Lieutenant Colonel Manners, who had been at Dieppe, ordered the Commando into a sandy hollow while he and his officers sorted out the confusion and eventually the Troops advanced, bayonets fixed. Only at one position was there a brisk battle in which two officers were wounded and then the Commando seized the objectives allocated to No. 40 (Royal Marines) Commando. When P Troop reached their objective, a machine-gun post on the air photographs turned out to be a derelict shed. 'Streeten', as ordered, returned to Commando HQ.

No. 40 (Royal Marines) Commando landed in the wrong place and intermingled with the Canadians, nevertheless by 5.00am, it had overrun its objectives, which turned out to be machine-gun posts, during which three officers and six other ranks were killed, and thirty-seven wounded. Generally, the Italians defended their positions until the Royal Marines closed with them and surrender was the preferred option. By 9.00am, the Commando was in contact with the Seaforth Highlanders of Canada and in the correct position. During the day, both units had moved about 2 miles inland and then after two days consolidating their positions were withdrawn to a beach rest area.

At the end of July, both Royal Marines Commandos in Catania were waiting to land at Scaletta next night to cut the railway from Catania to Messina when the town was shelled. Sergeant 'Streeten' and his team were setting up a prisoner reception and interrogation centre at the railhead at the railway station when it was hit by an 88mm shell. Lance Corporal 'Franklyn' was also severely wounded and 'Nelson' less so. Waking up in hospital in a Scottish General Hospital in Cairo, doctors did not expect 'Streeten' to live and yet he did, although troubled by shell splinters in his neck, legs, head and arms for the rest of his life, his talent as a long-distance runner abruptly ended. 'Anson' was on board the *Queen Emma* when it was dive-bombed in the harbour. Having survived the first attack, he was helping to lay an injured commando on a stretcher when he was so severely wounded by a splinter embedded in his head from a bomb in the second attack, that the medics on board thought he would not survive. Treated in a Canadian field hospital, he was resuscitated on one occasion and spent several weeks wearing a plaster caste helmet until he was evacuated to hospitals in Tripoli and Cairo. In December 1943, his skull was patched with a piece from someone's else's because the owner 'doesn't need it anymore'. Posted as a postal orderly to an infantry depot near Cairo, he met 'Franklyn', who was recovering and determined to join in the invasion of Europe.

When German forces crossed over to the toe of Italy and were reinforced by experienced divisions from France and Austria, they exploited the rivers flowing east and west, and the spine of the Apennine Mountains, to create formidable defences. On 3 September, the day that Italy surrendered, XIII (British) Corps landed near Reggio Calabria, hoping to draw the Germans south, and then land at Salerno six days later behind their lines, hoping to trap them. Nos 2 and 41 (Royal Marines) Commandos and their 3 (British) Troop detachments faced formidable resistance. Meanwhile Eighth Army landed at Brindisi and Taranto and linked up with the beachhead on the 17th. After the capture of Naples and its port wrecked by expert demolition, the Allied advance to Rome was brought to a sharp halt by the defensive Gustav Line consisting of a series of stop lines on high ground stretching across Italy from north of Naples to Ortona, thereby preventing advance up the Liri Valley, and incorporating the Garigliano and Sangro rivers. The defence was hinged around Monte Cassino and was studded with pillboxes, dug-in tanks and obstacles. Autumn rain flooded the low ground and watercourses.

On 10 September, the seven officers and eighty-seven other ranks of 4 (Belgian) and nine officers and eighty-six men of 6 (Polish) Troops left

Eastbourne bound for the Mediterranean as an independent unit and were accompanied by Captain Lutyens as the Commando Liaison Officer. He took a letter from Lieutenant Colonel Lister to Brigadier Laycock expressing his regrets at losing them. Three days later, the Belgians, on the MV *Athlone Castle*, and the Poles on the SS *Cameronia*, along with No. 9 Commando (Lieutenant Colonel Ronnie Tod), joined a convoy at Glasgow. Disembarking at Algiers on 23 September, the commandos were sent to the Reception Camp P at Birtouta where the abundance of fresh fruit, a rarity in wartime Great Britain, was too much of a temptation and within three days many of the commandos were ill with upset stomachs. Fortunately, Second Lieutenant Boleslaw Switalski, the Polish Medical Officer, obtained medicine from 15th (Scottish) General Hospital and within a week the men were training hard and acclimatizing. The Poles then found another distraction in the Elbiar district of Algiers when they met about 200 families of Poles serving in the Middle East, the first Polish women and children most of the commandos had met since being evacuated from France. Many had been in Soviet prison camps when the Germans overran Poland and, after being released when Hitler attacked Stalin in 1941, had made their way through Eastern Europe to Egypt where General Anders formed the 2nd (Polish) Division. The commandos arranged a dance and a play, and then, when a frail old man dressed in Arab clothes with a Holy Cross around his neck, appeared at their camp turned out to be a Polish missionary who had spent most of his adult life among the Arabs, they arranged a field altar and invited the families and some Polish-Americans from a US unit to celebrate Mass. When he heard about Poles in Algiers, the missionary walked the 25 miles from his house, reading Polish aloud to remind himself of the language – such was the emotion of the occasion that he wept when given the opportunity to use his mother tongue. A jeep loaded with gifts took him home.

On 23 October, Laycock was promoted to Major General and was appointed Chief of Combined Operations when Lord Mountbatten departed for the Far East. When Major General Robert Sturges then formed the Special Services Group to co-ordinate the activities of the proposed four brigades, in November, Brigadier Tom Churchill formed the 2nd Special Service Brigade at Molfetta from the Commandos in the Mediterranean theatre, namely Nos 2 and 9, and 40 and 43 (Royal Marines) Commandos. No. 3 Commando, depleted after Sicily, and No. 41 (Royal Marines) returned to Great Britain. However, it was hinted by Eighth Army that No. 10 (Inter-Allied) Commando was not yet ready to fit into its order of battle.

On 6 November, fifteen men from 7 (Yugoslavian) Troop commanded by Second Lieutenant Tripovic, and twelve men from 3 (British) Troop commanded by Lieutenant 'Bunny' Emmet, arrived in Algiers from

Eastbourne to form the Half Troop that supported 2nd Special Services Brigade operations in the Mediterranean. Emmet was the Commando Administration Officer and had previously served in the RAF and Royal Tank Regiment. Others who arrived were a 3 Troop detachment to support No. 9 Commando commanded by a sergeant. The sergeant was German, had arrived in England before 1939 with his parents and had studied law at Cambridge. Sent to Canada on the *Ettrick*, he first enlisted in the Pioneer Corps where he dug trenches near Bristol and then joined the RAOC preparing rusty weapons for service before volunteering for No. 10 (Inter-Allied) Commando. When linguistic difficulties led to Captain Lutyens, now promoted to Acting Major, being appointed to command of the No. 10 (Inter-Allied) Commando detachments, and also several hospitalized No. 9 Commando, he persuaded Brigadier Churchill that his Troops would be useful to his brigade. On 23 November, the detachment travelled to Phillipeville and then spent five days on the French tramp *Ville d'Or* before landing at Taranto, and then travelling by train and truck to join HQ 2nd Special Service Brigade at Molfetta. On the 5th, Nos 3 (British) and 7 (Yugoslavian) Troops were divided among the Commandos in the brigade, and Lutyens and Emmet returned to Eastbourne, arriving in the New Year.

While No. 9 Commando was at Castello de Rudolfo in Pozzuoli Bay, the sergeant joined Sergeant Brown on a jaunt to Procida Island. It appears that Brown's Italian girlfriend had complained to him that the island authorities were alleging that her father was using explosives to fish, and were intending to confiscate his boat and threaten the family income. The two commandos acquired a boat, and, after kicking in the door of the harbourmaster, threatened a full-scale invasion. After a relaxing and social lunch, the two commandos returned to the mainland.

On 4 December, Brigadier Churchill wrote to Lieutenant General Sir Miles Dempsey suggesting that the Belgians and Poles join his XIII Corps to gain front-line experience. Dempsey replied that since he was held up by the Gustav Line, he was limited to patrolling, nevertheless when Churchill visited Dempsey, he agreed to deploy the Troops with 5th Infantry Division, undertook to review their activities and ensure that they were administered properly. Churchill visited HQ 17 Infantry Brigade at Pescopennataro, nearly 6,000 feet above sea level, and a former pretty ski resort, now dirty and unkempt from the rigours of warfare. From a hotel window, he could see the River Sangro below him with, to the north, the massive hills of the Gustav Line, and learnt that the demolished bridges were covered by the formidable German 1st Parachute Division. By the time both Troops moved up on 13 December, 78th Infantry Division (Major General Charles Keightley) had taken over the Pescopennataro sector. Bitterly cold, deep snow covered the mountain meadows and the Sangro was about 4½ feet deep of uninviting, freezing, mountain water spewing between its banks. Both Troops were placed under the command of the 56th Reconnaissance Regiment at Bojano, whose tactical frontage extended from Villa Santa Maria to Castel di Sangro.

After a short shakedown, 4 (Belgian) Troop, taking with them the German Private 'Harold Kendal' from 3 (British) Troop, was placed on the left flank of 56th Reconnaissance Regiment in San Pietro, a village wrecked by German engineers in order to deny Allied troops shelter 3 miles south of the Sangro. On some walls was scrawled 'Hello, Tommy. Hope you enjoy your winter billets.' A Section (Lieutenant Meny) initially established themselves in tents in the village cemetery, while B Section, also under canvas, moved on to a bleak snowy hillside, however the winter was coldest on record and within days the Belgians resorted to sheltering among the shattered buildings. A wing of the shattered church was Troop HQ. Although the Regiment provided radios for the Troop HQ, there were no section radios because it had few to spare. Damp cloud shrouding the hills reduced visibility to 30 yards, except when sudden exposures for a few minutes revealed magnificent mountain views extending about 15 miles. German patrols were active and at night sentries were doubled; from 6.00am to 7.00am and 6.00pm to 7.00pm, the entire Troop stood to in its defensive positions. The first day was spent observing German activity and then Captain Danloy began a programme of despatching two or three patrols per night, each consisting of an officer and six to ten men, depending on the task, to collect information about the area and enemy dispositions. Tethered yellow RAF rubber dinghies were used to cross the Sangro. White flowing robes worn by local men at funerals were used as winter camouflage.

On 14 December, at 9.00am, Lieutenant Meny, Sergeant Artemieff and Private Wilmotte crossed the Sangro on a recce patrol and returned at 1.00pm, reporting that they had crossed a railway line and had found woods to check but there was no enemy activity. At 4.45, dusk, a ten-man fighting patrol led by Meny set off. Covered by Lieutenant Dauppe with his Bren gun section of Privates Thonet and Seeger, Lance Corporal Beauprez and Private Dellacherie stripped, swam across the icy river and tied a rope to a tree to tether the dinghy. Two at a time, the commandos hauled themselves across, then the patrol crossed the railway and searched a house about a mile north of the river, but still found no sign of enemy activity. After eight hours, the patrol crossed back over the Sangro. On 22 December at 8.00pm, Lieutenant Albert Deton and a seventeen-man fighting patrol crossed the Sangro to capture a sniper who had been firing at the Belgians the previous day. Deton, aged twenty-six, had fought in the Belgium campaign in 1940. With no sign of German activity, the patrol pressed on along a track for about 400 yards and was about to return when someone was heard coming along the track, and then the order 'Halt!' There was a brief burst of firing in the darkness and when Deton ordered a right-flanking attack covered by his Bren gunners, two Germans were seen scurrying through the undergrowth; a third soldier was found badly wounded. But Lance Corporal Marcel Mairesse, who was Deton's batman, was bleeding badly from a wound in the thigh. Carried on a makeshift stretcher along paths slippery with ice, and across the Sangro to the shelter of an abandoned farm, every step was agony for him, however he remained silent. Since the Troop still lacked radios, Sergeant Dedeken made his way to San Pietro, but by the time he returned at 4.00am with Lieutenant van Peperstraete, the Troop Medical Officer, and Father Corbisier, the Chaplain, Mairesse was dead from loss of blood and shock. He was the first Belgian killed in action. Aged twenty-seven, he had fought in Libya with the Free French.

When another patrol crossed the Sangro to recce Carceri, a village badly damaged by the retreating Germans, a house was seen to be occupied and the Belgians invited the Germans to surrender. The subsequent exchange of fire resulted in a German standing in a doorway being killed and Sergeant Count Annez de Toboada being knocked over when a burst of fire from a Schmeisser hit the Thompson magazine loader in his pouch. He later showed Brigadier Churchill his bruised stomach and the damaged magazine. Near the end of the deployment, a patrol 2 miles north of the river encountered a German patrol moving along a track from the south. When both sides opened fire, the Belgians heard the Germans shouting 'Imbeciles, don't fire on your own men!' Men were wounded on both sides.

On 30 December, the Belgians joined three companies of the 2nd London Irish, from 38 (Irish) Brigade, in the village of Montenero, on the extreme left flank of the Eighth Army. The Brigade was part of 78th Infantry Division. When thick snow made it difficult to supply the troops, vital supplies were transported by mules, weather permitting. 'Kendal' learnt the only way to release one from a snowdrift was to dig out each foot separately. On 9 January, the Troop was withdrawn into a divisional rest area at Castelonorato on the banks of the River Garigliano.

When the Belgians moved to San Pietro, 6 (Polish) Troop moved into Pescopennataro on the right flank of 56th Reconnaissance Regiment, taking with them the German Privates 'Marshall' and 'Merton' of 3 Troop, and Corporal Anton Banko and Private Franz Trebizon of 7 (Yugoslavian) Troop. Also determined to stir up the Germans, Captain Smrokowski despatched a recce patrol that night and next day led a fighting patrol across the Sangro to search buildings thought to be used by the enemy. Lieutenant Andrzej Czynski provided fire support. When the patrol came under heavy fire from the buildings and withdrew, the Germans followed and isolated Senior Rifleman Franciszek Bogucki, a Polish-American from

Pittsburgh. Seeing that Bogucki had been wounded in the thigh, Czynski crossed the open ground and carried him on his back to safety. Faced by a determined enemy, Smrokowski withdrew across the Sangro, but Bogucki died at about 10.00pm, after the Poles had reached Pescopennataro.

At about 5.00pm on 20 December, Brigadier Churchill was visiting the Troop when an Italian civilian, who apparently crossed the opposing lines regularly, reported that two Jaeger mountain companies were planning to attack a British battery east of Capracotta during the night of 21/22 December. Claiming the plan was to cross the Sangro at San Angelo del Pesco at about 7.00pm, eject the Poles from Pescopennataro and then capture the guns, the man said that three days earlier he had been asked about British deployments in the Capracotta and Pescopennataro area and had then been press-ganged into guiding them. Eight 25-seat buses had arrived at the German position the previous day and he claimed that several officers had been shown their tasks from the forward mountain slopes. Although this information could not be assessed for accuracy, at 7.00pm, British gunners shelled the St Angelo crossing point, nevertheless within the hour the Poles were attacked from the east by two Jaeger platoons, each about forty strong, and by two more from the west until, by midnight, they were surrounded. Greatly helped by accurate shelling, the Poles held their position and then at 3.00am, after a lull, a heavy attack was beaten back when British gunners brought fire down to within 30 yards of the Polish position. After nine hours of desperate night fighting, at about 5.00pm, with dawn due within a couple of hours, the Germans withdrew. As dawn broke, five Polish patrols cleared the Pescopennataro locality while a 56th Reconnaissance Regiment squadron cleared the area between the village and Capracotta, and checked several approaches to the Sangro without finding any trace of the Germans. Incredibly, the Poles suffered just one killed, Lance Corporal Stanislaw Stadnik, and three wounded. Captain Smrokowski was awarded the MC for his exemplary leadership and Major General Keightley sent this despatch:

> On the occasion of your first encounter with the enemy, I express my thanks to you, your officers and other ranks for a decisive and good fight to keep and retain the position assigned to you. Your service is in accordance with the tradition of the Polish and British Armies, therefore in the name of the soldiers of the 78th Division, I am sending my thanks for a good result of fighting.

It had been a source of some dissatisfaction to the Poles that while the Jaegers ranged far and wide on skis, they were restricted to foot patrolling. Officer Cadet/Sergeant Adam Bachleda was a skier of international recognition and when four sets of cross-country skis were found in an abandoned house, Private 'Kendal' negotiated with the mayor for more skis, bindings and poles. After about two days of training, Bachleda led a ski patrol to a plateau in the Luperian Mountains. Dressed in white funeral robes, the patrol came across several Jaeger mountain troops with a light mortar near a stone hut in deep snow. When they opened fire, the Poles beat a hasty retreat down the mountain slopes, complete with several spectacular falls. As far as can be determined this was the only Eighth Army ski patrol during the Italian campaign.

When 4 (Belgian) Troop joined 2nd London Irish, the Poles occupied San Pietro Avellano, a prospect that filled them with disquiet because the wrecked houses afforded little shelter. At Pescopennataro, they had decent shelter, indeed 'Kendal' sometimes slept on the church altar. His irritable nature made him a most effective interrogator! Heavy snow trapped them on New Year's Day and it was only when Bachleda skied to Capracotta on 5 January 1944 that supplies were dropped by parachute on the 7th and the 9th. Two days later, the Troop was rested in a school at Troia and then trucks took them to the X Corps Reception Camp to await orders, and have their first hot bath in weeks, followed by the inevitable party.

On 28 December, when Brigadier Churchill was instructed by X (British) Corps, which was held up about 20 miles north of Naples by the River Garigliano, to supply a Commando for an amphibious operation on the west coast, he selected No. 9 Commando and moved them to Baia. Operation Partridge was intended to focus enemy attention on the lower reaches of the Garigliano, in the 56th (London) Division sector, while X Corps massed upstream ready to cross the river. Although farmers had built bunds to prevent serious flooding, the low-lying ground was icily soggy and activity was largely confined to patrol clashes. The Germans had strongpoints on Monte Argento about a mile and half north of the estuary, and at a Roman amphitheatre about a mile upriver near a demolished bridge carrying the Appian Way to Rome. In effect, the Germans dominated both banks. Lieutenant Colonel Tod split his force into three:

- Force X – to destroy an enemy post and then defend the bridgehead through which the Commando would withdraw.
- Force Y – to attack Monte Argento.
- Force Z – to attack the post in the amphitheatre.

In support was 2nd Scots Guards, from 201st Guards Brigade, with orders to advance north to the river and dominate enemy positions. 3rd Coldstream Guards was to attack the area of the bridge and prevent German forces interfering with the attack on the amphitheatre. Nine Royal Army Service Corps DUKWs and three tethered rubber dinghies crewed by Royal Engineers would evacuate the commandos; artillery support was provided by the Royal Navy and X Corps.

During the morning of 29 December 1943, No. 9 Commando, in its first action, embarked on the LSIs *Royal Ulsterman* and *Princess Beatrix* and left Pozzuoli Bay at 6.00pm. With the Commando due to land at 11.00pm, the Guards battalions began their diversions at 9.00pm, during which the Scots Guards suffered several casualties from shelling, but since they were critical in covering the withdrawl, they held firm. But there was no sign of the commandos. Poor guidance by US patrol boats led to the launching of LCAs about 2 miles south of the Garigliano and it was not until 12.35am on 30 December, ninety minutes behind schedule, that the LCA ramps splashed onto a beach about 800 yards south of the selected one. The Force Y attack on Monte Argento alerted the Germans, who then shelled the river banks, causing more Scots Guards casualties. Although behind schedule, Tod decided to attack the amphitheatre, as planned. Stumbling across icy, flooded meadows and negotiating ditches, Force Z was deflected by marked minefields and it was not until 5.00am that they attacked the amphitheatre. Too late to withdraw through the DUKW bridgehead, the commandos constructed a toggle rope bridge and were south of the river by 7.55am. Downstream, the DUKWs collected Force X and Y and twenty-six prisoners, one of whom had been captured by a 3 Troop Intelligence sergeant. Of the nine killed, the bodies of five were brought back.

The next night, Brigadier Churchill met Brigadier Fitzroy McLean, who had fought with the SAS in North Africa and had then been appointed by Prime Minister Churchill to lead the British Military Mission to the communist Partisans in Yugoslavia, at the Brigade New Year's Eve dance. McLean explained that although the Partisans lacked supplies, weapons and clothing, they were tying down several German divisions, however the advance through Italy had prompted the Germans to occupy the Dalmatian Islands. Asked by McLean if he could spare troops to support the Partisans from the island of Vis, Churchill assigned No. 2 Commando, which was commanded by his brother, Jack.

Meanwhile, when 2nd Scots Guards reported they could see two dead commandos from Operation Partridge, Lieutenant Colonel Tod instructed Lieutenant Wilson to recover them. On 4 January, the 3 Troop Intelligence Sergeant was in Naples at the Teatro San Carlos listening to the famous Russian pianist Leff Pouishnoff when he was summoned to return to No. 9 Commando and joined the patrol. On a cold night with a fitful moon and scudding clouds, the patrol crossed the river in a tethered dinghy and divided it into two, with Wilson using the riverbank as a guide to the reported bodies, but found nothing. Instructed by Tod to search toward the sea, the patrol followed a track until the lead scout reported a German helmet in front of him. Wilson was about to climb over a low fence when the 3 Troop Sergeant saw a sign, 'Minen'. As the patrol skirted around the helmet, the sergeant stepped on a mine, which shattered his lower leg. The

61

patrol was then mortared, wounding him in the wrist. Wilson now had the problem of evacuating a badly wounded man from enemy territory, south across the river, with a patrol too few in numbers for him to be carried. Supported by two commandos and in inconsiderable pain, the sergeant hopped and was supported to the riverbank before being whisked to 14th Mobile Casualty Clearing Station, where his lower leg was amputated. There was considerable criticism of Tod's attempt to recover dead commandos, in particular from Brigadier Churchill who had regarded the patrol as the 'height of pure folly to risk lives'. On being discharged, the sergeant became a Circuit Judge in South-East England.

By January 1944, in the first offensive on Rome, the Fifth (US) Army attempted to outflank the Gustav Line by landing parts of VII (US) Corps at Anzio. Nos 9 and 43 (Royal Marines) Commandos landed with their 3 (British) Troop detachments on 21 January, advanced across a flat plan criss-crossed with gullies and shallow ravines, killed a few Germans and then linked up with the 3rd (US) Rangers until they were withdrawn three days later. In atrocious winter weather, the French Expeditionary Force crossed the Rapido during the night 11/12 January and, advancing through the mountains north of Cassino, the Moroccans and Algerians came close to breaching the Gustav Line, but ran out of men in dogged fighting with the determined German 5th Mountain Division. Quite apart from the wounded, frostbite and trench foot added to the casualty list; the soldiers were issued with one blanket each and no winter equipment. X (British) Corps on the left flank crossed the Garigliano on 17 January with the 56th (London) Division on the left and 5th Infantry Division on the right. As a direct consequence of their amphibious skills, 2nd Special Service Brigade joined X Corps.

On 15 January, 4 (Belgian) Troop, at the X Corps Reception Camp at Villa Literno, was placed under command of 201 Guards Brigade and two days later assembled at Lusciano, 8 miles south of the front line and part of the 46th Infantry Division (Major General John Hawkesworth) on the British left flank. When the Troop crossed the river with the Guards, it lost Private van Vooren, badly wounded when he stepped on a mine, and then went into reserve at Sobello, south of the river. Two nights later, it again crossed the Garigliano and joined 2nd Green Howards on Monte Tremensuoli, which was one of the most advanced British positions. Battalion HQ was at Minturno.

Attached to 169 Infantry Brigade, which was part of 56th (London) Division, in an operation spearheaded by No. 40 (Royal Marines) Commando and in spite of the northern banks being shelled from 8.00pm to 9.00pm, the Poles crossed the Garigliano under intense fire at 8.30pm on 17 January with orders to press on and ambush enemy rear areas around Creno and Autonia. Lance Corporal Tadeusz Rozankowski, who spoke good English, was awarded the only MM given to the Poles, when, after the two leading platoon commanders of 2/6th Queens Royal Regiment (West Surreys) were wounded by mines shortly after landing, he encouraged the infantry to keep going, irrespective of casualties, cut the barbed-wire defences and joined the leading platoon assaulting enemy positions. The Poles followed a white tape laid by the Queens until it stopped near an orange orchard, which was found to be mined after four Poles were slightly wounded. By 3.30am, the Troop had reached its rendezvous point with the Queens for an attack on the ridge above the village of Sujo, which was thought to be held by tough veterans of the Battle of Stalingrad, but there was no sign of the infantry. The Poles therefore clambered up steep bush-covered and precariously balanced rock slopes and, within the hour, charged the enemy positions. As dawn broke at 6.00am, they were relieved by No. 40 (Royal Marines) Commando and the Queens.

Later in the day, 6 (Polish) Troop was tasked to seize Monte Valle Martina, which is to the north-east of Sujo, and to patrol the Valle Zintoni. Captain Stanislaw Woloszowki, the Troop Second-in-Command, led the Valle Martina patrol and captured a German section after a brief firefight, however the skirmish alerted an enemy platoon higher up the mountain near a farm and the Poles were soon taking casualties, including Woloszowoski shot dead while treating a casualty, who was also killed. Even though his Thompson had jammed, Senior Rifleman Konrad Braulinski convinced several Germans to surrender by a noisy charge. Meanwhile Lieutenant Czynski leading the Valle Zintoni patrol with his Section Second-in-Command, Lieutenant Antoni Zemanek, overran a six-man mortar team in a ravine and captured a forward artillery observation post. While they were resting, they heard the battle in Valle Martina and were then joined by Captain Smrokowski and a Troop HQ. Hurrying through a wood, they reached open ground and when Smrokowski saw that Woloszowoski's patrol was in trouble, he instructed Czynski to seize the summit. Czynski reached it shortly before the Germans. When Smrokowski committed his third Section (Lieutenant Stefan Zalewski), the Germans withdrew and by 10.15am the Poles had cleared Monte Valle Martina, but at a cost of four killed and twenty-two wounded. The Germans left thirty dead, such had been the ferocity of the fighting in which at least one Polish commando is reputed to have used his commando knife.

Meanwhile, Brigadier Churchill, who was organizing the build-up of No. 2 Commando to Vis, was briefed on 30 January by Lieutenant General McCreery that X Corps was held up north of the Garigliano in front of the Gustav Line, and that 46th and 56th Infantry Divisions holding the northern sector on the Corps bridgehead were exhausted after fighting through the bitterest Italian winter on record, with cleverly dug-in German machine-gun posts protected by minefields and bunkers contesting every yard. McCreery said that he wanted to place Nos 9 and 43 (Royal Marines) Commandos and 4 (Belgian) Troop, under command of 56th Infantry Division, in the counter-attack role while the two Divisions rested. Lance Corporal 'Ross' was with 9 Commando and Private 'Barnes' was with the Royal Marines. Both were German. Churchill assembled Brigade HQ and the Commandos at Sessa with HQ 56th Infantry Division. After joining the Green Howards, 4 (Belgian) Troop settled into the ruins of Minturno; two patrols on the night of 20 January clashed with German infantry escorting engineers laying mines, while a third attacked a light mortar position. On the 22nd, the Troop returned to Brigade reserve at Sorbello and joined the X Corps Reception Camp at Villa Literno until Churchill was told by McCreery that 2nd Special Service Brigade was to go under command of 46th Infantry Division for an attack on Monte Fuga, in order to extend the Corps perimeter and deny the Germans observation of bridges over the Garigliano. Major General Hawkesworth ordered Churchill to seize the forbidding 3,000-foot-high Monte Ornito and the 3,730-foot Monte Faito and Monte Tuga, south of the main objectives. There was little intelligence. Churchill was puzzled because his units were half the size of British battalions and even if they captured Monte Faito, Monte Ornito might be beyond his capabilities. Hawkesworth mentioned that he did not regard the assault on Ornito as an exploitation task. On call was the Divisional artillery.

With guides supplied by 6th York and Lancs, Churchill could see that the brigade would be advancing up 2 miles of rugged hills devoid of cover. Digging in was impossible, the only shelter being boulders and sangars that the troops managed to construct. Churchill opted for a night attack with No. 43 (Royal Marines) Commando attacking Monte Ornito, while No. 9 Commando seized Point 711, a small feature to the south-west of Monte Ornito. After travelling 60 miles along muddy roads cluttered with military traffic, often under shelling, and two days without sleep, the commandos used mules to take their stores to the concentration areas. Churchill persuaded Hawkesworth to postpone the attack for twenty-four hours to allow his brigade some rest, and then next day his men man-packed their stores and ammunition to their assembly areas in a dry river bed because the route was too steep for mules. Joining the forward company of the 6th York and Lancs, the Belgians defended Brigade HQ in a small pigsty and were the reserve. When the infantry reported that two German platoons had moved on to a feature in between Monte Tuga and Point 711, Churchill altered his plan. No. 43 (Royal Marines) Commando would move around the east of Monte Tuga and attack Point 711, while No. 9 Commando would pass to the rear of the Royal Marines, capture Point 803, in between Monte Ornito and Monte Faito, and exploit to Monte

Faito. The final mid-afternoon commanders' recce was dogged by thick mist shrouding the objectives, nevertheless Brigade HQ was mortared and four Belgians were wounded.

At 6.30pm, in bright moonlight, No. 43 (Royal Marines) Commando in denims and cap comforters, started climbing, followed an hour later by No. 9 Commando, in battledress and green berets. The artillery began diversionary shelling and the infantry opened fire on enemy positions on Monte Tuga. At about 8.00pm, the Royal Marines clashed with enemy outposts and by 7.00am next day, after a night of fighting, had seized Mount Ornito and Point 711. 'Barnes' was severely wounded when Commando HQ was mortared. Not expected to live, he was evacuated next day by Private 'Kendal', who gave him his last lollipop. When No. 9 Commando went firm on Point 803, it had suffered such heavy casualties, including Lieutenant Colonel Tod wounded, that it was unable to attack Monte Faito, which was thought to have been augmented by troops falling back. Lance Corporal 'Ross' was knocked unconscious by mortaring while interrogating a prisoner. When he surfaced and saw that he was surrounded by several Wehrmacht, he thought he had been taken prisoner, but they were Czech conscripts surrendering to him. Persuading them to carry him to the RAP, he was evacuated to a military hospital in Pompeii on the day that Vesuvius erupted. During shelling that day, the Belgians were lucky when a large shell that crunched into the middle of their positions failed to explode. Captain Danloy characteristically described it as 'a large champagne bottle'. During the evening, a German reserve company, identified from interrogations to be based in the village of Cerasola, a mile to the north on Monte Ornito, attacked No. 43 (Royal Marines) Commando from a small hill below the feature and was driven off after close-range fighting. Churchill instructed the Belgians to seize a small feature in between Point 711 and Monte Ornito, which they did against no opposition. After dark, they drove off an enemy patrol sniffing around Monte Tuga, and shortly after midnight on 3 February, 5th Royal Hampshires took over the Commando positions. During the attack, the commandos had 198 casualties. 46th Infantry Division twice tried to capture Monte Faito. It was eventually seized when the Germans were outflanked by the French Expeditionary Corps advancing through the Aurunci Mountain in May.

After nearly two months of continuous operations, on 6 February, 2nd Special Service Brigade rested in a rest camp at San Adreas di Vivo Equense, south of Naples. Training continued with landings, patrolling and range work. The eruption of Vesuvius and the dust filtering south made life miserable for a few days.

Meanwhile the Anzio landing was bedevilled by inept US leadership that allowed the Germans to bottle up four Allied divisions, including 56th

Infantry Division. After two weeks rest, as No. 9 Commando and No. 40 (Royal Marines) Commando were warned that they would be reinforcing the beachhead, Lieutenant Colonel Tod visited Lance Corporal 'Ross' in hospital and said that he needed him. On 2 March, both Commandos landed and the Royal Marines were sent to the battered 169 (London) Brigade while the Army Commando was attached to 167 (London) Brigade to the west. On 19 March, in three Forces, the Army attacked a ravine, used by the Germans for forming up, in the first offensive action from the beachhead for some time. But coming under intense fire, they were pinned down all day until the evening when a determined German attack reached Commando HQ. Driven back by a bayonet charge, 'Ross' shot a charging German with his Thompson, but as the man fell 'Ross' was stabbed by his bayonet and hospitalized for a month. The Commando then withdrew from the ravines under a creeping barrage. The day's fighting cost nineteen killed, fifty wounded and four missing. 'Ross' was wounded for the third time within the month when the field general hospital in which he was being treated in Naples was bombed.

Chapter 8

Cassino and the Adriatic

With the invasion of Europe imminent, Lieutenant Roger Taymans, the 4 (Belgian) Troop liaison officer, returned to England with a joint request from Captains Danloy and Smrokowski that their Troops return to Great Britain. The Belgians were keen to liberate their country and the Poles had just one ambition – defeat the Germans and get at their real enemy, the Russians.

Lieutenant General van Strydonck and Major General Kopanski, the Polish Commander-in-Chief in London, welcomed the suggestion, particularly as both Troops had performed well in Italy. On 17 February, Major General Sturges, commanding the Special Services Group, wrote to Major General Laycock emphasizing their experience would be a valuable addition to the Special Service brigades. Laycock replied that Prime Minister Churchill had instructed that no Commandos were to be withdrawn from the Far East or the Mediterranean without his express permission. General Montgomery had been given the eight Commandos of the 1st and 4th Special Service Brigades for his 21st Army Group. Laycock then helpfully suggested that requests for the Troops to take part in Operation Overlord should come from the men and their governments, and that Sturges should approach 21st Army Group confirming that No. 10 (Inter-Allied) Commando, minus 2 (Dutch) Troop in the Far East, was available.

After Yugoslavia had been routed by the Germans in April 1941, resistance was, at first, divided until two strong personalities emerged. Colonel Draja Mihailovitch supported the exiled King Peter. His followers were mainly Serbs who had evaded captivity when the Yugoslavian Army surrendered and were known as Chetniks. Josip Broz was the Secretary of the Yugoslavian Communist Party and is better known as Tito. Appearances deceive and his tough Partisan army of men and women were dedicated to replacing the monarchy with Tito's brand of communism in a socialist republic for the diverse nationalities within the borders of the future Yugoslavia. Although ideologically bitter opponents, at first both factions combined to resist, but by the time Hitler invaded the Soviet Union in June 1941, they were sworn enemies and a deadly civil war developed. Unlike the Italians who sought an understanding with Mihailovitch, the Germans were ruthless. Prisoners were a nuisance. The British initially supported Mihailovitch but, faced with increasing American influence in the Mediterranean at the 1943 Teheran Conference, when the Allies agreed to back Tito, the Communist Yugoslavian National Liberation Committee banned King Peter from returning to Yugoslavia until the people had decided his fate. When Italy surrendered, Tito's Partisans seized several Adriatic islands and parts of the Dalmatian coast, but the Germans reacted swiftly, recovered Dalmatia and suddenly the islands became strategically important. The Allies needed them to cushion the German threat to their right flank in Italy and the Germans knew if they seized them, they could threaten the progress of the Allied advance. On 23 December, the mountain-trained 118th Jaeger Division and the German Navy began operations to prevent the seizure by the Allies of the islands as naval bases from which to launch commando and ground force operations.

Meanwhile, the Allies had responded to Fitzroy McLean's appeal to help the Yugoslavian Partisans by sending Force 133 (Brigadier Miles) to the island of Vis. Eighteen miles long and 8 mile wide, it is about 100 miles north-west of Dubrovnik and 20 miles from the mainland. Units arriving from 16 January included Tactical HQ, 2nd Special Service Brigade, No. 2 Commando, which was still recovering from its experiences at Salerno, a Royal Artillery 75mm mountain gun battery and first-generation Greek- and Yugoslavian-Americans of the US Operations Group. Attached to No. 2 Commando was Corporal 'Anson', now recovered from his wounds, while Corporals 'Scott' and 'Merton' were attached to Brigade HQ. The commandos were soon raiding German-held islands with the Americans involved from mid-February.

On 20 February, the 118th Jaeger Division, a detachment of the Brandenburg Division, a SS rifle battalion and an amphibious sapper battalion threatened Vis, however the force were inexperienced in amphibious operations and Hitler suspended further operations until his General Staff reviewed the strategy and resources. No. 43 (Royal Marines) Commando arrived and raided Solta and several other islands near the mainland. An intelligence problem faced by Miles was the disregard the Partisans had for prisoners and their potential intelligence, nevertheless Vis became a thorn in the German side. On 4 March, HQ 2nd Special Service Brigade arrived as part of Force 226, which later included 11 Field Regiment and the RAF Regiment with anti-aircraft guns. When it became apparent that No. 10 (Inter-Allied) Commando was not included in the Operation Overlord order of battle, as we have seen, the Poles remained in Italy while 4 (Belgian) and 7 (Yugoslavian) Troops joined the Brigade on Vis in March.

So far, Lieutenant Tripovic's detachment had done well, but when it deployed to Vis its presence antagonized the Partisans because the Troop had been raised from the Royal Yugoslavian Army in Egypt, and the commandos were wearing the insignia of King Peter on their berets and epaulettes – a red rag to a bull. Captain Monahan, the Troop Officer, then discovered the Yugoslavians were split politically and interfaction fighting broke out with those sympathetic to the communists abandoning their green berets and joining the Partisans, an act regarded with considerable disgust by the British commandos, who looked upon them as deserters. On one occasion, British and Belgian commandos broke up a nasty clash in Komiza, and in another incident, Tripovic was rescued by a priest after being pursued into the town church by Partisans. Meanwhile Lieutenant Kerovin and ten Yugoslavian commandos had left Glasgow on 17 February with orders not to wear their green berets until out of sight of land. By the time that they reached North Africa, Tripovic's section had been sent back to Rear HQ 2nd Special Service Brigade in Molfetta, Italy after the antagonism on Vis became too sensitive for the Troop to be allowed to function in the Adriatic. There was only one solution, and on 15 April Major General Sturges reported that 7 (Yugoslavian) Troop was to be disbanded. No records exist about its fate. Within ten days, Monahan, a good French speaker, had transferred to SOE and four months later dropped with Jedburgh 'Arnold' into France to help the Maquis.

4 (Belgian) Troop was assigned to support the six MGBs and MTBs commanded by Lieutenant Commander Morgan Giles RN, who was the Senior Naval Officer, Vis with his HQ in a waterfront house overlooking Komiza harbour. The Royal Navy were using the island as a forward operating base to: attack German schooners and landing craft; land Partisans to cut coastal railways and roads; deliver war stores to Partisan groups; and evacuate the wounded, escaped prisoners of war and homeless Partisan families. When the Germans reacted to British domination of the sector between Zara and Dubrovnik by increasing convoy protection with powerful E-boats, coastal batteries and air patrols, Giles ordered his boats to operate at night, whenever possible, and keep close to the shore to take advantage of the shadows from cliffs. Considerable reliance was placed on Partisan intelligence of German movements.

The Belgians relished the piratical adventures of the MTBs. Private Seeger was on MTB 95 (Lieutenant Commander Tom Fuller DSC** RCNVR) when it stopped the 200-ton schooner, *Libbechic*; sixty-five barrels of Danish butter, flour and ersatz coffee were found and taken back to Vis to be distributed throughout the garrison. On the night of 14/15 April, Lieutenant Roman and five men joined the same MTB and, after being shown around by a petty officer, followed by an excellent meal, left Vis with MTB 99 and lurked in a shadowy bay off the island of Murter. At

3.30am, a lookout reported a destroyer and, at full speed, the MTBs attacked. Soon after the navy gunners had opened fire and flares had rocketed into the night, the enemy sounded its siren in surrender. The 'destroyer' turned out to be an armed tug 'piggy backing' a lighter and towing two others. Covered by MTB 99, Fuller went alongside and a commando ordered its mixed German and Italian crew to assemble at the bow. Several others were pulled from the water and four lay dead on the deck. Commandos searching the tug were unable to close the sinking tug's steam safety valve or release the jammed wheel. Meanwhile, MTB 99 sank two of the lighters carrying concrete and petrol, and the third was towed to Vis where its cargo was not the expected fresh food but hay, nevertheless valuable feed for the mules.

On 10 May, Lieutenant Meny and fifteen men protected HQ 2nd Special Service Signals Section during the raid on Solta by 1,500 Partisans and two mountain gun batteries. Landing shortly after midnight near Uvala Tatinja Bay, the commandos waited until 4.25am while the Partisans deployed in front of the village of Grohote, the target of the raid. After shelling the village from 5.30am until 7.00am, the Partisans eventually overwhelmed the German defences in fighting that lasted all day and the force withdrew at 11.30pm.

Meanwhile, pressure being exerted by the Belgian Government-in-exile, particularly by Premier Pierlot, to permit 4 (Belgian) Troop to return to Great Britain, led to a letter dated 15 April in which Major General Sturges noted that it was an officer and nineteen other ranks understrength, and the prospects for replacing its casualties from the Belgian Brigade were remote, however the Troop had no desire to remain in Italy while Belgium was liberated. A week later, after Ambassador Emile Cartier de Marchienne agreed, the CIGS relented and three days after the Solta raid, they left for England.

6 (Polish) Troop was then ordered to join II (Polish) Corps and, on 4 April, it was taken by truck to Busso where they were then visited by General Sosnkowski, who had arrived from London. Presenting awards and swords, he declared that the commandos had 'well served their Fatherland' and brought a morale-boosting message from President-in-exile Mr Raczkiewicz that all ranks were promoted by one rank with cadet officers being commissioned to second lieutenants. The Troop was not entirely enamoured with the transfer to Polish command, however they settled down quickly. On the 24th, their casualties were replaced by twenty battle-hardened desert veterans, who had not done the commando course but, after a short and intensive course, were deemed suitable replacements. The Polish Corps consisted of the 3rd Carpathian Rifle and 5th Kresowa Infantry Divisions, and the 2nd Independent Armoured Brigade. The

Carpathians had experienced tough fighting in North Africa, including at Tobruk.

After four attempts, Monte Cassino was still held by the Germans. With the arrival of spring, the plan for Operation Diadem was for II (US) Corps to advance north up Route 7 along the coast towards Rome, while the French Corps would attack through the Aurunci Mountains, west of Cassino, and protect the American right. VIII (British) Corps would cross the Garigliano to the west, envelope the feature and advance up the Liri valley toward Rome, while II (Polish) Corps was to cross the River Rapido, isolate Cassino and link with the British. Essentially the full weight of Fifth and Eighth Armies would assault the Gustav Line and then advance towards the Hitler Line, 10 miles north of Monte Cassino.

On 6 May, the Troop, supported by Sergeant 'Merton' from 3 (British) Troop, moved up to the front. At 11.00pm a week later, the Allies advanced with the French again making the best progress and VIII Corps managing to pass Canadian tanks over the Rapido. On the right, the bombardment of German positions was less effective than hoped and the Polish Corps faced three days of grim fighting during which the 3rd Carpathian Rifle Division seized Hill 593 but lost 20 per cent of its strength. When 5th Kresowa Division also suffered, attacking Colle San Angelo, General Anders withdrew his battered troops. By next day, the German defences were creaking under immense pressure and the American advance quickened. When the French tore holes in the Gustav Line and forced the German 94th Division to withdraw from Castelonorato, German Tenth Army reserves prepared to defend the Hitler Line. The 3rd Carpathian Rifle Division again suffered badly, this time attacking Cavalry Mount. By 17 May, the Germans were unable to hold Allied pressure except at Monte Cassino where the 3rd and 4th Parachute Regiments, from the 1st Parachute Division, and part of the 51st Mountain Corps, were stubborn defenders.

6 (Polish) Troop, which was temporarily commanded by Captain Zalewski, was assigned to the 5th Kressowa Division (Lieutenant General Nolodem Sulk). Sulk planned to attack Monte Cassino on a battalion-sized frontage with the aim of capturing Phantom Ridge, Colle San Angelo and Hill 575, and then advance west until he met with the 78th (British) Division. To give his drive some weight, he created a strong reserve of the 5th Wilno Brigade less the 14th Battalion; the 17th and 18th Battalions of the Lvov Brigade; and the Shermans of the 3rd Tank Squadron, 4th Armoured Regiment. 6 (Polish) Troop, reinforced by the dismounted assault squadron of the 15th Posnan Lancers and engineers, was to protect the right flank of the 17th Battalion, which was to capture Colle San Angelo by climbing Monte Castellone, cross 'Phantom Ridge' and attack the north-west sector of the German positions. The seizure of Phantom Ridge was to

be aided by tanks of the 3rd Carpathian Rifle Division, diverting German attention to attack on Hill 593.

By the time the Troop was ready to climb Monte Castellone, the 5th Kressowa Division had crossed the start line at 7.22am. The 13th Tank Squadron struggled up the southern slopes of Phantom Ridge to a point about 100 yards below the summit and shot in the 17th Battalion, then, crossing the ridge, seized the northern flanks of Colle San Angelo, but the German defence remained stubborn. Under heavy fire, the commando battle group advanced up the hill, but when it lost two killed, including Second Lieutenant Bachleda, the international skier, and several wounded, Zalewski withdrew and reorganized. At about 11.15am, the Troop was ordered to attack again and, by 1.00pm, the 15th Posnan Lancer squadron had joined the 17th Battalion on the northern slopes of Colle San Angelo. When 2 Section commander, Lieutenant Zemanek, and his sergeant, Senior Sergeant Bradowski, were among six wounded by heavy mortar fire, Cadet Officer/Sergeant Henryk Jedwab took over command, however, soon after midday, they were so short of ammunition that they threw stones and rocks in a vain attempt to stop a German counter-attack at 2.00pm recovering the southern peak.

After creating a reserve from his echelons and others not directly involved, when General Rudnicki said he had nothing left, Anders told him not to worry as the German defence was beginning to collapse along the entire Allied front. Rudnicki then launched the 16th and 18th Battalions and the Polish Troop up Colle San Angelo, and by 6.00am, the hill was in Polish hands, although the Troop casualties were again high – an NCO killed and eleven wounded, including three officers, one of whom was Captain Zalewski. When command passed to Captain Czynski, he handed his 1 Section to Second Lieutenant Victor Rzemieniecki. The Troop now numbered seven officers and forty-five men.

During the day, XIII (British) Corps made significant progress up the Liri Valley when a gaping hole in the German defences opened. In the east, the 4th (British) Division crossed Highway 6 to Rome and the 78th (British) Division was within 500 yards of the railway station at the Colle d'Anguano. With the monastery almost isolated, the 3rd and 4th Parachute Regiments withdrew in the direction of Piedmonte, leaving small rearguards. At 8.00pm, a patrol led by Cadet Officer Bartosiewicz reported that the ridge and Hill 575 were clear of enemy. 3rd Carpathian Rifle Division patrols found only small rearguards. At 4.15am next day, the 4th, 5th and 6th Battalions swept these away and, by 10.00am, the red and white regimental pennant of the 12th Podolski Uhlan Lancers, improvised from handkerchiefs and a medical Red Cross flag, was flying over the ruins of the shattered monastery. Thirty badly wounded men from the German Parachute Regiment was all that was found inside.

At midday, 6 (Polish) Troop filed down Colle San Angelo ridge in the knowledge that they had taken part in an epic battle. Among the II (Polish) Corps casualties (3,779 casualties in six days of fighting, of whom 1,150 were killed), the Troop had lost two killed and twenty wounded, all of whom were serious enough to warrant evacuation.

After a rest, with 25 per cent of its strength casualties who were extremely difficult to replace, the Polish Corps was moved east to lead the advance up the Adriatic Coast. 6 (Polish) Troop remained with the Corps and was located in Oratino with 111th Company, which was a unit of Italian volunteers recruited to protect local bridges. Already game for any fight with the Germans, the Poles fitted them out with uniforms and insignia, and provided officers and NCOs. In an action with the Company, the Troop cleared Monte Freddo near Ancona, however, during a raid by 1 Section on German rear areas near La Montagnola to capture a prisoner, Private Rudolf Klimzak was killed in a clash with a German patrol. He was one of the desert veterans.

On 15 July, the Troop joined 2 (Polish) Armoured Brigade, which was on the left flank of II (Polish) Corps, and, as infantry, crossed the River Musone before climbing Monte Polesco, from where they could see across a maize field that the next village of Case Nuove was heavily defended. A deep ravine from the river divided the village from a brick factory and its distinctive tall chimney. On the 17th, the Troop advanced across the field but lost five killed and three wounded before it even reached the outskirts of the village. When 2 Section moved left to attack the brickworks, they found the complex had been converted into a heavily defended position and four more Poles were killed before Captain Smrokowski ordered it to withdraw. Meanwhile, 1 Section had cleared the village by 10.00am without further casualties. The tanks reduced it to rubble during the afternoon. The Troop were next loaded onto tanks and transported to the next objective, the town of Castelferretti, an uncomfortable experience in which they were shelled and mortared. Private Jan Fiedorczuk was killed near Augugliano before the Troop were told to take shelter inside the tanks. Castelferretti was occupied without loss. During the three days, the Poles had captured fifty-six prisoners but at the cost of eight killed, including Corporal Antoni Kaliwoszka, another desert veteran, and nine wounded. Corporal Hieronim Rink died of his wounds suffered at Case Nuove on 7 August.

During the Italian campaign, 6 (Polish) Troop lost eighteen killed and seventy wounded, in other words 80 per cent of its strength, most during the fighting around Ancona; 176 awards and decorations, including the Polish equivalent of the Victoria Cross, were made to the Troop, of which just two were British. On 3 August, the Poles were transferred from No. 10 (Inter-Allied) Commando to become the 1st Independent Commando

Company, one of five Troops in the 2nd Commando Motorised Battalion, and later took part in the battle for Bologna.

The departure of the Poles left the 3 (British) Half Troop attached to 2nd Special Service Brigade as the only No. 10 (Inter-Allied) Commando representatives in the Central Mediterranean Force (CMF). In August, Sergeant 'Merton' joined No. 2 Commando when 2nd Special Service Brigade landed near the port of Sarande in Albania in September, and although hindered by hostile terrain and very heavy rain, by 8 October had defeated the German defenders. When it was rumoured that there were some Germans on Corfu, Corporal 'Anson' landed with a patrol from No. 45 (Royal Marines) Commando. It turned out that there were no Germans and for the few weeks they were billeted there enjoying gourmet meals conjured up by Spiro, the chef.

In January 1945, Lieutenants Bartlett, Shelley and Stewart, fresh from OCTU, arrived and joined the CMF to establish a Troop for 2nd Commando Brigade. Selecting sixteen soldiers, including two Swiss ex-French Foreign Legion, a Yugoslav, a Pole and the stateless Pte 'Warwick' who had enlisted into the Essex Regiment in Nairobi, the men underwent a two-month commando course run by the existing Half Troop at a school in the town of Minervo in southern Italy. In April, they joined the Brigade as interrogators and interpreters in the fighting against the Georgian Brigade, conscripted into the Wehrmacht, around Lake Commachio. The rounding up of thousands of prisoners meant that the Troop was very busy selecting those for interrogation, during the course of which Sergeant 'Anson' upset a German general by telling him to carry his own baggage. Their job completed, the Half Troop had a leisurely rail journey to Naples before returning to England and being billeted in Seaford.

Chapter 9

Raiding the Atlantic Coast

By the spring of 1943 and in preparation for the invasion of Europe, GHQ Home Forces needed to convince the Germans that a landing in the Pas-de-Calais was a probability by launching small-scale commando raids from the Dutch/Belgian border to northern France. There were no definitive rules, which led to the author and commando, Evelyn Waugh, declaring that the operation was 'to raid for raiding's sake'. Raid commanders were not told of the strategic nature of the operation but were instructed to gather intelligence, capture prisoners and leave evidence of visits with beach navigation markers, as opposed to the usual in and out without leaving a trace. It was also intended that aircraft should fly low over the beaches, weather permitting, to give further credence to the imminent landings.

HQ Combined Operations, under operational command of either Commander-in-Chief Portsmouth or Vice Admiral Dover, were responsible for the planning of Operation Forfar. Fresh from raiding Norway, 12 Commando was used. Commanded by the recently promoted Major Fynn, it was reorganized into: an amphibious raiding Troop, called Fynn Force, of four officers and thirty-nine other ranks; the airborne No. 4 Troop, known as Rooney Force, of seven officers and sixty-two other ranks commanded by Captain O.B. Rooney; and the second amphibious Hollins Force of three officers and nineteen men commanded by Lieutenant Hollins.

The method of operation differed from Norway in that a MTB, sometimes with a Motor Gun Boat (MGB) or aircraft escort, ferried raiding parties of one or two officers and eight to ten commandos across the Channel. About a mile offshore, the raiding party transferred to a dory, manned by a Royal Navy coxswain and a commando signaller, with an S-Phone homing device and a radio set on the same frequency as a Patrol HQ radio on the MTB. Designed on West African models coping with Atlantic rollers, Camper and Nicholson Ltd of Gosport designed several variants. Typically used in Operation Forfar were 20-foot-long wooden

SN-6s fitted with an Austin motor car engine giving a speed of about 6 knots, and also equipped with long and tapered oars fitted into rowlocks shaped to hold the oar in case the rower lost his balance while breaching surf. For the final approach, the commandos transferred to a RAF dinghy tethered to the dory by a floating line with a telephone cable, and paddled in. Raiding forces were supplied with the latest equipment, such as walkie-talkies and US M1 carbines. When Combined Operations instructed No. 10 (Inter-Allied) Commando to form detachments to support No. 12 Commando, Major Laycock formed Layforce 1. The debonair Leading Seaman Laurent Casalonga and his colleague Pierre Bocccador were attached to No. 12 Commando from 1 (French) Troop as interpreters. 3 (British) Troop provided interrogators from its base in a large house near Littlehampton. The German Sergeant 'Drew' participated in several raids.

Forfar Easy took place on 3/4 July when Lieutenant Hollins and ten men landed near Onival south of the River Somme and brought back examples of barbed wire. Two nights later, three operations were launched. Forfar Dog landed at Biville but the cliffs were blocked by thick barbed-wire entanglements along the top. Forfar How, which was due to land at Quend Beach, north of the River Somme estuary, and Forfar Beer were unable to land because of a patrolling armed trawler and heavy surf. Forfar Beer 2 and Easy 2 were repeated during the night of 31 July/1 August but again were aborted, as was Forfar How 2 on 2/3 August. When Major Fynn argued that if prisoners were going to be captured, the raiding force needed time ashore, Forfar Beer 3 landed at Eletot on 3 August and the commandos spent a day concealed in the folds of a cliff top hoping for a prisoner. Forfar Love targeted Dunkirk pier on 3/4 August but again took no prisoners.

Fynn launched Forfar Beer 4 on 1/2 September, which included Corporal Casalonga. Leaving Dover, the raiding party of two officers, Fynn and Lieutenant I.D.C. Smith, and seven other ranks were ferried by MTB 250 (from the 14th MTB Flotilla at Portsmouth) and landed between Elelot and St Pierre-en-Port. Hoping to capture a prisoner from an observation post at the top of the cliff, Fynn found the climb barred by an overhang. At 2.10pm, he instructed Lieutenant McGonical, who had remained with the dory, to go back to the MTB and return during the early hours of 4 September. Smith and Casalonga, sent to recce the approaches to St Pierre-en-Port, reported that they reached the casino and had seen a German sentry post. With the tide on the ebb, Fynn rested his men until 2.30pm and, because there had been no enemy activity during the day, then sent three men to find a way off the beach up a gully, while he, Smith and Casalonga tried a route that Smith had seen, but had no success. When several French fishermen with nets then arrived on the beach, Fynn instructed Casalonga to contact them, which he did by whistling sharply.

Explaining that he was a French commando and that his two colleagues were British officers, he said that he wanted to go to St Pierre-en-Port but had been prevented by barbed wire. One fisherman said a green dory indicated the gap in the wire and a path past the casino led into the village. There were no sentries and he did not know about mines. Casalonga arranged to meet the fisherman at 7.30am next morning.

At 8.00pm, Fynn sent Lieutenant Smith, Sergeant Major Sam Brodison and Casalonga on another recce to St Pierre while he and two commandos tried another route, however the caked mud and chalk forced them to abandon the attempt at 10.30pm, even though they had pitons and crampons. When the recce had not returned by 12.30am, Fynn and a commando set off to check another climb. Meanwhile, Smith's patrol had found the dory but, having spent an hour observing the village and a sentry post west of the casino near some tennis courts, they were unable to get closer because of noisy shingle. As they withdrew, there was a challenge from the courts, followed by another challenge, a rifle shot and an uncomfortably close burst from a Spandau on the cliff top. During the night, the patrol wrote duplicated reports of their findings, which were attached to the canisters of two pigeons, but when they were released they were attacked by five peregrine falcons and one was killed; the other one failed to reach England. Next morning two Fokker-Wulf 190 fighters approaching from the west circled their position, which suggested to the commandos that the Germans were suspicious.

Not surprisingly, the fisherman failed to make the rendezvous until later in the day. He was clearly very brave as Casalonga learnt from him that he had been questioned by the Germans, who claimed that a British patrol had landed during the night but had since left. The fisherman then said that a friend dressed in the blue overalls typical of French fishermen would leave some photographs near the fishing nets at the base of the cliff. During the early evening, the second fisherman appeared by the nets; when approached by Smith and Casalonga, he welcomed them warmly and produced photographs of St Pierre-en-Port viewed from the sea. He also provided an extensive brief detailing artillery and machine-gun posi-tions, minefields, HQs and billets and the fact that the village was occupied by forty men. There were no sentries near the casino but a post on the cliff top was equipped with a navigation beacon. It was probably from this post that Smith's recce had been seen the previous night. Two more fishermen then appeared, including the brother of the first fisherman, and more photographs were produced. When the brother added that there was an anti-aircraft gun manned by ten men in an underground bunker, Casalonga suggested they would attack it that night. One fisherman told them of a route up the cliff but refused to lay ropes from the top – it was too dangerous. They also reported that the Germans in St Pierre were demoralized. When the fishermen asked for weapons so they could be ready to attack when the time came, Casalonga replied that they had none to spare.

During the night Fynn failed in another attempt to climb the cliff and then, at 11.00pm, he and five men set off to the village with the intention of capturing a prisoner, while his signaller arranged for the dory to pick them up. Arriving on the outskirts, he deployed a covering party while he and Sergeant Major Brodison crawled to the barbed-wire entanglements with the aim of breaching it. At this point, Fynn was told by the signaller that the pick-up would be delayed because several E-Boats were lurking in the area – the commandos had seen them earlier. It was now about 2.15am and since the wire was too thick to cut, Fynn exploded a Bangalore torpedo poked through the entanglements, hoping that the Germans would investigate and give the patrol the opportunity to capture a prisoner. But there was no reaction, even when one of them fired a silenced Sten in the direction of the navigation light post. Disappointed and tired after three days of intense activity and anxiety, the patrol returned to the beach at 2.30am to find Lieutenant McGonical waiting with the dory. As the swell of the high tide was causing a good deal of surf the patrol had to wade up to their necks to the dory and were hauled in. The presence of E-boats meant that the MTB was some distance out to sea and it was not until 4.45am that they clambered on board; two hours later they were back in Dover.

At the same time as Operation Forfar Beer 4, Forfar Item took place on 2/3 September near St Valery-en-Caux. It was different from the other Operation Forfar raids in that the raiding force of eight Rooney Force were to be dropped from one of three 298 Squadron Halifax bombers regularly used for leaflet operations over northern France, while the other two provided a diversion. Extraction was to be by MTB. The aim was to check a new searchlight position seen on air photographs. Included in the drop was Corporal 'John Wilmers'. Poor weather prevented the drop for several days, on one occasion the commandos were actually sitting in the aircraft only for the operation to be cancelled when the Royal Navy reported that the English Channel was still too rough for small-boat operations. Conditions improved during the evening of 2 September and Squadron Leader Minnie, who was piloting the patrol's Halifax, took off from RAF Thruxton at 6.45pm.

Soon after 10.05pm, the three aircraft having attracted searchlights and anti-aircraft fire while dropping leaflets, Minnie arrived over a stubble field near St Valery-en-Caux and the commandos dropped through the hole in the floor. Setting their compasses and carrying their parachutes, whilst at the same time trying to avoid barking dogs, they assembled on top of the cliffs carrying a man knocked unconscious during the drop. Offshore, a slow German convoy was hugging the coast. Already behind schedule, while some commandos abseiled down the cliffs, 'Wilmers' and an officer inspected the searchlight position, cut telephone wires, removed an optical sight and chucked building material over the cliff. By the time the commandos had abseiled down the cliff, the dory crew reported that they had been washed ashore in heavy surf and needed help to refloat it. Picking up their equipment, parachutes and the optical sight, they stumbled along the shingle for about 3 miles before they saw that the dory had been beached at least 50 yards from the sea. The crew reported that MTB 249 had run into the German convoy and, during the approach to the coast, the dory crew had stopped the engine when they believed they had been seen from the cliff tops. As the dory careered through the heavy surf, the engine was damaged beyond repair. By now it was getting light so everyone stripped naked, but when the dory was hauled back into the sea, it was found to be leaking badly which meant jettisoning everything, including the sight. Paddling madly, the naked commandos eventually arrived alongside the MTB and returned to Newhaven, fortified by rum, tea and blankets.

The last Operation Forfars were during the night of 3/4 September with Forfar Pound in the Ushant area. Eighteen commandos and two US Rangers attacked an enemy post at Porz/Ahech and claimed two German killed, while Fynn led another raid to the Eletot area.

By mid 1943, with the invasion of Europe figuring strongly in Allied political, diplomatic and military strategy, and finally settled on Normandy, the CIGS issued instructions that all raids were to be co-ordinated by the Chief of Staff to the Supreme Allied Commander (COSSAC), with the Small Scale Raiding Committee at Combined Operations HQ planning them. When No. 10 (Inter-Allied) Commando was tasked with Operation Hardtack, again targeting northern France and Belgium, Major Laycock was placed in operational command of Layforce 2, reporting direct to Lieutenant Colonel Ian Collins and Major Godfrey Franks at HQ Special Service Group. Lieutenant Colonel Lister selected the French, not only for their local knowledge, but he also wanted to mollify their disappointment at not being sent to the Mediterranean. Lieutenant Kieffer selected twenty men from 1 and 8 (French) Troops for an intensive programme of vertical cliff climbing at Dover during the last two weeks of September, but they returned to Eastbourne when both French Troops were required at full strength for the invasion of Corsica – Operation Crossbow – an event that never happened. On 9 December, the French moved into billets in the Seaford, Newhaven and Peacehaven area and trained in small boat handling, identification of German equipment and raiding techniques. In November, 12 Commando, its role no longer relevant, was disbanded and the airborne raiding role of its 4 Troop was taken over by E (Airborne) Section, 3 (British) Troop. In preparation for their new role, the three officers and forty-six men attended Basic

Parachute Course 86A at Ringway from 7 to 16 October, which included jumping from a Halifax bomber with all equipment, including abseil ropes, strapped to the body. Inevitably, some of the RAF parachute jump instructors tried to find out why these foreign commandos were being taught how to parachute.

Operation Hardtack commenced with Hardtack Dog at Biville during the night of 24/27 November, followed by Hardtack 11 which first set out on 23/24 December but was cancelled when the MTBs were diverted to attack a convoy. Hardtack 23, commanded by Lieutenant Kieffer, was also cancelled the same night. Hardtack 11 was repeated the following night with the same objective of recceing the beaches between Calais and Gravelines by five 1 (French) Troop commanded by Warrant Officer Pierre Wallerand. He was supported by Sergeant John Parks of 2 SBS, the dory coxswain, and the Russian Corporal 'Jones' of 3 (British) Troop, the dory signaller. Also on board MTB 25 (Lieutenant Clarkson RM Reserve) was a French Army medical officer, Captain Villiere, the Layforce Signals Officer, Major A.J. Leahy and an American observer. The MTB was from the 4th Flotilla based at HMS *Wasp* in Dover.

At 2.30am on 24 December, MTB 25 hove to about 700 yards from the beach on a dark night. The breakers made sufficient noise to drown the dory engine as Parks navigated it to the point where the commandos transferred to the dinghy, however Wallerand instructed him to close to the beach and as the patrol waded ashore, although the boat was heavy, Parks and 'Jones' managed to stop it being beached. They then found that the engine would not start and, after 'Jones' had sent the signal 'Donkey' ('Engine stopped – am using oars'), this was misunderstood by the patrol HQ radio operator as 'Sunk', so it was therefore of some surprise when the dory bumped alongside the MTB from astern. After the dory had been drained, the MTB moved a mile out to sea and hoisted it on board to repair the engine, but it refused to start.

Ashore, Petty Officer Roger Caron, Leading Seaman Gaston Pourcelet and Able Seaman Joseph Madec checked a machine-gun emplacement and then covered Wallerand, Petty Officer Rene Navrault and Leading Seaman Albert Meunier as they recced a minefield a short distance from the beach. At about 4.00am they watched a two-man German patrol plodding along the beach and were then joined by Meunier carrying a mine, followed at 5.20am by Wallerand and Navrault, each carrying a French anti-tank mine. The patrol returned to the beach where Wallerand waded out to a sand-bank and signalled 'X' for the dory with his blue-shaded torch. Rowed ashore by Parks, 'Jones' and Royal Navy Telegraphist Chapman, their plan was for 'Jones' to land and collect the patrol while Parks and Chapman stood off. However the dory had again shipped a significant amount of water. When the patrol helped to bale it out before wading out up to their

80

necks pushing the dory, just in case another German patrol appeared, as they were trying to embark, the dory broached in a breaker and again filled with water. Everything was then emptied into the sea and an attempt was made to tip the water out, but when this failed Parks and Wallerand swam out to sea with grapnels to prevent it being driven ashore. At 5.35am, those on the MTB saw the dory disappear and then received the message 'Maroon' ('Dory sunk/wrecked'). Ashore, Wallerand decided that he was going to swim to the MTB to see what was going on and disappeared into the waves.

On board the MTB, when swimmers were seen and shouts of 'Aidez-moi! Help!' were heard, Lieutenant Clarkson edged the MTB so close inshore that the distance between the keel and sea bottom was just 5 feet. Dropping scrambling nets over the port side, however, he had difficulty in keeping station, particularly as the swimmers had made little progress and eventually returned to the beach. Wallerand, who was a strong swimmer, reached the MTB, but just as ropes were thrown to him, the MTB was knocked by a wave and the exhausted commando disappeared. Clarkson waited close offshore until 6.00pm in the hope that the commandos would appear and then with dawn not far off, he returned to Dover with Major Laycock reporting one commando missing, believed drowned, and five missing. When Clarkson returned to the beach the following night, which was standard operating procedure, he slowly cruised a mile offshore without seeing anything. Within days, the Germans, no doubt collecting the equipment discarded from the flooded dory, issued a communiqué that a commando raid had been wiped out at Gravelines. It was later reported that 'Jones' and Chapman were both seen making Churchillian V-signs from the back of a German lorry.

Although Hardtack 11 had been a disaster, more so because none of the raiders returned and their fate was unknown, it did not deter further raids. Hardtack 2 was mounted during the night of 24/25 December at Gravelines. During the night of 26 December, in Hardtack 7, Lieutenant McGonical of 12 Commando and five members of 1 (French) Troop left Dartmouth, and landed on Occupied Sark. McGonical had commanded the dory on Forfar Bear 4. Landing on rocks near Derrible Bay, they spent several fruitless hours trying to climb the cliffs and re-embarked in the dory on a beach recced by McGonical and Leading Seaman Boccador. Apart from Boccador believing he had seen a sentry and a box of fuses, nothing was found and the patrol was back on board the MGB by 4.25am.

The same night in Hardtack 28, Captain Philip Ayton (Argyll and Sutherland Highlanders) and four members of 8 (French) Troop landed in a cove near Petit Port on the north coast of Occupied Jersey, after being brought from Dartmouth by a MGB intending to capture a prisoner. Ayton was serving with 2 SBS. After recceing a deserted village and an unoccupied bunker, they knocked on the door of a farmhouse, however the woman who opened it was clearly very frightened. The patrol moved to another farmhouse and once again the commandos were met by a frightened farmer until his brother came downstairs and calmed things down. Over a glass of milk, having told the commandos there was no Resistance, the brothers then guided the patrol to a military strongpoint at Les Platon to capture a prisoner, but were unable to find a way through a minefield that surrounded it. At 4.45am, Ayton abandoned the prisoner snatch and while walking along the cliff back to the dory, as he crossed a fence, he stepped on a mine which blew him down the cliff into an entanglement of brambles. The French signalled the MGB and, after recovering Ayton, carried him with great difficulty to the dory on the beach. Sadly he died before reaching Dartmouth. So far, Operation Hardtack casualties had been heavy with an officer killed on Jersey, seven French and three British missing near Gravelines, and Wallerand missing believed drowned. A considerable amount of equipment had also been lost and very little intelligence gained.

The first Hardtack 4 was mounted during the night of 24/25 December, the intention being to land Lieutenant I.D.C. Smith and eight members of No. 4 Commando to recce beaches near Biville, but it was cancelled because of poor weather. This patrol included Able Seaman Felix Grinspin of 8 (French) Troop. Two nights later, the patrol landed near Creil-sur-Mer, two men climbed the cliffs and dropped ropes. Grinspin, the lightest man, was selected to climb, but just as he was being hauled over the lip, a patrol of fifteen Germans was seen and Grinspin rapidly descended. After Smith and another man had joined the two on the top and the rest were recceing the beach, the Germans saw the MGB hovering offshore and opened fire, forcing it out to sea. While the commandos were returning to her in their dory, a flotilla of E-boats heading east passed by very close. At the same time that Hardtack 2 was repeated at Gravelines during the night of 26/27 December, Hardtack 13 was mounted the same night to recce the area of Benouville, just east of Etretat. Captain Kennard of 2 SAS led the patrol, accompanied by Sub Lieutenant Jean Pinelli and nine 1 (French) Troop, but they were unable to find a way up the cliffs and returned to England without incident.

A third operation on the same night, Hardtack 21, another entirely French patrol commanded by Sub Lieutenant Francis Vourc'h and five men from 1 (French) Troop, recced a 500-yard stretch of beach at Quineville and penetrated a few hundred yards inland. Landing at 11.50pm, the patrol moved inland and encountered a patch of marsh. After extricating themselves, they cut some barded wire and halfway between a small dune and another flooded area discovered an anti-tank obstacle, later identified as Element-C, about which COSSAC needed details. A mobile steel lattice of vertical and horizontal rails sunk into a concrete base positioned individually and fitted with rollers, Element-C, or Belgian Gate, was an anti-tank obstacle developed by the French in 1933. Linked together, it was a formidable barrier. Many of those used by the Germans were from captured stock. Vourc'h carried out a detailed survey of the obstacle and, after taking some mud samples from the floored area, lay up for half an hour in the hope of capturing a prisoner. They boarded the dory at 3.00am on the 27th, but since a searchlight was sweeping the bay from Port St Marcouf it took four hours to reach the MTB. The patrol did not know that they had landed on Utah Beach over which the 4th (US) Division would land on D-Day. For this patrol Vourc'h was awarded the MC, the first to be given to No. 10 (Inter-Allied) Commando, however French bureaucracy delayed approval until Major General Laycock eventually presented Vourc'h with his award when he visited the French soon after D-Day.

Hardtack 7 was repeated during the night of 27/28 December on Occupied Sark by Captain McGonical and a 1 (French) Troop patrol accompanied by the Hungarian Private 'Sayers' from 3 (British) Troop, landing at Derrible Point. Sayer had served in the French Army and had previously been awarded the Croix de Guerre. After climbing a 200-foot sheer cliff and a steep 100-foot slope, they were confined by thick undergrowth to a path, but Leading Seaman Robert Bellany was killed when he stepped on a mine and Able Seaman Maurice Le Floch was wounded. Le Floch looked after the French Troop mascot, a terrier known as Diane. The patrol then ran into two more mines that exploded, wounding McGonical and killing Ordinary Seaman 'Tarzan' Dignac, who had also been wounded by the first explosion. As the patrol withdrew, Ordinary Seaman Joseph Nicot was wounded by another mine, leaving Leading Seaman Boccador the only man left unwounded to help McGonical back to the beach. McGonical was awarded the MC and Boccador was Mentioned in Despatches. Within days, a German communiqué referred to a raid by Anglo-French commandos.

On the same night, another attempt was made to mount Hardtack 23 but the MTB ran aground. Hardtack 26 was launched from Dover after dark on 20 January, the target being Middelkerke, near Ostend. The patrol consisted of Warrant Officer Paul Chausse and six members of No. 8 (French) Troop; although the dory was launched, the engine malfunctioned and put them behind schedule. As they approached the shore, Chausse spotted a vessel and, with the sea becoming rougher, he aborted the raid. A series of Hardtack 14 raids scheduled for January 1944 were cancelled by COSSAC, keen to avoid drawing attention to Normandy until Admiral Bertram Ramsey, who was the Naval Commander, Allied Expeditionary Force to Combined Operations, requested the operations should continue, but not in Normandy. Major General Freddy de Guingand, who was Chief of Staff to General Montgomery, felt that raiding anywhere along the Atlantic coast would give the Germans sufficient intelligence to calculate that the invasion would be in Normandy. When Ramsey's request was placed before the SHAEF Raids and Reconnaissance Committee, it agreed that all raids, except Combined Operations Pilotage Parties activities, were to be banned along the entire French and Belgian coast. Pilotage Parties, normally of canoeists and swimmers, were landing and taking samples of sand, rocks and inspecting the assault beaches.

Major Laycock was then instructed by Naval Intelligence to plan Operation Premium – the reconnaissance of the Wassenaarse area north of Scheveningen on the Dutch coast. The background was that in the spring of 1942, Deputy Director Operations Division (Intelligence) had conducted numerous operations using coastal craft to land and recover agents and material on behalf of MI6 and SOE, however the Germans had become so alert to the activity that their internal security operations were preventing agents from using the coast. The SOE was unaware that an agent named Herbert Lauwers, from N (Holland) Section, had been captured in 1941 carrying ciphers and information, and was handed over to the Abwehr where he was turned by Major Hans Giskes. Although Lauwers sent codes in his messages that he was transmitting under duress, these were ignored and over the next eighteen months, Giskes fooled the British into dropping fifty-four of fifty-nine agents straight into German reception parties. Some were turned before being executed. The Germans dubbed the deception 'Englandspiel' (England game). The Resistance group most affected was the Orde Dienst (OD – Order of Service), whose former officers and civil servants, supplanted by Nazi officials and Dutch collaborators, collected intelligence and developed plans for administrative services and civil order after liberation. A sub-group was the Geheim Dienst Nederland (GDN – Dutch Secret Service). The losses of Lysanders flying in agents to Holland, Belgium and France led to SOE exploring new infiltration routes. Deputy Director Operations Division (Intelligence) had mounted four Operations Madonna by No. 4 Commando under the command of Captain Porteous VC, but each had failed for various reasons. The essential elements of Operation Premium were:

- Establish the possibility of penetration inland as far as the Aankver Canal and find a crossing point.
- Establish if the beach and coastal obstacles encountered during the penetration can be circumnavigated by an individual of Dutch nationality.
- Gain a description of obstacles and identify landmarks and cover.
- Calculate the time it would take an individual to land, cross the beach and be inland.

Major Laycock assigned the fiery Lieutenant Trepel, the French second-in-command, for the operation. Trepel had been upset when his recce in Hardtack 14 had been cancelled and he was denied an opportunity to strike back at the Germans. He had travelled to London and had persuaded the Free French to allow him to lead Hardtack 36, which was originally going to be led by Sub Lieutenant Leopold Hulot; it was also cancelled. Part of Layforce 2, Trepel selected his patrol of five from 8 (French) Troop for Operation Premium. The dory coxswain was Quartermaster Grossi and two French commandos, Able Seaman Grinspin, the radio operator, and Able Seaman Etienne Bougrain. The MTB signaller was the German, Lance Corporal 'Farr', and the dory signaller Private 'Sayers', both of No. 3 (British) Troop.

At 4.00pm on 24 February 1944, MTB 682 (Lieutenant William Beynon) left Great Yarmouth accompanied by four MGBs to screen the purpose of the operation and, if the opportunity arose, hunt enemy shipping. Landing conditions were good, however when his navigation equipment developed a fault, Beynon told Trepel that he would be unable to find the exact landing point, and since none of the MGBs could help, nor could a Dutch naval navigator, he must return to port. Two MGBs diverted to deal with E-Boats in the Humber Estuary were damaged. On 27 February, the direction-finding equipment was declared repaired and the MTB and the MGBs left Great Yarmouth at 4.00pm in good weather, however the equipment intermittently malfunctioned and the flotilla was diverted around a German convoy. By the time the MTB reached the landing point at 1.30am, the recce was two hours late, nevertheless Trepel's patrol quickly transferred to the dory and set off. Ten minutes later, those in the MTB watched red flares burst over the beach and fall between two known bunkers. Thirty yards from the beach, the patrol transferred to the dinghy at about 1.50pm, and although three flares – red, green and white – were fired from a large bunker to the north of Trepel's proposed landing point, they landed while Trepel paddled to the dory to collect a mooring anchor, aiming to return to the dory by 4.30am. More flares were fired, with those from the large bunker falling around the landing point while those from the right bunker were being fired out to sea. Two landed close to the dory and when, ten minutes later, a flare fell into it, Grossi moved about 100 yards out to sea and re-anchored. Those in the dory then heard shouting, as though someone was attacking, but no shooting. More flares lit up the wintry night and German soldiers could be seen using torches around the smaller two bunkers. By now it was 3.30am and when another flare landed near the dory, Grossi took it a further 50 yards out to sea. At 4.30am, 'Sayers' was told by the MTB that the dory should remain in position until 5.00am. The flares ceased at 4.45am, but nothing was heard from the patrol. When Lieutenant Beynon returned to Great Yarmouth he reported the entire patrol missing. Lieutenant Commander David Bradford, who commanded the MTB Flotilla, told him to prepare to return to the beach next night but was instructed by London to countermand the instruction. Although Laycock later wrote this was because of unfavourable weather conditions, the fact was that the wind was favourable for a beach recovery.

On 30 December, E (Parachute) Troop, 3 (British) Troop were moved into the sealed Tarrant Keynston House, near Blandford, in preparation for Operation Hardtack Item, to drop near the village of Le Tot, capture a prisoner and withdraw by MTB. A suspected searchlight position was also to be examined. On 27 February, when the Troop was warned for the operation, Lieutenant Colonel R.L. Broad of Combined Operations watched Exercise Carburettor in which a patrol simulated a parachute drop, carried out a recce and then lay up until a dory collected them after a night abseil. He was satisfied the Troop was ready. On 3 March, on a pitch black and moonless night, Private 'Carson', a German, was abseiling down the Seven Sisters, rehearsing extraction, when his rope twisted in his harness, spun him around and then jammed tight around his chest, making breathing extremely difficult. Drifting in and out of consciousness his only option was to cut the rope with his commando knife. Falling 80ft onto the shingle beach, he shattered his knee, elbow, foot and nose. After a year of operations, he was discharged from the Army. Later, living in Scotland, he qualified as a rugby referee and in 1997, fifty-three years after the fall, he completed a 120-foot abseil down the Holiday Inn, Edinburgh, in aid of the McMillan Cancer Foundation. Two days after 'Carson' fell, Lieutenant W.T. Matthews, the Commando Signals Officer, was severely injured in another fall when he was testing a new type of nylon rope with Captain Hilton-Jones.

Chapter 10

D-Day Preparations

Following his inspection of the Atlantic Wall in January, under Führer Directive 51, and believing that the Allies would land on the long Norman beaches, Field Marshal Erwin Rommel formed Army Group B to defend Normandy and northern France, with Seventh Army responsible for Normandy and Fifteenth Army defending north of the River Orne and northern France. While operationally responsible to Army Group B, the administration of the newly-formed XLVII Panzer Corps was subordinated to Panzer Group West. Field Marshal Gerd von Rundstedt, Commander-in-Chief West, was unable to assure Rommel that he could commit the strategic reserve of the 12th Waffen-SS 'Hitler Jugend', Panzer Lehr and 17th Waffen-SS Panzer Grenadier Divisions without the authority of the High Command of the Armed Forces, in effect Hitler.

The divisions of LXXXIV Corps defending Normandy consisted of two regiments, each of three battalions, made up of veterans of other campaigns commanding German and occupied country conscripts, older men not suited to fighting a major battle, and men unfit after service on the Russian Front. Each also had an Ost (Eastern) battalion of mostly Russian prisoners of war escaping the murderous brutality of prison camps. Shortage of food in Germany had reduced the physical prowess of recruits to the extent that marches over 11 miles usually resulted in casualties. Supplementing diets with local milk was ignored. With the need to develop the Atlantic Wall, military training, which was largely based on the Russian Front experience, took second place to construction work; nevertheless in May, Hitler instructed that the invasion be contested to the last foxhole and the last bullet. Divisional tactical areas were formed into Fortresses from which regiments, companies and platoons fought from Strongpoints while infantry sections occupied Points of Resistance. In addition to the coastal artillery emplacements still evident today, the beaches became a network of beach, underwater obstacles and minefields. 'Rommel's Asparagus' of spikes and wire were planted on potential parachute and glider landing zones. Internal security was by foot, bicycle and motorcycle patrols.

The 352nd Infantry Division was responsible for Coast Defence Sector Bayeaux and consisted of three Grenadier regiments, each of two regular battalions, and the 352nd Fusilier Battalion. The 716th Infantry Division was a static formation raised in Bielefeld. It consisted of 726th and 736th Grenadier Regiments, with the 441st Ost Battalion, supported by artillery, engineers and the usual service support, defending Coast Defence Sector Caen, which stretched 35 miles from the River Dives estuary to La Riviere. The 736th Regiment straddled the River Orne.

Defending the ground between the River Dives and River Seine was LXXXI Corps, which had responsibility for the ground east of the River Dives. Raised in 1942, the 711th Infantry Division first manned the demarcation line between Occupied France and Vichy France before being converted into a fortress division. Lieutenant General Joseph Reichert assumed command in April 1943 and strengthened his weaponry from captured British and French equipment. Although ammunition stocks were diminishing, he exercised quick reaction forces using military vehicles, requisitioned trucks, buses and bicycles. The 155mm artillery battalion was horse drawn and Divisional Recce had not yet been formed. Under interrogation, he said that in spite of Allied activity targeting his sector in May 1944, he was convinced that the Allies would land on the Cotentin Peninsula to take advantage of the port at Cherbourg. The 346th Infantry Division (Lieutenant General Erich Diestel) was raised in October 1942 as a fortress formation until, in December 1943, it was transferred to Fifteenth Army as the army reserve positioned north of Le Havre. The Division consisted of 857th and 858th Grenadier Regiments. Its roles were to counter airborne landings behind the Le Havre fortress; provide counter-attack forces between Fecamp and Le Havre; and be prepared to transfer at short notice to reinforce the defence of the Pas de Calais area. It was not considered to be a major threat.

Brigadier Lord Lovat now commanded 1st Special Service Brigade, which was essentially an Army formation consisting of Nos 3, 4, 6 and 45 (Royal Marines) Commandos, the latter having the least battle experience. In February, he briefed Lieutenant Colonel Robert Dawson, who had assumed command of No. 4 Commando from him in April 1943, at his HQ in Scotland on the invasion of Europe. Lovat told him his Commando was to secure the left flank of Sword Beach by neutralizing coastal batteries, as it had done at Dieppe. Lovat knew the Commando to be highly motivated, nevertheless he was aware that No. 10 (Inter-Allied) Commando had not been committed and offered its two French Troops. The French-speaking Dawson enthusiastically accepted the proposal. He knew them from Dieppe and had been on the 3rd Infantry Division exercise in Scotland during the month when the French had landed with his Commando near Burghead to attack a battery in conditions close to those expected in France. Lieutenant Colonel Lister had previously supported the suggestion.

On 16 April, both Troops joined No. 4 Commando at Bexhill-on-Sea with 1 (French) Troop absorbed as 5 Troop and 8 (French) Troop as 6 Troop. On 11 March, a third French Troop, designated 9 (French) Troop, of five officers, a warrant officer and sixty-three other ranks had joined No. 10 (Inter-Allied) Commando. Lieutenant Kieffer, appointed by Dawson as Senior Officer, French Troops and promoted to Major, formed the 1st Marine Fusilier Commando Battalion and appointed Lieutenant Lofi to take over 5 (French) Troop. Replacing their No. 10 (Inter-Allied) Commando shoulder flashes with those of the Army Commando, the French named themselves Le Franco-Britannique Commando and adopted Army ranks. Differences in drill were resolved when Dawson and Regimental Sergeant Major Bill Morris simplified British movements to suit the flamboyant French system. With traditional phlegm, the British commandos, most of whom knew little about the French activities, were suspicious until the French trained with equal expertise in nearby neighbourhoods; suspicions were forgotten when some French-Canadians pulled a knife on a Frenchman at a Belgian dance in the Lamb Inn in Eastbourne. During the fight, when a French-Canadian fetched a Bren gun, the British waded in on behalf of the French. Lieutenant Pinelli was the French duty officer and had to sort out the inter-Franco differences. Pinelli originated from French Caledonia in the Pacific and had recently married a young widow. On 10 May, the French replaced the Cross of Lorraine cap badge with one designed by Corporal Chauvet of a sailing ship under full sail, over which was superimposed a commando dagger on a bronze shield. In the top left corner was the Cross of Lorraine and on a scroll on the bottom, between two French naval anchors, was inscribed '1er Marine Commando'.

Meanwhile, Captain Hilton-Jones had been lobbying sceptical British officers that 3 (British) Troop be given more recognition. His men had proven themselves in Italy and some were sufficiently well educated that in most British units they would have been commissioned. The German Lance Corporal 'Saunders' came from an aristocratic Jewish family, the Salingers, who lived in Munich. When, in 1937, the Nazis arrested such families, a SS general who arrived in a black Mercedes at the family house turned out to be the groom of Mrs Salinger. Advising the family to leave Germany, he arranged for SS soldiers to pack their belongings in three railway trucks. When the family arrived in England, 'Saunders' was sent to Gordonstoun where a classmate for two years was Prince Philip of Greece, the future husband of Princess Elizabeth. In 1940, the family were interned and 'Saunders' was sent to Canada. Several men had fought in the Spanish

Civil War, including the Hungarian Private 'Swinton' and Czech Corporal 'Latimer'. Hilton-Jones's persistence paid off and on 26 April, Sergeants 'Streeten' and 'Dwelly', Corporals 'Kingsley' and 'Wilmers', and Lance Corporals 'Griffith' and 'Kershew' passed the War Office Selection Board and were posted to No. 165 Officer Corps Training Unit to undertake a shortened course. Lance Corporal 'Firth' was selected for the long course. During the next month, Hilton-Jones promoted two men to sergeant, three to lance sergeant, three to corporal and seven to lance corporal. On being commissioned, 'Wilmers' transferred to the SAS, which had formed a Half Troop of German-speakers.

In April, in preparation for D-Day, Bomber Command softened up German defences and transportation infrastructure by attacking a coastal battery near Houlgate; a bomb exploded on the beach which resulted in several explosions. When photographs were shown to the brilliant communist Professor Desmond Bernal, who was a scientific adviser to Combined Operations, he suggested the Germans might have developed a new mine. Fortunately, the British were tolerant of dissenting scientists and thus kept him wedded to defeating Nazism. A founder of the philosophy of Operational Research and the complexities of warfare, he had analysed the effectiveness of RAF raids on Germany and was playing a crucial role in planning Operation Overlord. The existence of a new mine worried the planners and, in spite of the embargo of raids in France and Belgium, General Montgomery and Admiral Ramsey were sufficiently anxious to authorize Operation Tarbrush in which No. 10 (Inter-Allied) Commando was instructed to carry out four nights of beach recces during the dark period between 14 and 19 May. With D-Day barely three weeks away, secrecy was essential.

When, on 13 May, Hilton-Jones was promoted to Major and appointed Second-in-Command of the Commando, he handed 3 (British) Troop to Lieutenant 'Lane', who had returned from instructing on dories at the Combined Operations centre at Warsash on 24 March. Lieutenant Emmet, the Troop Administration Officer, was promoted to captain and took over as Commando Intelligence Officer and Assistant Adjutant. Two days later, almost on the eve of battle, Lieutenant Colonel Lister handed command of No. 10 (Inter-Allied) Commando to the newly promoted Lieutenant Colonel Peter Laycock, brother of Major General Laycock.

Major Hilton-Jones was appointed Military Commander of Operation Tarbrush and assembled 'Hiltforce' at Dover. The operating procedures were as for Operation Hardtack. Lieutenant 'Lane' selected the best dory coxswains. Technical examination of the mines was the responsibility of a Royal Engineer officer and NCO, both volunteers and experts in mine warfare from 21st Army Group, who would relay their findings through the dory signaller to the MTB. Bernal explained they should be looking for a mine, but its triggering device was not known and could be contact, acoustic, magnetic, remotely electrically controlled or voltaic.

During the night of 15 May, Tarbrush 3, commanded by Lieutenant I.D.C. Smith, were unable to land at Bray Dunes because the sea was too rough. German naval activity forestalled Tarbrush 5, commanded by Captain McGonical, who had recovered from his wounds. Next night, when Tarbrush 8, under the command of Lieutenant E.L. Smith landed at Quend Plage, the Royal Engineer officer slipped from a beach defence and grabbed the mine that he was examining to prevent him being swept out to sea. Nothing happened and the mine was later identified to be an anti-tank Teller 42. Tarbrush 10 landed at Onival the same night, but the MTB had faulty navigational equipment and the dinghy beached too far to the south. Lieutenant 'Lane' commanded the patrol and his dory coxswain was the Dane, Private 'Davies'. The next night Tarbrush 3, 8 and 10 tried again. Lieutenant I.D.C. Smith landed at Bray Dunes undetected and, although a German sentry was seen smoking only 150 yards away, the two Royal Engineers identified the mines as Tellers. Lieutenant E.L. Smith had been ashore for about twenty minutes when they were challenged and a brief firefight broke out before they withdrew. They reported that there were no mines attached to the four rows of beach posts sunk into the sand and the water. Tarbrush 10 turned back from Onival because of deteriorating weather.

From the patrol reports, Professor Bernal concluded that the mines tied to the underwater posts were insufficiently waterproofed, and the sea had corroded the firing pins making the mines sensitive; thus, when the bomb had hit the water, its shock waves detonated the mines. Nevertheless, Lieutenant 'Lane' was instructed to return to Onival on 17 May. It was his third raid in three nights. On board the MTB was Major Hilton-Jones and the dinghy party consisted of 'Lane', 'Davies' as coxswain and the signaller, Corporal King, Royal Marines. The sappers, Lieutenant Roy Wooldridge and Sergeant E. Bluff, were equipped with an infrared camera to take photographs of Element-C, known from air photographs to be near Ault, to the south-west

The patrol landed on time and the two Royal Engineers swept the path with a mine detector to the beach defences of four rows of posts. 'Lane' then accompanied Wooldridge surveying the beach defences, noting the absence of mines and no evidence of Element-C. At about 1.40am on 18 May, 'Lane' sent the two NCOs back to the dinghy with instructions that he and Wooldridge would search for an Element-C, and that if they were not back by 3.00am, they were to return to the dory. The two officers kept in shadow by walking between the second and third row of beach defences, and although it then rained heavily, they moved at a brisk pace, stopping to examine some Tellers strapped to wooden obstacles designed to damage landing craft. By about 2.15am, still some distance from Ault and with the summer dawn not far off, they decided to return to the dinghy.

Meanwhile, King stayed with the dinghy while Sergeant Bluff evaluated the beach defences. Soon after the officers had left, they saw a red flash and assumed it to be the officers taking photographs, but then heard a scream and three shots. Flares from German positions and starshells from the MTB illuminated the rainy night. Taking cover in folds on the beach, they watched a patrol splash along the tide line and detonate a line of illumination canisters. Cut off from the sea and exposed by a flare, the NCOs came under fire from a patrol, however the Germans did not approach them, something Sergeant Bluff later commented upon when he was debriefed, as useful in assessing the quality of the troops in that sector. By 3.00am, they were paddling to the dory, as instructed, when they realized that they were leaving Lane and Wooldridge without any means of escape; they therefore returned to the beach, dragged the dinghy to firm sand and swam to the dory. Bluff was forced to drop the mine detector because it was too heavy. Even as 'Davies' made for the MTB, they were fired on. The rumpus ashore alarmed the MTB commanding officer and although he had weighed anchor for a quick withdrawal, he waited until the dory came alongside at 3.09am. After debriefing two NCOs, Major Hilton-Jones asked the commanding officer to return to his original position and then sent 'Davies' inshore in case the officers had found the dinghy. The MTB could not wait beyond 4.15am and when the dory returned at 3.58am minus the two officers, Hilton-Jones agreed that they should return to Dover, and posted both officers as missing. The success of Operation Tarbrush in solving a puzzle that could have a significant effect on landing troops is reflected in that six MCs, one each to Hilton-Jones and 'Lane', and two bars were awarded, five MMs and four Mentions in Despatches.

Giving his orders for the landings, Brigadier Lovat instructed that 1st Special Service Brigade was to land on Queen Red and then reinforce 6th Airborne Division (Major General Richard Gale), which was to seize the high ground around Breville north of the River Orne during the night and help protect the invasion left flank by slotting in to defensive positions between Franceville Plage and Amfreville. The 6th Airlanding Brigade was scheduled to arrive on D-Day evening. During his inspection of the Atlantic Wall, Field Marshal Rommel had stood in a field beside the crossroads in Breville and noted that Breville had a commanding view of long, wide beaches to the west and to the plains stretching east to Caen and the River Dives to the north.

Sword Beach stretched 5 miles from Lion-sur-Mer north to Ouistreham and was overlooked by the village of Breche. The area was dotted with defended holiday homes and tourist establishments behind a seawall. The strongpoint codenamed WN-20 by Allied planners, nicknamed Cod, covered the beach and the logistic Roger Beach to its left and consisted of an 88mm and three 50mm anti-tank guns, three mortars and six machine guns in an area covering roughly 300 yards wide and 150 yards in depth. Also covering the beach was WN-18, which consisted of a 75mm field gun and a 50mm anti-tank gun. The sector was defended by 10 Company, 3/736th Grenadier Regiment.

1st Special Service Brigade was to land behind the 2nd East Yorkshires, the amphibious Duplex Drive (DD) Sherman tanks of the 13/18th Hussars and the Centaur tanks of 5th Independent Battery, Royal Marines Armoured Support Group. Sherman Crab Flail tanks from A Squadron, 22nd Dragoons were to punch holes through minefields while sappers and Armoured Vehicles Royal Engineers (AVRE) from 79 Squadron, 5th Assault Regiment were to tackle the beach defences. Sexton self-propelled guns of 33rd and 76th Field Regiments on landing craft were in close support. Brigadier Lovat hoped that the infantry would have dealt with much of the opposition before the Brigade landed. The Brigade priority tasks were:

- Nos 3 and 6 Commandos – reinforce 6th Airborne Division in the Breville area.
- No. 4 Commando – clear Ouistreham of the enemy.
- No. 45 (Royal Marines) Commando – seize Franceville Plage and secure the approaches to Cabourg.

Dawson gave his orders that No. 4 Commando would assemble at a wrecked children's holiday camp about 250 yards inland from Breche. The French would lead the advance into Ouistrehem and then divert to attack the Riva Bella strongpoint WN-10.

The Germans had flattened the Riva Bella casino and replaced it with a formidable position consisting of a two 75mm guns and machine-gun bunkers, individual Tobruk weapon pits connected by trenches over-looked by a water tower, and protected by field defences. When the French saw the air photographs, they knew exactly where they were going. Corporal Chauvet:

A month before the opening of the Second Front, we studied air photographs and plans in detail of where we were to land. Very quickly, we knew the ground by heart. The German defences con-sisted of blockhouses and pillboxes along Boulevard Aristide Briand with a strongpoint at the Casino. Between the Casino and the port, there was an anti-tank ditch and some flame-throwers. The mission of the two French troops was to clear out about twelve pillboxes along the Boulevard Aristide Briand as far as the Casino.

The aristocratic Sergeant Count Guy de Montlaur was reportedly delighted because, as he reminded Kieffer, he had lost several fortunes in the casino.

The British were to destroy coastal battery WN-08 and ensure that the Orne Canal sluice gates remained intact. Air photographic interpreters had identified WN-08 to consist of six 155m French guns in open emplacements between 50 and 80 yards apart across the northern corner of Ouistreham covering Sword and Roger Beaches, and protecting the harbour entrance and lock. The complex was defended by at least two 20mm Flak anti-aircraft guns, machine-gun posts and field defences. Both batteries was connected to a tall tower in the middle of Ouistrehem

Since it was not known how many wireless operators would survive the landings, or the extent of the German jamming radios, Captain Kieffer donated a British hunting horn to Dawson to rally the Commando. To increase the firepower of the Heavy Weapons Troop, Lovat gave Dawson eight Vickers .303 aircraft K-type machine-guns, firing 950 rounds per minute from circular magazines adopted for the ground role. Since the French lacked Vickers machine guns, Dawson gave four to Kieffer, who assembled them in the 24-strong K-Gun Section commanded by Lieutenant Pierre Amaury. Attached to the French were six Royal Signals handling rear link communications to HQ 1st Special Service Brigade, and two RAMC orderlies supporting the Medical Officer, Captain Robert Lion.

4th Special Service Brigade (Brigadier 'Jumbo' Leicester) was essentially a Royal Marine formation:

- No. 41 (Royal Marines) Commando – land on the right flank of Sword Beach, destroy defences at Lion-sur-Mer and link up with No. 48 (Royal Marines) Commando.
- No. 48 (Royal Marines) Commando – land on Canadian Juno Beach and at St Aubin, and destroy coastal defences at Langrune.
- No. 46 (Royal Marines) Commando – assault coastal artillery batteries at Houlgate and Mont Canisy if they threaten the landings.
- No. 47 (Royal Marines) Commando – land on the right flank of British Gold Beach, capture Port-en-Bessin and link up with the US left flank landing on Omaha Beach. The port was designated as the US logistic funnel with Mulberry Harbour A. The British used Arromanches.

Attached to the two brigades were the forty-four men of 3 (British) Troop. With the Half Troop with the 2nd Special Service Brigade in the Mediterranean and others on courses, this was the balance of the Troop. Hilton-Jones divided the Troop into sections and, sceptical that Commandos had sufficient knowledge of the German Army, he instructed them to 'Make yourselves useful. If a CO won't use you, keep nagging until he does' and prove that their German linguistic skills would be useful to Intelligence Sections. Their deployment is not known, however a suggestion is at Appendix 5. Since most Royal Marines Commandos were still unblooded, the arrival of the Troop was welcomed, however, it seems that some of the Troop was unimpressed with the standard of Royal Marines training. Many of the battle-experienced Army Commandos, however, viewed the Germanic-accented and in some cases educated soldiers with suspicion. Some Commandos were assigned to Troops while others were kept at Commando HQ. The five commanded by Corporal 'Nichols' attached to No. 6 Commando were dismayed because the unit had the reputation of being a 'bullshit' unit led by regimental disciplinarians to the extent that chevrons were highlighted with white blanco, with Lieutenant Colonel Derek Mills-Roberts (Irish Guards) insisting on parade-ground smartness, even in the field. They believed that Hilton-Jones had appointed a corporal as a detachment commander to avoid a sergeant being demoted. Corporal 'Nichols' remained at Commando HQ. When Lance Corporal 'Masters' was sent to 1 (Cycle) Troop, which was commanded by Captain Robinson, an experienced commando, he found that balancing his rucksack (containing two days of dehydrated rations, spare clothing, a blanket and pickaxe), his Thompson, 200 rounds of ammo, four hand grenades and 200 feet of hemp rope on his bicycle was difficult. He had hoped to dash cross the beach.

On 3 June, the newly commissioned Second Lieutenant 'Griffith' was appointed as the Commando Mechanical Transport Officer and then, four days later, when Lieutenant 'Lane' was confirmed missing, he took command of 3 (British) Troop. Second Lieutenant Emmet took over as the Administration Officer.

With each man issued with an 'Embarkation Tag' showing his name and number, and a tear-off slip marked 'Disembarkation Tag' for the dead and wounded, on 25 May, 1st Special Service Brigade assembled at the closed American-administered Camp C18, near Titchfield at the mouth of the River Hamble. Here the commandos were given detailed briefings and orders, and then on 4 June, after a religious service followed by an address from Lord Lovat, the French were taken by truck to Warsash where they embarked on two LCI(S) of the 201st Flotilla, 1st LCI (Small) Squadron:

- LCI 523 (Lieutenant Charles Craven RNVR) embarked 6 (French) Troop (Lieutenant Alex Lofi), Troop Headquarters and two K-Guns. Craven commanded the pair of LCIs.
- LCI 527 (Sub Lieutenant Jack Berry RNVR) embarked Battalion HQ, 5 (French) Troop (Lieutenant Guy Vourc'h) and two K-Guns.

Disembarkation from the landing craft was by gangplanks lowered from the bow. For heavily loaded infantry, this was precarious and overbalancing into a ducking was not uncommon.

Major Kieffer asked Craven that the two landing craft should land as close together and as far to the left of Sword Beach as possible, so that his 177 commandos would land in strength. His men included the Luxemburger big game hunter, Lance Corporal Jean Reiffers, the Belgian brothers, Lance Corporal Antoine and Private Jean Neuwen, and the French-Canadian Sergeant Paul Briat. Briefed that mines and booby-trapped obstacles would be cleared, Kieffer's navigation way markers ashore included Ouistreham Church spire, which was about a mile inland, a modern square grey villa on the foreshore marking the eastern limit of the Red sector of Sword Beach, and a round water tower beyond indicating the WN-20 strongpoint in Breche.

When General Eisenhower uttered those immortal words at his HQ at Southwick House 'OK, we go' at 8.15pm on 5 June, a day behind the original D-Day schedule, the message flashed around the invasion forces and 6,939 vessels of all shapes, sizes and tonnages set a course to a mid-Channel assembly area and then split into their various flotillas – minesweepers, escorts, landing craft and warships on the gun line. The sea was still rough and most of the commandos were seasick, even those who were experienced sailors. Overhead, the 6th Airborne Division headed toward their DZs near the bridges of the River Orne and its canal, and Merville and Ranville. Captain Kieffer had visited the commandos on his landing craft and, after a few moments going over final details, they knelt in prayer as he repeated the words of Sir Jacob Astley before the Battle of Newbury: 'Lord, I shall be very busy this day. I may forget thee, but do not thou forget me.'

Chapter 11

Operation Overlord: 6 June 1944

No. 41 (Royal Marines) Commando landed in some disruption 300 yards from their intended beach at Lion-sur-Mer. Wading ashore under heavy fire, Sergeant Major 'Gray' and Corporal 'Latimer' encouraged inexperienced Royal Marines to get off to the beach and into the shelter of the dunes and grassy knolls. The interrogation of prisoners by Sergeant 'Gray', who would be wounded five times on D-Day, enabled Lieutenant Colonel Tim Gray to direct his Commando through a minefield to the forming-up place where they divided into two columns to attack the chateau and Strongpoint WN-21, codenamed 'Trout'. Moving west to attack a château near Lion-sur-Mer, Gray was killed and contact was lost with its Royal Marines Armoured Support Group and artillery support. While clearing a house, 'Gray' encountered an old Arab using an ancient muzzleloader to snipe at the Germans and he was adopted by 3 (British) Troop until later wounded. The Royal Marines were subjected to several counter-attacks by 3/736th Grenadier Regiment and forced to withdraw to Lion-sur-Mer.

No. 48 (Royal Marines) Commando suffered heavy casualties landing at St Aubin from bunkers at Langrune. Even with the Royal Marines Armoured Support Group, it was unable to link up with No. 41 (Royal Marines) Commando.

As No. 47 (Royal Marines) Commando approached Juno Beach with orders to seize Port-en-Bessin, the Austrian Sergeant 'Fuller' commanding its 3 Troop detachment astonished the men in his LCA by sitting on the stern, telling everyone the landing was fantastic. As the Commando approached the beaches, five LCAs were sunk and seven damaged. The Austrian Lance Corporal 'Terry', aged nineteen, and Private 'Andrews' both landed, but Corporal 'Webster' was killed when his LCA was sunk. Spread across 1,500 yards of beach, the landing turned into a shambles. Since many men had swum ashore, weapons were taken from British casualties. 'Fuller' persuaded a surrendered German position to hand its captured weapons to the Royal Marines. At midday, as the Commando headed to Port-en-Bessin, it was clear 231 Infantry Brigade was having a tough time clearing Le Hemel. 'Fuller' and 'Terry' joined a recce patrol commanded by Corporal Thornton and, after a short, sharp exchange of fire in La Rosiere, persuaded about twenty disenchanted Poles conscripted into the Wehrmacht to carry the Royal Marines' equipment. During the afternoon, they captured a cyclist who turned out to be a Regimental Sergeant Major, insisting on being treated in accordance with the Geneva Convention. He said that he was cycling to an Ouistreham brothel and then intended to surrender trusting he would be sent to Canada where he wanted to live. Both commandos were excited because on the Intelligence courses they had been told that Regimental Sergeant Major was a rank rarely used in the German Army. The prisoner had fought on the Russian Front where he had been wounded and had been discharged, but had been recalled to the colours on light duties, commanding a prison camp of refugees from Franco's Spain.

By nightfall, the Commando had seized Mont Cavalier (Point 72) south of Port-en-Bessin. Next day, after a patrol sent to Escures captured a medical bunker, 'Terry' translated a message to be taken by a captured medical captain to the Port-en-Bassin commander suggesting surrender by 3.00pm. When the mayor of Come-de-Fresne reported a wounded RAF Spitfire pilot hidden in the village, 'Terry' joined Corporal Thornton to rescue him. Capturing several Polish prisoners on the way, they were greeted as liberators in St Come until a sniper opened fire. 'Terry' ran upstairs and captured four more prisoners. In the event, the pilot wished to remain in the village but as the patrol returned to Point 72, a Royal Marine was killed by a sniper. During the night, before 'Terry' joined Corporal Thornton who had been ordered to return to La Rosiere to collect stragglers, he learnt that Sergeant 'Fuller' was missing, believed captured. On the way, 'Terry' was shot in the thigh by a sniper. At La Rosiere, Thornton found about 10 Royal Marines, one carrying a Lewis gun from a wrecked landing craft, however, as the patrol was rejoining the Commando, it became separated into several groups. By now, 'Terry's' wound was painful and he spent the night with a French family. Meanwhile, the Commando captured Port-en-Bessin. Next morning, escorted by several captured German naval personnel, he was wheeled in a cart belonging to the family into the port where his arrival was greeted with considerable amusement by the Royal Marines and by the ever-cheerful Sergeant 'Fuller'. 'Terry' refused evacuation until he collapsed next day and was evacuated to England, complete with souvenirs, including a pair of binoculars, and had an emotional meeting with his parents. While waiting for the landing craft, he met the German Regimental Sergeant Major who was complaining about the lack of food and poor sanitation.

After being captured by German paratroopers near Point 72, 'Fuller' briefly escaped only to be recaptured by a column of German cyclists, who took him to a château where he was searched. Finding a rubber London Underground handgrip, which had been issued to commandos as coshes, they told him coshes were against the Geneva Conventions and proceeded to hit him with his, although not too hard, then locked him in a cell with the promise of a court martial. In the confusion of No. 47 (Royal Marines) Commando's attack, he escaped.

On 7 June, Nos 41, 46 and 48 (Royal Marines) Commandos were tasked to neutralize the Douvres radar complex. The complex housed two radar bunkers, was four storeys deep and had formidable armoury of three 50mm anti-tank guns and six 40mm flak guns, supported by strong field defences. The previous evening a company from 192nd Panzer Grenadier Regiment, 21st Panzer Division, moved in to bolster the defence. In a long operation, the Commandos disrupted the radar, but with the Royal Marines in demand elsewhere, by 9 June, only No. 41 (Royal Marines) Commando was still in the area. Late on 11 June, Sergeant Major 'O'Neill' was part of a fighting patrol breaching a minefield. He marked the positions of one S-mine with his white handerkerchief and placed his hand over the spikes of a second one, nevertheless a Royal Marine stepped on the first and the patrol withdrew under fire. When it seemed next day that the smaller bunker might have been evacuated, a fighting patrol, which included 'O'Neill', blew holes in the fence with Bangalore torpedoes and then laid white tape along a cleared route for Royal Engineer AVREs to use and shell the bunker. However, they were forced to withdraw under heavy fire, leaving an AVRE tipped into an anti-tank ditch. On the other side of the complex, Corporal 'Latimer' was involved in a diversionary attack and clubbed a German with his pistol, but injured his finger in the process. Eventually on 17 June, supported by AVREs, mine-lifting flail tanks and artillery, the Royal Marines captured the complex. 'Latimer' threw a phosphorous grenade into a ventilation shaft, which quickly induced the occupants underground to surrender. Sergeant Major 'O'Neill' was later returned to his unit after a disagreement with an inexperienced junior officer on a patrol.

Off Sword Beach, at 5.00am, *Princess Astrid* and *Maid of Orleans* hove to 9,000 yards from the assault beaches, and No. 4 Commando scrambled down the nets into their LCAs. On LSI(S) 523, a sailor poked his head into the troop compartments and quietly told the French 'It's time.' The 25-man Sub-Sections were squeezed in the compartments surrounded by their equipment. At about 5.30am, Major Kieffer had a small breakfast in the wardroom, including, in his opinion, poor coffee and then joined Battalion HQ and Lieutenant Guy Vourc'h and 6 (French) Troop. All was silent, except for the swishing of the waves against the hull until at 5.40am, the early morning tranquillity was shattered by the warships opening fire. Twenty minutes later Allied bombers rumbled overhead heading for the French coast. Corporal Jean Couturier was the signaller to Lieutenant Lofi:

> During the crossing it rained, it was cold, the sea was very rough and most of us were sick. We occasionally heard the bagpipes of Bill Millin, the piper of Lord Lovat. I did not know Bill personally, because he did not speak French, but we began to understand the power of his instrument and its sound became a signature of the Commando. With Hitler condemning us to die in the event of capture, the bagpipes brought us together in the Commando brotherhood and increased our confidence. As day broke and the fleet approached the Normandy coast, I was impressed by the balloons attached to the boats, hundreds of them and as far as the eye could see. It was incredible. It was then I realised the gigantic operation in which we were taking part. It was almost unreal.

On the upper deck, as the Troop Medical Officer, Captain Robert Lion, reported the BBC had announced that the Allies had entered Rome, the French were acutely aware that they were going home. Some would not survive. About a mile from 'Queen Red', an E-boat torpedoed an escorting Norwegian destroyer.

At 7.20am in the grey early morning, the two LCI(S)s, on the right of No. 4 Commando, approached Sword Beach. Ahead, 13/18th Hussars DD Shermans had hauled themselves ashore at 7.25am after a 7-mile swim, just as the ramps of the 8 Infantry Brigade landing craft splashed into the water and the leading infantry companies of 2nd East Yorks charged ashore, straight into heavy, accurate fire from WN-20 and WN-18. Speed after landing is critical, but the withering fire, casualties and shock of action experienced by the inexperienced infantry commanders at all levels led to inertia. With a stronger prevailing wind, a tide flowing quicker than expected, and casualties, the Royal Engineers of 79th Assault Division had trouble clearing paths through the beach obstacles. Sherman Flail tanks of the 22nd Dragoons were also being picked off.

When Lieutenant Craven saw that the beach defences were largely intact, he hailed Sub Lieutenant Berry and suggested they land further south, however Berry, having guessed where there were probably mines, said that he was taking LCI 523 straight in. Engaging full speed ahead, his coxswain drove the landing craft through the obstacles so hard that when it beached at 7.32am, its bridge was level with the tide line. Berry dropped the bow ramps and ordered, 'Troops out!' Kieffer's first question was, 'Are we at the right beach?' When he saw they were, Lieutenant Lofi shouted, 'Ready to disembark!' whereupon the heavily laden 6 (French) Troop negotiated the narrow ramp, dropped onto the sand and quickly advanced inland through the carnage of the first wave. Corporal Couturier:

> At 7.30, No. 4 Commando landed opposite Breche. We charged down the ramps with our 120lbs of equipment. A mortar shell hit LCI 527, wrecking the ramp. As far as I am concerned, 8 Troop landed without much reaction from the Germans and crossed a barbed wire entanglement. Others remembered a savage response from the enemy. It was a very personal experience. I ran, as quickly as I could, my prime objective to survive. I have little recollection of what was happening around me, however, there were losses.

Craven followed Berry but his propellers fouled an underwater obstacle and her ramps were wrecked by the direct hit. Stranded several yards off-shore and with some crew wounded by machine-gun fire, the scrambling nets were lowered, some members of 5 (French) Troop dropped into the water up to their chests and struggled ashore. When Berry went astern and came alongside, commandos clambered onto his landing craft and then he beached a second time. Corporal Otto Zivohlava, an Austrian who lived in Paris, had been torpedoed twice in the Atlantic during his escape to England and had the alias 'Jean Gautier' to outwit the Gestapo:

> Pinelli is the first to move. Opposite the ruins of the distant holiday camp, I follow Casalonga and Piauge. The water is up to my chest and, with my Thompson held above my head, I wade with some difficulty through the waves. The air is full of the sound of bullets, all seemingly directed at me. On the beach, there are a dozen bodies of Royal Engineers from the 5th Assault Regiment quietly moving backwards and forwards as the waves ebb and flow. The Germans have knocked out some special tanks of the 79th Armoured Division. The water was cold but no one really remembered this. The air was alive with bullets and ricochets and all, it seemed, concentrated on us. When we arrived on dry sand, a large pond barred our way. Lieutenant Pinelli plunged straight in with about a dozen men, however not wishing to get my feet wet a second time, I went around to the right. This was fortunate because a mortar fell among Pinelli's men. When the blast cleared, among the wounded was Casalonga, who was celebrating his birthday and Pinelli was stretched out on the sand, his legs peppered by splinters. When he noticed his friend, Lance Corporal Pepe Dumenoir, stomach ripped open, was dying, Pinelli groped to him on his elbows but there was no question of helping. Orders were orders. The assault had to be carried out and I had only fifteen minutes to reach the holiday camp.

Corporal Chauvet was with Battalion HQ:

> Royal Engineers, with their white-ringed helmets, were with us. After 25 or 30 metres in waist high water, we had to cross sand and pools of water to reach dry sand, all swept by machine-gun fire from the left. I do not remember being wet. As I ran across the sand, there were already several casualties. I saw Captain Kieffer had been wounded in the thigh and was being treated by a French medical orderly. Where the sand started to be covered with vegetation, there was a network of barbed wire through which there was a 2-metre gap. We had to pass through in single file and it was while I was waiting that I was told of the casualties.

Meanwhile, No. 4 Commando had pushed through the 2nd East Yorks while C Troop had tackled several pill boxes and trenches near WN-18 and crossed the coast. They had taken forty casualties, including Lieutenant Colonel Dawson wounded in the leg, and Corporal 'Franklyn', killed by a mortar splinter who, after being wounded in Italy, had been determined to take part in the landings. Sergeant 'Howarth', also landing with No. 4 Commando, was so seriously wounded in the chest and stomach from mortar splinters that he required seven operations. As he drifted in and out of consciousness, he persuaded a group of prisoners that he was their ticket to England provided they injected him with morphine, nevertheless it was a day before he was evacuated. Dawson was wounded a second time, this time in the head, while trying to find the 2nd East Yorks Battalion HQ.

When the French reached the holiday camp, Battalion HQ had suffered two wounded on the beach, Major Kieffer hit by mortar fragments and Private Harcourt, a No. 4 Commando wireless operator. 5 Troop had lost three killed and eleven wounded, including Lieutenant Vourc'h, while 6 Troop had no casualties. With Lieutenant Pinelli wounded, Kieffer appointed Lieutenant Jean Mazeas, the Administrative Officer, to command 5 (French) Troop until he was seriously wounded on a recce a little later. Short of officers, Kieffer disbanded Battalion HQ and took command of 5 Troop with Sergeant Major Herbert Faure as his Second-in-Command. It was 8.15am.

Having contacted HQ 6th Airborne Division and established that the canal and road bridges over the Orne were intact, Dawson handed command over to his Second-in-Command, Major Ronald Menday, saying that he would catch them up, and instructed his Adjutant, Captain Donald Gilchrist, to get the Commando moving. Since the French were to lead the advance to Ouistrehem, Gilchrist ran over shouting, 'Allez! Allez! Vite! Vite!' Somewhat perplexed, the French thought that he was shouting

'Allah! Allah!' Nevertheless, they rose and Second Lieutenant Leopold Hulot's Section in 6 Troop led the advance along Avenue de Lion-sur-Mer, keeping the narrow-gauge tram railway on the right until the column arrived on the outskirts of Ouistrehem, having been bracketed by mortar fire while breaching a minefield.

6 Troop and Lieutenant Hubert's K-Gun Section had been ordered to deal with a blockhouse on the western sector of the Riva Bella WN-20 sector and, leaving the column, it headed towards the beach through the side streets, using Boulevard de Maréchal Joffre as the axis. 5 Troop continued to lead the advance until it reached Avenue de Pasteur that led direct to the casino. At the next junction, No. 4 Commando turned right and filtered through Ouistrehem to attack the battery WN-08, only to find that the guns had been moved inland several days earlier and had been replaced by telegraph poles.

Darting from house to house, 6 Troop arrived at the chateau. Just as Lieutenant André Bagot's Section entered the grounds, they came under mortar fire, however Second Lieutenant Hulot found a break in the perimeter wall and led the Troop through another minefield, past several abandoned machine-gun posts and continued advancing along Boulevard de Maréchal Joffre, taking more casualties from mortars, including Hulot. Bagot then took over the lead and, as they approached the defences and its network of trenches, machine-gun fire wounded four French. Houses provided some cover and as Bagot was deployed to attack, the wounded Hulot arrived to rejoin his Section; however Lofi ordered him to join the Sub-Section commanded by Sergeant Major Chausse which was taking up position on a dune to the left, ready to give covering fire. Chausse was Second-in-Command to Bagot. As Bagot advanced, Chausse's men opened fire with everything they had – rifles, two PIATs, Brens and the K-Guns – and although Hulot managed to get within grenade-throwing distance, the barrage had little impact on the defences. Barbed wire was proving a major obstacle and since the Bangalore torpedoes had been rendered useless by being soaked, the attack ground to a halt.

When a German section began to outflank the two K-Guns commanded by Sergeant Robert Saerens providing support from a bomb crater, Lofi instructed Bagot to link up with Saerens. Lieutenant Hubert was killed trying to signal Saerens to join him and then matters became critical when both guns developed stoppages. Saerens ordered they be taken to a house to be stripped and cleaned. Taking advantage of this, the German section worked their way toward the crater, however, as soon as the K-Guns were ready, Saerens reoccupied the crater and was joined by Bagot. With casualties being treated by the Algerian Lance Sergeant Ouassini Bouarfa, Lofi sent his runner, the wounded Lance Corporal Guy Laot, to ask Major Menday for tank support. He had just ordered 6 Troop to withdrew when the house in which he and several commandos were taking cover was hit by an anti-tank shell fired from the Riva Bella WN-10 strongpoint, collapsing it in a dusty heap. During a pause in the fighting, at about 11.00am, Dawson arrived and told Lofi that he had done a good job and must return to the holiday camp to prepare for the Commando's next task.

As 5 Troop advanced toward WN-10 down Avenue de Pasteur, an elderly, white-haired gentleman sporting a magnificent moustache appeared at the front of the column. 'Stop! The houses are full of Germans. Give me a rifle! I fought in the last war.' Pierre Lefevre, veteran of the First World War, was a member of the Resistance. Kieffer sent Lieutenant Amaury and two K-Guns to find a fire position to support both Troops, which they did in a house in Boulevard d'Angleterre. Guided by Lefevre, 5 Troop cautiously approached a house known to be a German machine-gun post but, short of the junction with the coastal Boulevard Aristide Brian, they were confronted by a concrete wall across the road about 100 yards from WN-10, blocking their progress. The wall had not been mentioned in the briefings but in the middle was a hole. Going over the top was suicidal, so the Troop took cover in waste ground; as they did so, Lance Corporal Emile Renault was killed by a sniper from a house on the left. With the Troop's depleted firepower enhanced by several Thompsons collected from casualties, the commandos burrowed into shelter out of sight of snipers.

Knowing that he had to dominate the German position and with no alternative but order a frontal assault, Kieffer, Sergeant Major Faure, Sergeant de Montlaur and Lance Corporal Nicholas Poli found a fire position for the two PIATs on the first floor of a house overlooking WN-10, but it was quickly rendered untenable by snipers and a 20mm cannon on the water tower. When Kieffer then heard over the radio that 5th Royal Marine Armoured Support Battery Centaurs had landed, in an action dramatized in the film *The Longest Day*, he and his batman, Private Ferdinand Devager, went to find one. On the way Kieffer shot a German with his revolver when two Frenchwomen indicated the man was in their house. At about 9.25am, after some difficulty in persuading the Battery to provide support, they returned riding on the back decks of the Centaur commanded by Sergeant E.R. Woods. Kieffer:

> I decided to keep the wall as protection and go with the tank through an adjacent courtyard and we set up in front of the casino and commenced firing under my direction. The first two shells went into the casino which stopped its two guns firing. At that moment, having just been wounded in the right arm by a rifle bullet, I dropped from the tank and went forward five metres behind a wall and directed the tank's firing by hand signals.

Blasted by the shock waves as the tank fired, Kieffer directed Woods as he lobbed explosive canister shells into the German positions; a steel cupola proved impossible to silence. Meanwhile the Troop had been divided in two equal-sized Sections by Troop Sergeant Major Faure. Kieffer planned that they should filter through the hole and assault WN-10 with Sergeant de Montlaur's Sub-Section on the left and Sergeant Major Abel Lardennois on the right. It was then that he learnt that Captain Lion had been killed at the Regimental Aid Post at 47, Avenue de Pasteur. Assisted by the 5 Troop medical orderly, Private Gwenn-Ael Bollore, aged eighteen, Lion was administering morphine to Lance Corporal Paul Rollin, who had been shot in the head, when he was shot dead by a sniper. Bollore and de Montlaur dragged the wounded Rollin into a bomb crater but he later died in England. When Lardennois's Section came under fire from the water tower, the Centaur wrecked it with four shells. Pulverized by the pre-landing naval bombardment, shelled by the Centaur and cut off from escape as the French began to breach the defences, the men of 2/736 Grenadier Regiment began to surrender – dusty, grey faced and uniforms in tatters. Sergeant Louis Lanternier was escorting a dozen prisoners, which included several Poles, when one was unwise enough to throw a grenade, which wounded two Frenchmen. Retribution was swift with three prisoners killed.

Monsieur Lefevre, who had been given a rifle and ammunition, told Sergeant Major Faure that he knew where telephone lines linking the WN-10 battery command post in the water tower to the German Command Post in the 52-feet high bunker in the centre of the town, and to Caen, were buried. Faure and Lance Corporal Nicot dug a hole and fractured the cables with two 8lb pack charges of plastic explosive (PE). An earlier attempt made by No. 4 Commando to attack the Command Post was repulsed by machine-gun fire and grenades thrown from the top. It was not until 9 June that Lieutenant Bob Orrell of 91 Field Company, Royal Engineers, and a demolition team blew in the armour-plated door and took the surrender of two officers and fifty men.

By 11.20am, the fighting around WN-10 had largely died down and the French were in control of western Ouistreham. When Father de Naurois mentioned to Kieffer, 'These men are magnificent,' the attack had cost Battalion HQ one killed – Captain Lion – 5 Troop had lost two killed and three wounded, one evacuated, while 6 Troop had one killed and sixteen wounded. The K-Gun Troop lost three killed and one seriously wounded. Some civilians were surprised to see that the British were actually Frenchmen. Arrangements were made to evacuate Madame Odette Mousset to Roehampton Hospital after she lost a leg in bombing and Corporal Zivohlava distributed two kilos of sweets he had brought among frightened children.

The nature of cinema creates legends and so when a Sherman tank was used in *The Longest Day*, this became part of the story. In his report on the attack, written on 13 June 1944 to Rear Admiral d'Argenlieu, Major Kieffer notes the excellent conduct of the commander of the Royal Marine Centaur, and also refers to collecting a Centaur in his memoirs, *Les Berets Verts Francais du 6 Juin 1944*.

At about 11.30am, Lieutenant Colonel Dawson ordered No. 4 Commando to reassemble at the holiday park. By 12.40pm, the two French Troops had reorganized and redistributed ammunition, stores and equipment, and after a 25-minute rest, although most had not eaten since the previous evening, they hoisted their rucksacks on their backs and followed No. 4 Commando toward Colleville-sur-Mer.

No. 6 Commando landed with Brigade HQ in ten LCI(S) at 7.40am on 'Sword Beach, Queen Red Beach' with orders to reinforce Major Howard's D Company, 1st Oxfordshire and Buckinghamshire Light Infantry and Bucks at the Orne Bridges. The LCI(S) carrying Brigade HQ took a direct hit and spun out of control. Private 'Drew' stormed ashore alongside Brigadier Lovat with his Thompson loaded with just one round. Thompson magazines had been adapted for D-Day to take thirty-two rounds, as opposed to twenty, and his, as they habitually did, fell off – into the shallows. As 'Drew' crossed the sea wall, he told two Germans soldiers who surrendered to him that Nazi propaganda was misleading and that the Allies were 10 miles from Rome – they told him the city had been entered that very morning. Managing not to fall off the ramp, 'Masters' dragged his bicycle through the shallows and, seeing Major Hilton-Jones landing with Brigade HQ, saluted him, possibly the only salute in the landings. Hoisting the bicycle onto his shoulder, he followed Captain Robinson across the beach, which was curiously empty of infantry, past sappers sweeping for mines and across the tram track to a ploughed field bisected by 6-foot ditches of thick mud topped by water. Robinson indicated the assembly point at the corner of a flat field about 800 yards away, on the edge of Colleville-sur-Mer. Cover was sparse and scaling ladders were laid across ditches until snipers forced the commandos to cross and recross a muddy stream several times. 'Masters' was waiting to drag his bicycle along a ditch when a Sherman rumbled up and shot up the snipers with its 75mm main armament and Browning machine gun.

By the time that 'Masters' reached the assembly point, the Commando was about twenty-five minutes behind schedule, nevertheless Lord Lovat instructed him to interrogate two shell-shocked prisoners about the location of German artillery. However, when 'Masters' checked their paybooks, one turned out to be a Pole conscripted into the 736th Infantry Regiment, and the other a Russian – as neither spoke German Masters suggested to Lovat that since French was the second language of Poland,

106

he might like to question the Pole. Punching holes through the 736th Regiment, the Commando advanced through Colleville-sur-Mer decked in signs welcoming 'les Tommies' and along roads of excited French people. Leaving C Company, 1st Suffolks and C Squadron, 13/18th Hussars to mop up some pillboxes and a multi-barrelled mortar, No. 6 Commando and Brigade HQ again set off at a fast pace past exposed Teller mines on the side of the road, lifeless parachutists hanging from trees, and dead and injured cattle, most of the time under intermittent sniper and mortar fire, through Aubin d'Arquenay to La Port.

Nos 3 Commando and 45 (Royal Marines) Commandos had landed at 8.10am and although the Army lost twenty men when their LCI(S) was hit, there was little opposition and both caught up with Brigade HQ and No. 6 Commando, which had been greatly assisted in their advance through St Aubin d'Arquenay by the 13/18th Hussars. As 1 (Cycle) Troop approached the high ground overlooking the River Orne, the lead cyclist was killed by a Spandau from a pillbox at the north end of Benouville. The Troop, many of them North African veterans with Captain Robinson, dismounted. Following Major Hilton-Jones's edict for 3 (British) Troop to nag, 'Masters' had done so with Robinson on several occasions, without success, and was not entirely convinced that he trusted him. Asked by Robinson to recce the village, 'Masters' was briefing him what he intended to do when it slowly dawned on him that he was to walk down the road, devoid of any cover, to a village not yet cleared of enemy, and, realizing that Robinson considered him expendable, draw fire. Remembering a scene from *Life in the Bengal Lancers* in which Cary Grant tells a dissident mob the immortal lines 'You are all under arrest', he walked down the slope and instructed the defenders to surrender. Not surprisingly, there was no response from the amazed defenders at the lunacy of this Austrian-accented British soldier, until a German armed with a Schmeisser sub-machine gun popped up from behind a wall, opened fire and missed. 'Masters' dropped to one knee to fire back with his Thompson but it jammed after one round, with two rounds in the breech. 'Masters' fought to clear the stoppage and when the German again missed, he scrambled into cover behind a grassy verge. When his predicament was seen by the Troop, a Bren gunner, Corporal George Thompson (Grenadier Guards), firing from the shoulder, led a bayonet charge and shot two machine gunners – a wounded man and a fifteen-year-old boy – left behind by the Germans. Both were questioned by 'Masters' before being evacuated.

Cycle Troop crossed Pegasus Bridge at 12.30pm, two minutes behind schedule, followed by Brigade HQ running down the hill. Accounts of Piper Millin blowing his pipes as they did so are legend, as the area was under fire from snipers, mortars and machine guns. Brigade HQ then linked up with HQ 6th Airborne Division at Ranville while No. 6

Commando headed cross country, joined the road to Breville and reached Le Plein at about 2.00pm. No. 3 Commando, held up by heavy shelling near Colleville-sur-Mer, crossed Pegasus Bridge at 2.00pm under continuous sniping, followed by No. 45 (Royal Marines) Commando about thirty minutes later. Commanded by Major Nicol Gray after the Commanding Officer had been wounded on the beaches, the Marines were to reinforce 9th Parachute Battalion, which had seized the strategically important Merville Battery during the night – only to find that the guns had been removed – and then attack the resort of Franceville Plage. The paras had been withdrawn to reinforce the defence of the bridges and a small German force reoccupied the battery. At 3.30pm, Lord Lovat instructed No. 3 Commando to defend Divisional HQ at Ranville, which meant that his plan to hold the line from Merville to Breville could not be achieved; he therefore shortened it by instructing the Royal Marines to occupy Merville. As Lovat then moved Brigade HQ to Ecarde, No. 6 Commando was mopping up German resistance lurking around Le Plein on the Brigade right flank in the gap to the left of 9th Parachute Battalion.

Bringing up the rear of the Brigade was No. 4 Commando. With the British leading, the thirsty commandos were offered cider and calvados by the villagers of Colleville-sur-Mer – a farmer also distributed cider and calvados at Saint Aubin d'Arquenay – the first time that many of the French commandos had sampled Norman drinks for four years. 6 (French) Troop seized the German HQ in the old chateau. As the column left the village, which was later renamed Colleville-Montgomery, a sniper broke Lieutenant Pierre Amaury's arm and he was evacuated by jeep to a Beach Dressing Station; he rejoined the Battalion a month later. With snipers regularly causing casualties, the French mounted two K-Guns on jeeps to give a stable platform for suppressive fire. Now without officers, Kieffer attached the K-Guns to his HQ, with Sergeant Saerens leading one detachment and Sergeant Georges Coste the other. Advancing towards La Port, the column used both sides of the road and, at about 3.00pm, whilst passing through the 7th Parachute Battalion, there was an outbreak of heavy firing from the bridges. The Commando quickened its pace, ready to help the airborne soldiers, and although his thigh wound was inflamed and swollen, Major Kieffer did not falter. Entering Benouville village square, the commandos saw the wreckage of a 21st Panzer Division Mark IV tank and several dead Germans on the road to Caen. Kieffer learnt that a boat load of Germans had just attacked the canal bridge and that 1st Special Service Brigade had crossed during the afternoon and No. 3 Commando was defending Divisional HQ.

He also learnt that No. 4 Commando had suffered casualties while crossing the bridge from a Spandau hidden in woods on the northern bank and snipers in a church spire. At about 4.15am, covered by a smokescreen

rlech, autumn 1942. Officers of No. 10 Commando. Left to right, Standing: Capt Lutyens (LO, ldstream Guards); Capt Clarke (Adjutant, Gordon Highlanders); Lt Col Lister (CO, The Buffs); j Peter Laycock (2 i/c, later CO, Notts Yeomanry); Capt Hilton-Jones (3 Tp, RA); Capt Hodges O, RAMC). Sitting: Lt Woloszowki (2 i/c, Polish Army (KIA in Italy)); Capt Mulders (Dutch ny); Capt Danloy (Belgian Army); Capt Hauge (Norwegian; Army); Lt Kieffer (French Navy). *korski Institute*)

nacarry. Commandos land from Goatley assault boats. (*Author's Collection*)

Newhaven, 19 August 1942. A 1 (French) Troop
SNCO, in the black peaked cap, possibly
Sgt de Wandaleur attached to No. 3 Commando,
waits to disembark from a destroyer after returning
from Dieppe. (*Author's Collection*)

Fairbourne. A Polish radio operator. The Poles were
the only Troop to prefer steel helmets to the Green
Beret. (*Sikorsky Institute*)

rbourne, 1942. Typically smart Polish commandos march past an inspecting officer. The wireless erators carry No. 38 radios. (*Sikorsky Institute*)

Polish commandos training in cliff assault. (*Sikorsky Institute*)

Fairbourne. Captain Smrokowski and Lt Col Lister alongside a Polish Army officer. Note the thickness of the toggle rope. (*Sikorsky Institute*)

Fairbourne. A Polish Bren gun team. (*Sikorsky Institute*)

ndon, 4 July 1943. An admiral inspects No. 1 (French) Troop. Carrying the Troop colour is
t Nassau de Warigny. Lt Kieffer is over the left shoulder of the inspecting officer. (*Anonymous*)

stbourne, 1943. 2 (Dutch) Troop on the ranges. (*Wybo Boersma*)

Eastbourne, 1944. 2 Troop shortly after returning from the Far East. (*Wybo Boersma*)

India, early 1944. Dutch commandos on exercise. Rear left in glasses is Lt Knottenbelt. (*Wybo Boersma*)

…iers, November 1943. Major Smrokowski shares food with the Polish missionary. (*Sikorsky …itute*)

French Navy Lt Trepel who commanded the 'Premium' patrol that disappeared on 27 January 1944 at Scheveningen. (*Albert Le Fevre*)

Italy, 30 December 1943. Operation Partridge. One of the German prisoners captured by No. 9 Commando. (*Author's Collection*)

Italy, January 1944. 4 Belgian Troop at La Vaglia shortly after being withdrawn for a rest. Troops usually lost weight in the front line and so meals were often substantial, in this instance including bread. Mess tins are rested on a jeep bonnet. (*IWM – 11806*)

The Belgian Troop leaves La Vaglia.
(*IWM – 11805*)

is, 1944. Commandos
board a MTB. (*Polish
stitute*)

Monte Cassino. A Polish
commando Bren gunner in
May 1944. (*Sikorsky
Institute*)

January 1944. Field Marshal Rommel arrives to inspect the Merville Battery. By D-Day, its guns had been moved inland to prevent them from being destroyed by bombing. (*Author's Collection*)

D-Day. LCpls 'Envers' and 'Moody' of 3 Troop debrief French civilians at St Aubin-sur-Mer. On the left is the 48 (RM) Commando Intelligence Officer, Capt Wilmot. Tucked into the assault jerkin worn by 'Envers' is a London Underground handgrip used as coshes by commandos. (*Anonymous*)

An RM Armoured Support Group Centaur that stands at the site of Pegasus Bridge. It was this type of tank that helped the French at the Riva Bella Casino. (*Author's Collection*)

Amfreville, 8 June 1944. French commandos fraternize with civilians. Left to right, Pte Poli (wearing shoes and with water bottle), Pte Guyard, Pte Zivohlava (wearing leather smock), Mme Nicole, M Potel, Mme Lefevre, Pte Floch, Sgt Lanternier (with bandaged hand) and Gabriel (also with a water bottle and an egg). All have the distinctive French commando beret badge. (*IWM – B5280*)

ne Bridgehead.
Senee poses with a ptured Spandau. He as later killed in Indo- ina. (*Author's* llection)

Orne Bridgehead. Sgt Louis Lanternier of No. 1 (French) Troop. He wears the distinctive beret badge designed by Cpl Chauvet and No. 4 Commando insignia. (*Albert Le Fevre*)

Arnhem, 18 September 1944. In Wolfsheze, Pte van der Meer and Cpl Italiaander of 2 Troop hold the Dutch national flag with Mrs Tjoonk and Miss van der Poel. (*Author's Collection*)

Arnhem, September 1944 Sgt Luitweiler (on right) hiding in woods near Boxel with several other Allied soldiers. (*Wybo Boersma*)

Italy, 1945. Lake Comacchio area. Six members of the 3 Mediterranean Half Troop pose with captured weapons, including a Panzerfaust anti-tank weapon. Second left is believed to be Capt 'Bartlett', who commanded the Troop. (*Dr Michael Arton*)

...shing, 1 November 1944. Uncle Beach across which No. 4 Commando, and their French, British ...d Dutch Troop detachments, landed. (*Author's Collection*)

...alcheren, 1 November 1944. HQ 10 ...mmando on Red Beach. With the ...arette is Lt Col Laycock talking to a ...rwegian Commando. (*Ivar Krugland*)

Walcheren. Cpl 'Latimer' of 3 Troop rounds up German prisoners in Zoutelande. (*Ivar Krugland*)

Walcheren, 3 November 1944. 3 and 5 Troop commandos question some of the 211 German prisoners captured during the day. (*Ivar Krugland*)

Walcheren. Lt Col Lis watches an attack. Behind the group are the two Shermans tha helped 10 Commando (*Ivar Krugland*)

Walcheren. Two commandos milk a cow. (*Ivar Krugland*)

alcheren. Two Norwegian commandos talk to traditionally dressed Dutch women, one holding a ɔg. (*Ivar Krugland*)

alcheren. Three Norwegian commandos sit on a wall. Behind them is a file of German prisoners. ʋar Krugland)

Germany. The charismatic Major Arthur de Jonghe wearing a smock talks to a Royal Marines officer. (*NAM – 102152*)

The Commando Memorial near Spe[a] Bridge. Inspired by Lord Lovat, it bears the words 'United we conque[r] and 'This country was their Trainin[g] Ground'. (*Author's Collection*)

put down by their 3-inch mortars, the Frenchmen doubled across, but as the last ten men from 5 Troop were crossing the smoke began to clear and Lance Corporal Yves Perone was badly wounded in the stomach and two others received minor wounds. Lance Corporal Bollore returned to treat Perone and then Corporals Henri Richemont and Zivohlava carried him to the Airborne first aid post in the Café Gondrée. The Troop followed the cross-country route taken by No. 6 Commando, crossed the road to Sallenelles and, on the road leading to Le Plein from Ecarde, linked up with No. 4 Commando. Resting in ditches they had a thirty-minute halt in defensive positions covering approaches from the north. Lord Lovat arrived, congratulated the French on their admirable conduct during the day and ordered Kieffer to take over a position forward of Le Plein from the 9th Parachute Battalion. Meanwhile, No. 6 Commando had been ejecting the remnants of the enemy units from the area. With bodies lying around the church and snipers harrying anyone in the open, Kieffer deployed the K-Guns and PIATs, and despatched patrols to the north and south. At about 8,00pm, with the Royal Marines on the left, No. 4 Commando occupying Hauger, and No. 6 Commando on their right, Kieffer instructed his men to dig in. It promised to be a long night, however morale rose at 9.00pm when the 6th Airlanding Brigade used the last daylight hours to land by glider in fields at Drop Zone 'N', between Amfreville and Ranville.

Of the 177 Frenchmen who had landed, Battalion HQ was down to twelve all ranks, 5 and 6 Troops were both down to fifty-four, and the K-Guns to nineteen. Nine of the eleven officers were casualties. Corporal Zivohlava, who had been left behind at the Café Gondrée, was following the route taken by No. 4 Commando when he watched a detachment of paras with a PIAT destroy a tank on the road from Sallenelles; two others reversed back to the village. At dusk, he arrived at Amfreville where he was debriefed by Lieutenant Tony Smith, the No. 4 Commando Intelligence Officer, and rejoined his Troop.

Chapter 12

The Defence of the Orne Bridgehead: 7–13 June 1944

As reports circulated of landings south of the River Orne, 711th Infantry Division was dealing with groups of paras, most from the British 9th and 1st (Canadian) Parachute Battalions. Two paras captured when they dropped in to Divisional HQ led Lieutenant General Reichert to believe his HQ was being raided, nevertheless he was able to drive from his Divisional HQ at Pont l'Evêque to 744th Grenadier Regiment at Franceville Plage without difficulty, except to take cover from marauding Spitfires.

At Le Havre, 346th Infantry Division had been alerted to landings in Normandy on 4 June, but when nothing happened, it was taken to be an incorrect intelligence assessment; nevertheless, since the moon was full, units remained alert for parachute and seaborne landings in the Le Havre area. Although at 1.00am on 6 June, 744th Grenadier Regiment was reporting increased enemy air activity, airborne landings and bombardments of coastal positions, LXXXI Corps, convinced that the landings would take place to the north, did not place 346th Division on notice to move. However the next night Corps HQ decided that the high ground between Touques and Dives was vulnerable to an airlanding and instructed the 346th Infantry Division to reinforce 744th Grenadier Regiment and seal off the landings by attacking the key Orne bridges; the leading elements started to arrive at 11.00am. 857th Regiment arrived without harassment having towed its cycle battalion most of the way. Reichert had overall command of operations and moved 346th Artillery Battalion to Varaville. In support were the 155mms of the coastal artillery which had been moved inland several days earlier. Artillery registration was confined to the line Franceville–Breville. Lining up 857th Grenadier Regiment to the south, 858th Regiment in the centre and 744th Regiment to the north, 2/857th Grenadier Regiment moved into Breville, while 1/857th Battalion moved to its right – opposite 1st Special Service Brigade. The third battalion was in reserve behind 2/858th Battalion to the south of Breville. In support was a company of Mark IV tanks from 22nd Panzer Regiment, while elements of the 12th Waffen-SS 'Hitler Jugend' Division were recceing British positions.

When dawn broke on 7 June (D+1), the French commandos were treated to picturesque Norman countryside of apple orchards, hedges, meadows, woods and hamlets congregated around sturdy, thick-walled farms, linked by tracks and roads topped with hedges and trees on banks. The grass had yet to be cut for silage and farm animals, startled by the previous night's fighting, nervously nibbled at the grass. Everywhere there was the debris of war – dead animals and soldiers, parachutes and wrecked vehicles. The commandos had spent a second night without sleeping – digging in, laying telephone lines and marking sheltered 'rat runs' for runners, resupply and casualty evacuation, interrupted by small German patrols probing positions, the ever-present sniping and the rumble of battle around the beaches. At 2.00am, three unarmed Germans fleeing from Ouistrehem strayed into the No. 4 Commando position and were interrogated by Sergeant 'Thompson' and Private 'Broadman' in the Intelligence Section. At 3.00am, No. 3 Commando rejoined the Brigade and, taking up positions along the Ranville–Sallenelles road at Le Plein, strengthened the perimeter between No. 6 Commando at the south end of the village and the French.

5 (French) Troop, dug in between east of Le Plein church and Amfreville, was reinforced by two Vickers machine guns from No. 3 Commando. The K-Gun Section was 100 yards to the right and 6 (French) Troop was in a small wood overlooking Breville. Battalion HQ was in a farm in Le Plein. Individual shell scrapes, dug to a depth of about 15 inches during the night, were deepened. Corporal Zivohlava spent the morning connecting his trench to that of Lance Corporal Guy Picou and Corporal Jean Kermarec, before adding overhead protection against shell splinters and rain, with logs and planks from wrecked houses, onto which they laid tufts of grass as insulation.

During the morning, although feverish with septicaemia, Captain Kieffer sent patrols to visit every house in Amfreville, and important documents found in the German HQ at the school were sent to HQ No. 4 Commando. When he learnt that his men were suspicious that the steeple of the church was being used by snipers, he demanded from the parish priest and the mayor details of suspect collaborators. Both claimed that any traitors had fled, but when Kieffer insisted that the priest must hand over the church keys and join him, he found the church door unlocked. Armed with Thompsons, Corporals Zivohlava and Georges Scherer searched the steeple. Scherer, who was from Alsace-Lorraine, had already suffered burns while crossing Pegasus Bridge and was eventually evacuated on 18 July. The commandos found it a strange contrast to the brutality of war

111

that amid the chaos of the fighting, French farmers herded their cows and brought in the harvest, while villagers refused to leave.

When it became evident from events during D-Day that the 6th Airborne Division perimeter was to be shortened and that the 1st Special Service Brigade was expected to hold the high ground around Le Plein, Brigadier Lord Lovat sent 1 (Cycle) Troop, No. 6 Commando to strengthen his left flank from infiltration from Sallenelles, and withdrew No. 45 (Royal Marines) Commando from Merville to take up positions covering the approaches from Sallenelles. During the morning, General Gale visited Lovat and instructed him to mop up the enemy around Franceville Plage in order to protect his left flank. Although Lovat believed that this would stretch his defences, he ordered the Royal Marines to attack Franceville, its original D-Day task. As a diversion, 4 and 5 Troops, No. 3 Commando, commanded by Major John Poole MC (Royal Artillery), were to seize Merville Battery, which had been reoccupied by a small but determined German force. Corporals 'Arlen' and 'Hepworth', who was one of two brothers with 3 (British) Troop, accompanied his force. With naval gunfire support available from the 15-inch guns of HMS *Warspite*, the Royal Marines advanced to the outskirts of Franceville where 'Arlen' unfurled a white flag and, walking up to a German machine-gun position, told the occupants that since there were three divisions behind him, further fighting was pointless. Not surprisingly, this invitation was met with a hail of fire. 'Arlen', furious about this rejection, returned to his position, grabbed a Thompson and charged. Not surprisingly, he was quickly cut down. Two Troops battered their way into the northern end of Franceville, but without Heavy Weapons Troop support, which had not survived the landings, their toehold was extremely vulnerable. Command and control then collapsed when the Brigade rear signallers and A Troop became separated, and Major Gray was unable to call for artillery support. At 9.00pm, after a day of hard fighting, he had no alternative but withdraw to Merville in the face of strong counter-attacks.

The two Army Commando Troops faced exactly the same problems experienced by the gallant 9th Parachute Battalion on D-Day. 'Hepworth' attempted to persuade the Germans to surrender but was met with contempt. After taking several casualties while struggling across a minefield, the commandos broke into the battery but were then subjected to heavy fire from a self-propelled gun, mortars and machine guns. Without heavy weapons, and taking casualties, including Major Poole killed, they were forced to leave their seriously wounded behind and abandoned the battery. The survivors crossed the minefield, sustaining yet more casualties, and joined No. 45 (Royal Marines) Commando.

The absence of No. 45 (Royal Marines) Commando increased the width of the gap on the left flank and Lovat therefore shuffled No. 4 Commando towards Hauger. The seriousness of the situation was compounded by Strongpoint WN-6, which was about half a mile north-east of Sallenelles near Moulin de Buisson farm. Since its presence would ease a German counter-attack from Franceville, Major Menday needed to know if the village was occupied. The French were the logical choice and Sergeant Lardennois entered Sallenelles undetected, with Lance Corporal Jacques Guyader and Private Gubin, and contacted several farmers, who said that the village was almost uninhabited. After the baker, who delivered bread to the German strongpoint, provided useful information on German dispositions, Lardennois was able to observe from a large house at the western limits of the village that WN-6 consisted of a concrete bunker on the edge of marshy ground and the sea, protected by minefields and a trench system. The traverse of its 88mm gun was restricted to firing towards the coast east of the River Orne and had no direct view of Sword Beach. The detachment of fifteen gunners was commanded by a competent sergeant major. Although the position was under threat of bombardment, several Germans were seen walking to and from Franceville. After debriefing Lardennois, Kieffer began planning to attack the strongpoint.

During the day, 711th and 346th Infantry Divisions began six days of spoiling attacks against 6th Airborne Division, however, instead of a concentrated blow at the numerous weak points, they pecked at the defences, supported by area shelling from mortars and artillery. Although these tactics had been successful in the desert of North Africa, they were inappropriate in countryside suited for defence by troops backed up by artillery and naval gunfire support. When Lieutenant Colonel Mills-Roberts, whose No. 6 Commando had been suffering near continuous mortaring, told Kieffer that he was going to attack 2/857th Grenadier Regiment in Breville, 6 (French) Troop advanced about 650 yards to protect the left flank of No. 6 Commando, raiding Breville at 11.30am and capturing six light guns and six machine guns, all of which were used to strengthen the Le Plein defences. Its 3 (British) Troop detachment interrogated several prisoners. At about 5.00pm, when six tanks accompanied by infantry were seen approaching Amfreville from woods near Le Mariquet, Kieffer placed his two PIATs some distance from his main position to attract the German tanks while the remainder dealt with the infantry from concealed positions, when the attack was broken up by two Marauders. As dusk fell, a flight of German aircraft machine-gunning Le Plein was a timely reminder that while there had been no casualties, the Luftwaffe, given the opportunity, would strike whenever and wherever it could, and did so throughout the next three months, generally in the evenings. As night fell, 1/857th Grenadier Regiment patrols infiltrated through No. 4 Commando across open fields into the woods behind their position at Hauger, while French patrols recced several houses in Bas de Breville. The area was alive – as it would be for the next sixteen weeks – with outbursts of firing, and tracer, flares and signal lights zooming into the sky before eerily floating to earth.

During the early hours of 8 June, the three No. 45 (Royal Marines) Commando signallers, who had become separated during the attack on Franceville Plage, turned up at Brigade HQ with the survivors of Major Poole's two Troops returning to Le Plein; they brought news of the unsuccessful attack and that the Royal Marines were in Merville. The three were instructed to rejoin the Commando, taking with them a reserve signals detachment, and to advise Major Gray that although a relief force would be assembled when men were available, in the meantime the village must be held in order to protect the vulnerable left flank.

At 2.00am, when tanks and half-tracks were reported to be advancing towards the French positions, Lardennois and a six-man patrol crept forward 100 yards as an early warning post in front of the defences. All was quiet, nevertheless Kieffer again redeployed the PIATs and Nicot with his 2-inch mortar crew to face the threat. As daybreak broke, rumbling tank engines and threatening squeals of tracks were heard, and then, more ominously, an armoured vehicle was briefly seen before it disappeared, moving south toward Breville, behind a small hill. The patrol sighed with relief as it seemed that the tanks were leaving the area. Soon after Lardennois returned at about 5.30am, mortar bombs landed with increasing accuracy on the French positions and the commandos took cover as snipers began to harass them. It was the first of many disruptive mortar 'stonks'.

Soon after the signallers left, and before Brigadier Lovat could organize a relief force, at 6.30am, 1/857th Grenadier Battalion launched the first of several attacks against No. 4 Commando with the clear intention of breaking through to the Orne bridges by infiltrating around the Commando from three sides. A Troop was driven from its forward positions in a wood, leaving their bergens behind. About a fortnight later, a patrol found them, intact and untouched – the Germans were seemingly suspicious of booby traps. During a lull in the morning shelling, a recce patrol led by Sergeant de Montlaur found two well-constructed trenches with overhead shelters linked by a zigzag passage several hundred yards from the French position and during a cautious search, two German grenadiers caring for a wounded man were captured. As the attacks had continued all day, Major Kieffer abandoned plans to attack Strongpoint WN-6. Meanwhile, six 21st Panzer Division Mark IV tanks threatening Brigade HQ were driven off by Typhoons. A No. 3 Commando counter-attack drove German probes back to Breville and No. 6 Commando broke up another attack before again storming Breville, shooting up a German platoon in the process. When a

114

patrol unearthed Germans infiltrating around their positions to the south, as a precaution, Breville and a nearby wood were mortared.

No. 45 (Royal Marines) Commando disrupted several German probes nibbling at the 1st Special Service Brigade left flank, including at least one in which anti-tank guns were used as field artillery. At about 10.15am, two German ambulances drove into Merville and were captured, giving the Royal Marines the opportunity to evacuate eight badly wounded and a German prisoner to the Brigade Casualty Clearing Station at Le Plein. Since their German drivers were to be used, Lance Corporal 'Saunders', who had been wounded in the leg by grenade fragments at Franceville, was put in charge. He told the drivers that they must do exactly what he asked, because the Allies were winning the war and they would die if they did not. Soon after leaving Merville, the ambulances were recaptured by the Germans, but the drivers did not mention that 'Saunders' spoke fluent German, and next day he escaped and reached the Commando.

When the Germans resorted to mortaring and shelling, by 5.00pm, Brigadier Lovat knew that the isolated Commando was low on ammunition, food, medical supplies and water, and in a perilous position, but he needed it to bolster his left flank and was given permission by Gale to withdraw them. At 8.00pm, encumbered by a large number of casualties, the Royal Marines slipped out of Merville. Sergeant 'Stewart' and Corporal 'Shelley' were trapped with some Royal Marines in a farmyard by some Germans who had entered the village from the east. When they started lobbing stick grenades into the yard, the two members of 3 (British) Troop collected grenades from the Royal Marines and, whenever a stick grenade landed, they threw a 36 grenade back in the same direction, thereby stemming the number of grenades being thrown into the farmyard. They then poked a Bren through a hole in a wall and sprayed the area to cover the Royal Marines as they withdrew. In the gathering darkness, a clash with Germans occupying a position on the left of No. 4 Commando was resolved by D Troop (Captain Porteous VC) clearing the obstruction. After losing 33 men killed since D-Day, No. 45 (Royal Marines) Commando filed off wearily to Hauger and spent the night in the church cleaning equipment, having their first decent meal in thirty-six hours and resting.

Next morning, Kieffer attended the morning Brigade Orders Group and was ordered by Brigadier Lovat to a First Aid Post to have his wounds treated, however he had several administrative matters to attend to and it was not until 5.00pm that he saw a doctor. Seeing that his leg was badly infected, the doctor immediately put Kieffer in a jeep with two wounded British soldiers, however he first had to be ordered by Lovat and Dawson to hand over command of the French Battalion to Lieutenant Lofi, before being evacuated to a general hospital at Lion-sur-Mer. Next day, he was ferried to Haslemere Hospital by a Landing Craft (Hospital) and was given penicillin before being transferred to Warwick Emergency Hospital on 10 June. Injected four more times with penicillin, he was lucky not to lose his leg. Lofi appointed Lieutenant Francis Vourc'h to command 8 (French) Troop and Warrant Officer Faure to lead 1 (French) Troop. Sergeant Coste took command of the K-Gun Section. Lovat meanwhile moved Brigade HQ to Le Plein.

By the end of the day, it was clear that the 6th Airborne Division was under significant pressure from the south-east and north as German forces struggled to break through to the Orne bridges. Ammunition, food and water were low and casualties had been heavy. The 857th Grenadier Regiment was threatening No. 6 Commando, HQ 3 Parachute Brigade was cut off and 9th Parachute Battalion was isolated in Château St Come to the east of Breville. Snipers remained a nuisance. Lovat suggested to Gale that capturing Franceville and Merville with his depleted resources was out of the question, and the Brigade needed to be prepared to meet heavier attacks which appeared to be imminent. Gale agreed that 1st Special Service Brigade perimeter should be shortened from the River Orne to the high ground at Hauger, south to Breville and link up with the airborne left flank.

9 June was quiet but tense as German patrols sniffed for weaknesses and plotted positions. After four days without sleep and snatched rest, the commandos were not at their most alert. Harassing shelling and mortaring, sometimes a barrage, sometimes a single mortar bomb, often at meals and causing a steady stream of casualties, kept everyone on edge. It was difficult to pinpoint firing points because the mortars were often in a cart drawn by a horse. A Sdkfz (Sonderkraftfahrzeug) 251 half-track mounting a six-barrelled Nebelwefer mortar, known to Allied forces as Moaning Minnie or Sobbing Sisters, allowed German gunners to fire a salvo and then rapidly leave the area before the retaliatory artillery or mortar fire. Static patrols were deployed to listen for the distinctive sound of a mortar being dropped into a tube and then blew whistles as an early warning. When German positions at Gonneville and Breville were subjected to periodic retaliatory shelling, civilians reported at least two lorries evacuating wounded.

After its short rest, No. 45 (Royal Marines) Commando moved into positions south-west of Amfreville to disrupt the enemy forming-up places for the expected counter-attack. At about 9.30pm, platoon-sized fighting patrols probed British positions and the mortars at Strongpoint WN-6 began registering. During the night, recce patrols reported that Bas de Breville had been reoccupied. Overnight, Lieutenant General Reichert finalized his plans to break through to the Orne bridges in a three-pronged attack with 744th Grenadier Regiment advancing from Merville, 857th Grenadier Regiment striking at 1st Special Service Brigade in the general direction of Bas de Breville and 858th Grenadier Regiment attacking from Breville.

As dawn rose on 10 June, heavy mortar fire straddled No. 6 Commando and then periodically shifted to the left, hitting HQ No. 4 Commando and its Regimental Aid Post, fortunately causing only a few casualties because the commandos had avoided digging in likely defensive positions. At 8.15am, the 736th Grenadier Regiment, supported by a self-propelled gun and covered by an artillery and mortar fire bombardment, attacked No. 6 Commando from Breville, but by 10.15am had been driven back into the village. Meanwhile, 857th Grenadier Regiment thrust at Nos 3 and 4 Commandos and when the depleted 9th Parachute Battalion was ejected from Chateau de Comte at about 10.30am, the 744th Grenadier Regiment attacked No. 4 Commando from Sallenelles; spilling to its left, by 11.15am, the door to the Orne bridges began to wobble. Even though 1 (Cycle) Troop, No. 6 Commando was rushed to help break up the attacks, the infiltrations continued and by 11.45am, the forward positions of No. 3 Commando had been largely overrun. No. 4 Commando was in serious trouble with Commando HQ at Hauger in danger of being overrun.

When the Germans threatened Amfreville and the road to Breville, every yard was contested in the knowledge that reinforcements were en route, including Sherman tanks. Desperate hand-to-hand fighting took place when the Germans infiltrated behind French positions at about 10.00am. Lance Corporal Laot fought three Germans and killed two before he was bayoneted. Sergeant de Montlaur manned a Bren gun when its team were both killed and naval gunfire support from the battleships HMS *Nelson* and *Rodney* shelled the attacks, nevertheless a Ferdinand self-propelled 88mm gun brushed aside the bombardment, and, churning through clouds of thick dust, shelled the K-Guns firing from the windows of a farm, killing Private Rene Gersel. Lance Corporal Louis Begot had his jaw smashed and face hideously shattered by a shell, although his eyes were mercifully unharmed. With blood gurgling into his lungs, he was carried across 50 yards of open ground to the Troop Aid Post. Given morphine, patched up and evacuated to England, his shattered face was rebuilt, but he suffered from graft rejections for the rest of his life.

The shelling increased at midday. Rest was impossible because magazines needed to be reloaded, wounded evacuated and damaged defences repaired. At about 2.00pm, a No. 4 Commando counter-attack to recover lost positions stalled within forty-five minutes when attacks developed from Sallenelles against the Brigade left flank as a Ferdinand SP gun and German infantry infiltrated the road from Sallenelles. The depleted and tired commandos were hard pressed to hold their positions. In one instance, two NCOs crawled to within 10 yards of a deep ditch being used by an enemy platoon, lobbed grenades and, after spraying it with their

Thompsons, captured eleven Germans; the remaining fourteen were dead. When an inexperienced German company advanced in three ranks, the French commandos held their fire and although unsettled by the silence, the opposing infantry pressed on and walked into a close-range volley. The second wave heard the shooting but not knowing what was happening wilted under withering crossfire as they crested the slope. German mortars bombarded the defences as a third company crossed the field, but it was beaten off.

At about 4.00pm, Sergeant Major Faure was called to Battalion HQ to be informed by Major Menday and Lieutenant Lofi about the situation and was ordered to install a blocking position at Ecarde with 1 (French) Troop to prevent further infiltrations from Sallenelles.

While Faure was being briefed at Battalion HQ, German patrols continued to probe British positions but 6th Airborne Division could do nothing but defend the flank in the knowledge that the Germans were preventing the British from reaching Caen. At 4.15pm, when No. 6 Commando came under heavy mortar fire and German troops slipped around the flanks of No. 45 (Royal Marines) Commando and a request for tank and self-propelled gun support was sent to HQ 6th Airborne Division, at 5.00pm, B Squadron, 13/18th Hussars arrived, having destroyed the Ferdinand. By 7.00pm, after eleven hours, the German attacks weakened and within the hour had reduced to desultory sniping, although the morale-sapping mortaring, shelling and sniping continued until 10.00pm. During the day, the French had suffered three killed and twenty-two wounded, seven of whom were evacuated. The dead of No. 4 Commando, including the French, were buried in the orchard of Hauger Chateau where Father Naurois said. Requiem and everyone enjoyed the relative tranquillity of the evening. During the night, No. 4 Commando went into reserve and handed over its positions to the 12th Parachute Battalion.

Throughout the fighting, 3 (British) Troop had been busy interrogating prisoners and translating documents, paybooks and notebooks to help with tactical intelligence. The 1st Special Service Brigade intelligence assessment concluded that the Brigade had faced a three-pronged attack by two battalions supported by tanks of the 21st Panzer Division aiming to attack the Orne bridges. The middle probe directed at the centre of the British defence was from Bas de Breville, and the southern attack was on a south-west axis from Breville. It was known from prisoners that the German forces were drawn from 346th Infantry Division. A German officer claimed that 2/857th Battalion had suffered heavy casualties against Nos 3 and 4 Commandos and had drawn on the reserve elements of its sister 858th Grenadier Regiment for replacements. Also identified was the 744th Grenadier Regiment, which had been deployed from Villers-sur-Mer to reinforce 857th Regiment during its attack on No. 4 Commando. The 21st Panzer Recce Battalion was confirmed as well.

The 11th of June was signalled by light shelling bracketing Brigade HQ and most units, causing more casualties and further damage to defences. At first light, a No. 45 (Royal Marines) Commando patrol passed through the 12th Parachute Battalion lines facing Sallenelles and found the village empty except for a few wounded who were brought back as prisoners. At 5.00am, when Sergeant Major Faure led 1 (French) Troop from the chaos of Amfreville down the hill toward Ecarde, the commandos welcomed the tranquillity and noted fretful cows staggering under the weight of full udders waiting to be milked. The tranquillity was disturbed by the 'plonk' of distant mortars and whistling bombs exploding around the column with unnerving accuracy, wounding Corporals Henri Richemont and Ferdinand Garrabos, and Lance Corporal Roland Gabriel. Hardly had the French ran for shelter in a barn when another barrage landed, killing Private Pierre Vinat and wounding three others. At the crossroads, the French occupied an empty, solid, two-storey hotel and Faure placed Troop HQ and an observation post in the attic, with good views towards Sallenelles. Saddened by the death of Vinat, concerned that tanks would accompany attacks, and ordered to dominate the area and clear DZ 'N' of snipers, at about 10.00am, a patrol commanded by Faure's Second-in-Command, Sergeant de Montlaur, drove about fifty Germans supported by two self-propelled guns back to Sallenelles. With the area relatively calm, as the patrol rested in rotation, the hotel proprietor appeared and agreed to Faure's suggestion that the commandos sample the wines and cider in the cellar, and slaughter several chickens clucking in the courtyard. Faure gave the owner a receipt, which was duly claimed several years later. Garrabos, Ropert and Corporal Georges Scherer put their culinary skills to good use and the Troop, including those returning from patrol, were treated to a feast. Major Menday joined the French while on a visit and evidently never failed to remind them about it at reunions.

A Royal Marines patrol discovered a quantity of enemy equipment in good condition near Amfreville at 11.00pm, including two 80mm mortars and identity discs from several dead 21st Panzer Recce Regiment. On another patrol, Lance Corporal 'Saunders' of 3 (British) Troop was captured on a recce. 'Stewart' and 'Shelley' stalked the Sdkfz 251 half-track mounting the Nebelwefer and, ambushing it behind German lines in a lane, threw grenades into the fighting compartment, killing the crew before driving it back to No. 45 (Royal Marines) Commando. For this and other acts of leaderships, both soldiers were offered immediate field commissions in the Royal Marines, which they accepted.

Since D-Day, the German pressure on the beachhead perimeter had been significant and the 6th Airborne Division defence of the Orne bridgehead was reinforced by the 51st (Highland) Division. General Gale believed that the attacks from Breville had probably reduced German combat effectiveness and therefore the village was vulnerable; however an attack by the 5th Black Watch, supported by the 9th Parachute Battalion and D Squadron, 13/18th Hussars, was defeated and the Battalion withdrew to Chateau St Cômte with heavy casualties. The desert veterans found the fighting in the fields, orchards and woods of Normandy markedly different from North Africa.

During the day, Brigadier John Durnford-Slater, Deputy Commander, Special Service Group, told Brigadier Lovat that HQ 4th Special Service Brigade and Nos 47 and 48 (Royal Marines) Commandos would be arriving. No. 41 (Royal Marines) Commando was still engaged in operations around Douvres radar installation and No. 46 (Royal Marines) Commando was supporting 3rd Canadian Division operations in the Mue Valley. Gale committed the 12th Parachute Battalion to capture Breville. Understrength, with just 300 men, but rested after a day in quarries near Ecarde, he reinforced the attack with the 22nd Independent Parachute Company, D Company, 12th Devons from 6th Airlanding Brigade, and B Squadron, 13/18th Hussars. In preparation for the attack, Major Hilton-Jones led a 3 (British) Troop listening patrol into Breville to discover German strengths, dispositions and intentions. That wet and sultry evening, 4th Special Service Brigade filed through 1 (French) Troop at Ecarde and set up Brigade HQ about 400 yards south of Sallenelles. No. 47 (Royal Marines) Commando moved into reserve in the quarries and No. 48 (Royal Marines) Commando took over from 12th Parachute Battalion at Hauger, immediately declaring their intention when British Troop bumped into an enemy patrol in Sallenelles, as Brigadier Leicester dominated the ground and expanded his perimeter to include the village.

At 3.00am on 12 June, Hilton-Jones's patrol returned reporting an infantry company defending Breville. A No. 45 (Royal Marines) Commando company fighting patrol clashed with a platoon on the western outskirts of the village and captured a machine gun. Shortly before dawn, when No. 6 Commando was shelled and reported tracked vehicles in Breville, it was suspected that the 2/857th Grenadier Battalion was about to attack and the village was shelled, as were the German guns in Varaville. At midday, No. 4 Commando returned to their positions at Hauger and as No. 48 (Royal Marines) Commando moved left to dominate Sallenelles, No. 3 Commando sent a diversionary fighting patrol to the abandoned Moulin du Buisson farm. The afternoon saw two hours of particularly heavy shelling of Nos 6 and 45 (Royal Marines) Commandos, but attempts to locate the artillery failed, suggesting that it was probably self-propelled guns. At midday, the 3rd Parachute Brigade was subjected to an intense mortar and artillery bombardment and then, at 3.00pm, a

120

German infantry company supported by tanks and self-propelled guns drove 5th Black Watch, less a platoon, and most of the 9th Parachute Battalion back to Bois de Mont. With the Germans exploiting a weakness in the defences, a 1st (Canadian) Parachute Battalion company relieved the Scots platoon holding out in the chateau.

At 9.00pm, a 'rogue' British gun shelled the 12th Parachute Battalion briefing for the attack in an Amfreville orchard. About forty-five minutes later, Corporal 'Nichols' and Lance Corporal 'Masters' were in Saulnier Farm in Le Plein watching the Devons file past the church when several shells burst, one exploding among a group of officers, seriously wounding Lord Lovat in the stomach, shattering the femur of Brigadier Hugh Kindersley, who commanded the 6th Airlanding Brigade, and killing the 12th Parachute Battalion commanding officer, Lieutenant Colonel Johnson. 'Masters' was collecting wirecutters from his kit stored in a barn to cut people free when two more shells collapsed it. Meanwhile, 'Nichols' had dashed through the shelling and carried Lovat into the farmyard, asking for the No. 6 Commando Medical Officer. Seeing him sheltering under several huge cider barrels near the captured Sdkfz 251, and in spite of objections that he would be needed later, 'Nichols' dragged the doctor to the barn where Lovat and Kindersley lay. The latter appeared so seriously wounded that Lovat sent his Catholic chaplain to administer the last rites until Kindersley protested that he was a Protestant. In retrospect, it seems likely the shelling was another friendly fire incident. Lieutenant Colonel Mills-Roberts, a former solicitor in command of No. 6 Commando, was promoted to Acting Brigadier and took command of 1st Special Service Brigade.

With flames from Breville lighting up the night, C Company, 12th Parachute Battalion took heavy casualties as they advanced at 10.00pm. The following Devons were shelled in a sunken lane, probably by Allied artillery. With command and control collapsing, Major Warren, the 12th Parachute Battalion Support Company Commander detailed to guide the Devons, collected several infantrymen from a ditch and was directed to Breville by a No. 6 Commando sergeant advising him the sooner he reached the objective the better – for everyone's sake. More by luck than judgment, Warren entered the village to find that the 12th Parachute Battalion had seized its objectives, although another communications failure had led the 51st Highland Division into believing that Breville was still in enemy hands and they therefore shelled it, causing more casualties. Next morning, 1st Royal Ulster Rifles, from 6th Airlanding Brigade, re-inforced the village. Between them, the 12th Parachute Battalion and 12th Devons lost nine officers and 185 killed, with the cost to the paras of 139 all ranks. The 3/858th Grenadier Battalion had been reduced from 564 men to 146 since 7 June, such was the severity of the three days of fighting. The capture of Breville meant that the Allied left flank was more secure. In Amfreville, the French HQ had been reduced to ten all ranks, while 5 Troop was down to fifty-two, 6 Troop to forty-five and the K-Guns to fifteen. The Battalion had been reinforced by two naval riflemen and four local Norman volunteers, two of whom had been wounded in the fighting.

Chapter 13

The Thin Red Line: 13 June to 3 September 1944

The fighting died down with spasmodic shelling causing casualties and damaging defences. Since 1st Special Service Brigade did not have organic artillery, Brigadier Mills-Roberts met senior Corps and Divisional Royal Artillery officers to agree harassing fire on registered targets and direct fire support.

Both sides settled down into the routine of static warfare among the hamlets, woods, apple orchards, wrecked houses and farms. The Commandos stand-to for an hour from about 4.45am, when dawn attacks were expected, was followed by tactical weapon cleaning, washing, shaving and centrally cooked breakfasts with a brew of welcome hot tea or, for the French, preferably coffee. Harassing fire always a risk, the morning was spent repairing positions, bringing up and issuing rations, treating light wounds, cuts and bruises, and cleaning equipment. When 'Masters' found a double bed in Breville, he and three colleagues dug a trench big enough to accommodate it. An important fatigue was to service the communal latrines usually located behind a hedge and consisting of a long pole over a deep trench. The discipline of the age ensured that officers and men were separated by about five yards. Rest was taken in the afternoon before briefings for patrols at night. Some commandos were lucky enough to leave the front line for a spell in a rest camp. Others bathed either in the quarries, the Orne or the sea at Luc. In a café at Le Perraque, before having a coffee or calvados, HQ 48 (Royal Marines) Commando patrols would ask if there were any Germans around, invariably to be told that they had just left.

The commitment of 3 (British) Troop to the defeat of Nazism was second to none and hardly a night passed without the Troop accompanying standing, recce and fighting patrols. One patrol returned from Gonneville with an embarrassed German machine gunner, who had been dozing in the sun with his MG-34 Spandau. When Private 'Drew' ran short of food, he returned to a house in Breville and was promptly detained by some British paras, who thought that he was German from his accent. However, casualties mounted and while other No. 10 (Inter-Allied) Commando Troops could replace casualties, the intelligence resource, linguistic skills and experience of the Troop was becoming vital and difficult to replace.

13 and 14 June were the worst days. Lance Corporal 'Moody' and Private 'Norton', both attached to HQ 4th Special Service, were killed by shelling, as was Lance Corporal 'Graham', who was attached to No. 4 Commando. 'Graham' was due to marry the sister of 'Michael Merton'. On a Troop recce patrol, Corporal 'Broadman' was wounded and then Sergeant 'Fuller' was killed by an American bomb while providing tactical air control from Moulin du Buisson farm to a US Army Air Corps Mitchell bomber attacking the WN-6 Strongpoint near Sallenelles. During the night, when Major Hilton-Jones assembled a patrol to infiltrate three Resistance members through German lines between Gonneville and Varaville, the commandos were shocked when the Frenchmen turned up because one was wearing a white shirt and another a light blue smock typical of French farmers. Leaving Breville after dark, to the commandos' frustration, the Frenchmen had little idea of night patrolling and frequently bunched. Their weak physical state, after four years of occupation, caused them to fall asleep nearly every time the patrol stopped. When significant German activity prevented infiltration through their lines, Hilton-Jones split the patrol and sent Sergeant 'Nichols', Lance Corporal 'Masters', Private 'Drew' and the two younger Frenchmen to the left, while he and Sergeants 'Stewart' and 'Shelley' took the third to the right. With his two Frenchmen still falling asleep, 'Nichols' searched for about a mile and a half for a route through the lines until the Frenchmen whispered they could not continue. With 'Masters' translating in his limited French, they asked to be left where they were and said that next morning they would walk into German lines with the story that they felt safer with them because the Allies had no food. It had worked before. 'Nichols' agreed and returned to Amfreville where his patrol spent a few anxious minutes because the French sentries usually muddled the nightly password and then opened fire after a brief challenge. It seems that the two Frenchmen later made it to Varaville. Meanwhile, Hilton-Jones was leading his group toward a T-shaped hedge when a Spandau opened fire at close range, wounding Hilton-Jones in the stomach. The group split up, as planned. When all was silent, Hilton-Jones shouted in German that he was an officer and would someone kindly collect him but the Germans, probably fearing a trap, left him until daylight, by which time he had lost a lot of blood and was considered by a medical orderly to be more dead than alive. 'Stewart' and 'Shelley' made it back through British lines, however, when the third

Frenchman approached Amfreville, the French were at dawn stand-to and, since he could not remember the password, he was shot dead. With Hilton-Jones posted missing, Sergeant 'Stewart' took command of the Troop and promoted 'Masters' to corporal. Next day, General de Gaulle landed in France.

During the night of 19/20 June, Sergeant 'Thompson', a German former teacher now attached to No. 4 Commando, accompanied Lieutenant Littlejohn to investigate reports that the Germans were having supply difficulties. Their plan was to pass through the German defences from La Grande Ferme du Boissons somewhere on the road from Gonneville to Longuemare and then observe the Varaville crossroads. Leaving at 2.30am, the pair crawled up and down the enemy front but were unable to cross the road and all next day hid in a ditch about 50 yards from enemy positions. Next night, as they tried to infiltrate between two weapon pits, when Littlejohn practically crawled down a rifle barrel, both commandos threw grenades to cover their withdrawal, however Littlejohn was shot in the leg. 'Thompson' hid in a bomb crater in the middle of a field. After about an hour, a German patrol found Littlejohn, who had the steely nerve to feign death, even when a bullet was fired into the ground beside him and a bayonet prodded his face. They then returned with 'Thompson' to Littlejohn, declared he was dead and removed his revolver and ammunition. A second German patrol took their boots, compass, watch and binoculars. By dawn, Littlejohn had crawled back the 2,000 yards to the British lines and reported that 'Thompson' was a prisoner. Littlejohn later joined the SAS and was murdered by the SS as a prisoner.

During the day, 'Nichols' was wounded in the face while cycling to the Longmarc crossroads on a recce. He was given an immediate battlefield commission on the strength of Brigadier Mills-Robert's recommendation, an unusual award because General Montgomery had ordered that the Army were not to give immediate field commissions, but did not return to the Troop. Private Snowden, a signaller attached to the French Battalion from No. 4 Commando, disappeared on patrol to Amfreville.

In spite of several prisoner-snatch patrols, No. 3 Commando needed to identify the German units facing them. Corporal 'Lawrence' had some success by crawling to a German position and whispering 'Komme mit. Come with me,' and invariably returned with a confused prisoner. He came from a prosperous family of shopkeepers in Darmstadt and had a brother in the Hampshires. During the night of 22/23 June, he left on another solo patrol to bring back a German paybook in order to identify the unit opposite, but about half an hour later there was shooting and distant shouted orders in German, and 'Lawrence' was never seen again. Mindful of casualties, Sergeant 'Bartlett' set up a loudspeaker in the trees and broadcasted the latest news, according to the Allies, suggesting to the

125

Germans that it was time to surrender. Although the loudspeakers were shot at, deserters trickled in to the Commando lines, including a Pole who mentioned that he had seen a British soldier being led away at about the same time as the shooting and shouting.

On 24 June, Brigadier Mills-Roberts initiated a daytime programme in which snipers and their observers crawled into the fields and woods to pick off German officers, wireless operators and others too casual to be careful. The snipers usually used Lee Enfield Mark 4 .303 rifles fitted with a No. 32 Sighting Telescope that magnified images from 200 to 1,300 yards. Since sniping demands an ability to use the lie of the land, snipers also guided patrols probing German positions and helped artillery forward observation officers find observation posts. Private Paddy Byrne, of C Troop, No. 4 Commando excelled in sniping and on several occasions worked with 3 (British) Troop patrols. Corporal 'Masters' frequently manned a static early warning patrol with Private Ducas, from the French commandos, at the Longmarc crossroads, and also selected targets for Byrne. Major Godfrey Franks, who had joined No. 10 (Inter-Allied) Commando from the Special Service Group as Second-in-Command vice Major Hilton-Jones, was on a patrol on 25 June when four green flares burst overhead and were followed by several mortar bombs. As they sprinted for cover, Lance Corporal Guy Laot was mortally wounded in the stomach. Never leaving their dead or wounded, Sergeant de Montlaur and Privates Scherer and Zivohlava carried him to the French lines.

As June passed into July, the shelling and mortaring of the French was impacting on morale, particularly as ammunition for return fire was rationed. Casualties and men taken ill nibbled at unit strengths and the ever-present difficulty of defending their sector. Intelligence assessments suggested the Germans opposite to be stronger than the two Special Service Brigades. To keep the French offensively minded, Lieutenant Lofi organized a programme of night-fighting patrols penetrating 2 to 3 kilometres behind German lines from the direction of Sallenelles and La Grande Ferme de Buissons. Most patrols were lightly equipped and took automatic weapons, some preferring the lighter captured Schmeissers to the heavier Thompsons. Interestingly, many Germans preferred the Sten with its sideways magazine. The programme developed into an inter-section competition as patrols gathered information and frequently clashed with the Germans. It displeased several British officers because of German retaliation.

First thing on 7 July, the order to move the Brigade to positions in Bas de Breville was received with little enthusiasm by the French because it had a bad reputation for ambushes and booby traps left among abandoned equipment and kit. They left their trenches with sadness because most had been developed into comfortable shelters from the shelling and poor weather – a home from home – and the business of starting all over again was distinctly unappealing. As the Battalion approached the wrecked hamlet, the smell of death was pervasive. In fields, dead cows and sheep lay on their backs, their legs stiffly raised and their rotten intestines attracting masses of flies. Sat on a horse rescued from a field, Lance Corporal Poli led the column followed by Lance Sergeant Coste on a Renault caterpillar tractor pulling a trailer piled high with the K-Guns and equipment, and some commandos with bicycles. Overhead, bombers struck Caen in a huge show of force that inspired but saddened the French. Two days later, the wrecked city was liberated by I (British) Corps.

In the late morning of 13 July, Major Kieffer returned and next day, Bastille Day, several French commandos attended a parade at Bayeaux. A memorial was consecrated on Le Plein village green to commemorate those who had lost their lives in Normandy, followed by a march past, which included a detachment of French veterans. On the 16th, General Montgomery visited 1st Special Service Brigade and presented the MC to Kieffer at a parade at Herouvilles. During the day, 3rd Division moved in to the 1st Special Service Brigade area in preparation for Operation Goodwood and, over the next few days, patrolling was reduced in order not to prompt flank attacks on the operation. The plan was for VIII Corps to punch through German positions south of Caen and trap them near Falaise against US forces approaching from the west. However, the Germans, alert to the increased traffic on the roads, bombed Le Plein and hit three ammunition trucks full of 25-pounder ammunition. The offensive faced determined opposition and on 20 July, the day that an attempt was made to assassinate Hitler, Operation Goodwood ground to a halt with substantial losses in men and equipment.

Since the middle of July, 1st Special Service Brigade intelligence suspected that the Germans opposite had either been reinforced or replaced, but there was no hard evidence until the 23rd when a deserter from 857th Infantry Regiment walked in to the No. 4 Commando positions and confirmed that 346th Fusilier Battalion had left about a week previously. In preparation for Operation Bluecoat, to support the US breakout from Saint Lo, prisoners were required and on 23 July, No. 47 (Royal Marines) Commando was instructed by HQ 21st Army Group to send a patrol from Moulin du Buisson, which by now was a wreck after being fought over since 7 June. Corporal 'Terry' was selected to guide the patrol of volunteers from B Troop, but he was distinctly unhappy about the concept of using the farm as the jump-off point, because the Germans knew British routes, a view he shared with the Commanding Officer, Lieutenant Colonel Phillips. A few hours before the patrol departed, three Polish deserters crossed into the Commando lines and mentioned to 'Terry' under interrogation that mines had been laid alongside a path usually used by British patrols. Soon

127

after dark, 'Terry' was woken by Phillips's Marine Orderly Assistant with a glass of rum. The patrol left Commando Headquarters at midnight following a tall hedge as far as a T-junction. Here, the patrol commander, Lieutenant Collett, split the patrol, taking one side of the hedge with six men, while Sergeant Gutteridge led the remainder on the other side. Soon after the patrol re-assembled at a gap in the hedge, Gutteridge stepped on a mine. There was silence for about a minute and as he began screaming in pain, the Germans opened fire at close range and the Royal Marines dived into cover. As a flare burst overhead, 'Terry' was startled to see a bunker about 30 yards ahead and was scampering to the hedge when he was knocked out by an exploding grenade. Coming to, he was crawling back to Moulin du Buisson when, 200 yards from the farm, a Canadian paratrooper shot him. Collapsing into a ditch and calling for help, he was rescued by the Brigade Major and Corporal 'Harris', who was usually attached to No. 45 (Royal Marines) Commando, and was evacuated to an English hospital. Next day, a 6 (French) Troop patrol was ambushed near Breville and Lance Corporal Georges Gicquel was captured. His body was later recovered with evidence of mistreatment.

On 1 August, Nos 4 and 6 Commandos and Brigade HQ were relieved by 6th Airlanding Brigade and took over 3rd Parachute Brigade positions in the Bois de Bavent. The paras moved on to the right flank of 1st Special Service Brigade. The air was filled with the sickly sweet smell of death from the weeks of fighting and at night, swarms of whining mosquitoes breeding in the reeds of the River Dives and surrounding flooded fields pestered the commandos. Nos 3 and 45 (Royal Marines) Commandos, which had also passed under command of 6th Airlanding Brigade during the moves, were relieved by 4th Special Service Brigade and rejoined 1st Special Service Brigade by taking over from 5th Parachute Brigade at Le Mesnil, with a frontage of about 2,300 yards of thickly wooded country. The Germans mortaring was better than in the Breville area, and the Brigade prisoner-of-war cage and Brigade Aid Post at Le Carrefour de la Madeline were hit. When a policy was adopted that as soon as the enemy mortars fired, the commandos would retaliate on sound bearings, the Germans used harassing fire to screen the redeployment of the mortars to new positions.

On 6 August, General Montgomery issued orders for Operation Totalize that the German forces were to be surrounded and prevented from retreating. Intelligence then suggested that increased German aggression against the Orne bridgehead was screening preparations for a general withdrawal. On the same day, Corporal 'Andrews' was killed by a S-mine while on patrol with B Troop, No. 47 (Royal Marines) Commando while investigating Moulin de Buisson. In 1937, 'Andrews' had spent several months in a concentration camp before being sent to England by his parents. When they were in a liner that docked at Southampton en route to Latin America, the British authorities would not allow them to have a reunion.

Next day, General Gale received orders to pursue the enemy and was reinforced by the 1st Belgian Independent Brigade and the 1st Princess Irene Brigade, which enabled him to form a broad front, his limit of exploitation being the River Seine. By 7 August, the attrition had reduced the French Battalion HQ to twelve all ranks, 5 Troop to forty-five all ranks, 6 Troop to thirty men and the K-Guns to nine. It was therefore of some relief to Major Kieffer when thirty-one reinforcements arrived, including twenty-seven men recovered from wounds and the rest from 9 (French) Troop, including Seaman Yves Vourc'h, brother of Lieutenant Vourc'h. A few of the reinforcements were evacuated a few days later after being found not yet fit. On 16 June, Lieutenant Willers had arrived and took over 1 Troop on 16 July.

Determined to keep the pressure on 711th and 346th Infantry Divisions, Gale ordered that during the advance, recces were to be kept to a minimum and units were to leapfrog through each other. The ground was a maze of small flat fields, woods and high hedges bordering sunken lanes – ideal for ambushes and retreating snipers. As 1st Special Service Brigade sniffed for enemy intentions, No. 4 Commando patrols discovered booby traps and tripwires, a sure sign of a withdrawal; nevertheless, during the evening of 11 August, as a thick mist descended across the battlefield, the commando positions were mortared. For the next six days, both sides played cat-and-mouse as the Germans struggled to camouflage the timing of their withdrawal.

Except for those forces trapped in the Falaise Gap, on 16 August, Hitler reluctantly agreed to a general withdrawal and next day, seventy-two days after landing, 6th Airborne Division broke out of the beachhead and advanced north across the flooded River Dives valley. 4th Special Service and 3rd Parachute Brigades reached Troan and, crossing the River Dives, advanced along the main road toward the village of Dozule, the next objective. Two miles north of the Dives valley and dominating the area was the sausage-shaped Brucourt Ridge rising to 400 feet, and to the west of Dozule was the Bois de Dozule. The Germans had demolished the bridges over the river. It was thought that the 346th Infantry Division, with its HQ at Putot-en-Auge, would delay withdrawal until prompted. Intelligence on the position was scanty, although it was believed that the German artillery had pulled out leaving a thin crust of two companies supported by mortars and machine guns. During 19 August, 6th Airborne Division ground to a halt when 3rd Parachute Brigade was held up at Putot-en-Auge and the 5th Parachute Brigade, which had been ordered to seize Bois de Dozule, had been driven back across the Dives twice. Vehicles and marching columns were strung along the road to Troan.

No. 4 Commando led the 1st Special Service Brigade breakout, laying white tape for 3 miles across fields, and liberated Bavent, where delighted villagers learnt their liberators were French. No. 3 Commando drove out a German rearguard from the German HQ at Varaville. With the mosquito-infested Dives valley flooded, the advance was confined to causeways, with the Germans conducting a careful withdrawal across ground ideal for defence, wholly or partially demolishing bridges. On 18 August, a No. 6 Commando patrol crossed the Dives near Bricqueville, drove a German rearguard from Robehomme and, reaching Pont de Vacaville, created a small bridgehead on the left bank of the Dives. A lightweight bridge designed by a Royal Engineer at Brigade HQ was laid between Divette and Pont de Vacaville by a REME Light Aid Detachment and by 10.00pm, the bridgehead was expanding. A No. 3 Commando patrol sent to the Vacaville bridges sighted a few Goliath midget tanks and tried to bypass the Germans by going cross-country, but found the going very difficult. Returning to the road, the patrol heard two large explosions thought to be bridge demolitions. When it then came under heavy fire from the area, it was obvious that an attack over the damaged bridges would be costly.

During the afternoon of 19 August, a No. 45 (Royal Marines) Commando patrol found a crossing over the Dives. With the two parachute brigades held up before Putot-en-Auge, at 5.30pm Gale issued orders for a general attack, with 1st Special Brigade outflanking the Germans by seizing Brucourt Ridge by dawn, and the two parachute brigades attacking Bois de Dozule, their right flanks protected by 4th Special Service Brigade. Knowing that a Royal Marines patrol exploring the western flanks of the ridge had drawn enemy fire and that the known bridges were passable only by infantry, Brigadier Mills-Roberts returned to his HQ in his jeep and, in a race against time, devised a plan that with the Germans dominating any approach across 2,500 yards of marshy, open ground, it meant a daylight attack was out of the question. The French were to seize L'Epine, a small feature between Brucourt and Belmare. Issuing orders at 7.00pm for a stealthy cross-country approach, Mills-Roberts wanted the advance to start at 11.30pm; however some units were held up several miles from the forming-up place at Plain Gruchet. When reports arrived that the bridge would not be usable until at least 11.30pm, lorries and jeeps ran a shuttle service as far as the bridge and then the commandos marched. The night was very dark, hot and heavy with the fragrance of roses.

An hour behind schedule, at 12.45am on 20 August, the 160 men of No. 4 Commando – from the 435 who had landed on D-Day – crossed the start line with 6 (French) Troop leading, and crossed the Dives on an impro-vised Infantry Bridge thrown across a damaged railway bridge. Twenty minutes later, the remainder of the Brigade followed the white tape laid by No. 4 Commando, with signallers playing a key role in reporting delays and obstacles. At the bottom of L'Epine, Lieutenant Lofi ordered 6 Troop into extended line and began climbing, followed by Battalion HQ and 5 Troop. At about 3.00am, two scouts reported an enemy position of several empty trenches, the foetid smell of stale straw, some weapons and equipment, two French 80mm mortars and a considerable quantity of ammunition. Another German position was seemingly unaware of the French, but a message sent to Commando HQ recommending an attack was ignored. Consulting his map, Lofi believed he was about 100 yards from a suspected German position at a crossroads and sent Sergeant Senee with two scouts to check. When they reported all quiet, Lieutenant Hulot's Support Troop deployed around a small hillock and covered 6 Troop as they descended in single file onto a track that snaked through the gully and turned left to follow a grassy bank. They were about to halt to wait for dawn when, 'Halt! Wer da? Halt! Who goes there?'

Expecting to be joined by 5 Troop, Lofi thought the challenge was 'Halt! La!' and told the challenger to stop fooling around. The answer was a MG-34 opening fire at a range of no more than 30 yards. As Lofi and Senee threw grenades in the general direction of the machine gun, slivers and splinters hit Lofi and Sergeant Georges Messanot. Corporal Zivohlava opened fire with his Schmeisser and the rest of the Troop dived into a soggy ditch. Fortunately, the Spandau was firing on fixed lines and its rounds cracked over the heads of the Frenchmen, except for Zivohlava who was wounded in the shoulder and bowled over as he dashed for the ditch. In spite of the pain, he shot a German determined to finish him off. The MG-34 gunner kept the Frenchmen pinned down until Hulot's K-Guns on the left, Brens on the right and 2-inch mortars opened fire, which allowed 6 Troop to retire a short distance. With surprise lost and a counter-attack vital, Lofi and Sergeant Major Chausse disappeared into early morning dimness to find a position from which to attack the German flank. Above them, Kieffer was not clear about what was happening and believed the French to be surrounded until Lofi radioed that he was organizing a counter-attack. With bayonets fixed and supported by covering fire, the twelve commandos of 5 Troop, in extended line, hurled themselves at the enemy, so often practised at Achnacarry, and, in spite of their fatigue, fought through the valley, knocking out one enemy trench after another in hand-to-hand fighting. Almost nose to nose with a young lieutenant already wounded in the leg, Chausse shot him in the stomach with his .45 Colt, and did not stop until he reached a small orchard where the Troop regrouped.

The furious attack shattered the defences and when the French rounded up the prisoners, most were wounded. The lieutenant was carried in by

131

two lightly wounded Germans, his broken right leg swinging uselessly and his hands red from compressing the stomach wound. Fearful of the French, when the lieutenant asked more than once to see a British officer, Major Kieffer told him that he was in command and instructed a commando to treat his wounds, but the German insisted that no Frenchman should touch him. Kieffer later went to the apple orchard where several prisoners were being interrogated by 3 Troop and saw the lieutenant leaning against an apple tree, his face pale from loss of blood, reciting in German a passage written by the French poet Rollinat bidding his parents and friends farewell. After Kieffer had told the young officer that he and his men had fought with courage and had covered the retreat of their division, he allowed a French orderly to treat him. Two wounded Frenchmen were evacuated. Zivohlava, weak from loss of blood, made his way to the French Aid Post and, in spite of getting weaker, staggered on to the Regimental Aid Post, where an orderly made him lie on a stretcher and hacked off his smock with a knife. After a British doctor told Zivohlava that he was lucky as the bullet had missed his vein, he operated on him and sent him to the General Hospital in Bayeaux.

By 6.00am, No. 4 Commando had reached the summit of Brucourt Ridge, capturing three Flak guns and forty-one prisoners. As the remainder of the Brigade filed onto the ridge, shelling caused casualties with No. 6 Commando suffering the most. Then at 11.00am, the Germans launched the first of four counter-attacks, their intensity prompting the need for a logistic and casualty evacuation route to Rear HQ at Plain Gruchet. No. 45 (Royal Marines) Commando tried to create it across the valley to No. 4 Commando but when they lost five killed, it became clear that resupply must wait until darkness. By 1.00pm, the Commando had seized the crossroads in Dozule and linked up with 5th Parachute Brigade. Shortly after the final counter-attack at 10.00pm, a convoy of jeeps brought in ammunition, food and radio batteries, and evacuated about forty casualties, several deserters and some prisoners captured by clearing patrols.

Meanwhile, 4th Special Service Brigade on the right of 5th Parachute Brigade, with No. 46 (Royal Marines) Commando leading, had become embroiled in fierce night fighting among the thick hedges, fences and coppices on Bois de Dozule. Corporal 'Harris' was wounded in the leg by a grenade and, staggering back down the hill to the First Aid Post, fell into a trench occupied by a soldier who he began to throttle, until the figure asked, 'Hans, is that you?' When 'Harris' said that he was not, the soldier said that as he was not German and wanted to surrender. After he had helped 'Harris' to Commando HQ, he gave him his watch in gratitude for saving his life. Next day, when 'Harris' was being evacuated, he saw the soldier lying dead on the side of the road.

132

With Brucourt Ridge, Dozule and Bois de Dozule in British hands, at first light on 20 August, 4th Special Service Brigade, with No. 48 (Royal Marines) Commando leading, attacked German withdrawal routes beyond the village. After ambushing several vehicles, they freed 6th Airborne Division to advance on two axes towards Deauville in the north and Pont l'Evêque in the south. Next day, 6th Airlanding Brigade took over the lead while 1st Special Brigade used lorries to leapfrog the rearmost Commando to the front of the long marching column. On 23 August, the Brigade moved right to support a night attack on Pont l'Evêque by 4th Special Service Brigade after a 5th Parachute Brigade assault had been held up by demolished bridges. Although surprise was lost, by 5.00pm next day, the Royal Marines had bypassed Pont l'Evêque and were supporting 5th Parachute Brigade, which was again held up. As No. 4 Commando filed through Beuzeville they witnessed several French civilians cutting the hair of young women accused of collaboration. With orders to seize two hills south-west of the village, at 8.00pm, the Brigade passed through 5th Parachute Brigade and with No. 6 Commando attracting the attention of the enemy, Nos 3 and 4 Commandos and Brigade HQ slipped north across countryside dark with woods and bocage, and, after ten hours of exhausting marching, seized both features.

When Pont l'Evêque was liberated, 3 (British) Troop were overjoyed to be told that among the hospital patients was Major Hilton-Jones. After being captured, the Germans believed he was fatally wounded and instructed another prisoner to dig his grave, however he refused to give up and was evacuated to the town, where a German surgeon specializing in stomach wounds treated him. When the Germans evacuated the town, the surgeon offered him the option of staying or joining the chaos of retreat. Hilton-Jones agreed that he was too ill to be moved.

By 25 August, 6th Airborne Division had advanced 40 miles in five days across flooded and heavily wooded countryside against the 346th Infantry Division, who fought and then withdrew in bounds covered by shelling and mortaring. At 9.00pm, both Special Service Brigades were ordered to seize the road from Honfleur to Pont Audemer, which was about 4 miles north of Beuzeville, and prevent the Germans from crossing the River Seine. Again, the commandos struggled in the darkness through the bocage with brief respites of a meadow or an apple orchard before encountering more woods or hedges; nevertheless, by dawn, with 4th Special Service Brigade on the right, 1st Special Service Brigade in the centre and 6th Airlanding Brigade on the left, the road was reached, but of significant German forces there was no sign and it was assumed they had crossed the Seine. No. 4 Commando liberated Saint Maclou during the afternoon and next evening were entertained by Monsieur and Madame Turquet with generous quantities of calvados in their chateau. In Boulleville, French commandos wrecked several shops when shopkeepers rather unwisely increased their prices. When orders then arrived from HQ 6th Airborne Division that all units were to rest since the Allies had air superiority, most units moved into barns and outbuildings for their first full night's sleep since 4 June.

In the eighty-three days of fighting since D-Day, of the 146 officers and 2,552 other ranks in 1st Special Service Brigade, which included the No. 10 (Inter-Allied) Commando detachments, eighteen officers and 183 other ranks were killed, fifty-six officers and 636 other ranks were wounded, and two officers and seventy-one men were missing. Of the 177 Frenchmen who had landed on Sword Beach, only forty Frenchmen were unscathed. 3 (British) Troop lost a total of twenty-seven killed, wounded or taken prisoner. All members of No. 4 and 47 (Royal Marines) Commando detachments were either killed, wounded or captured.

On 6 September, a long column of trucks transported 1st Special Service Brigade to Arromanches where they boarded the *Ulster Monarch* at Mulberry Harbour and reached Southampton late next day. The Brigade were accommodated at the Special Service Group Reception Camp at Petworth where the commandos collected leave passes, rail warrants and money, and went on leave for fourteen days. For the French, some had formed relationships with British families and girlfriends and stayed in Great Britain while others were reunited with their families in liberated parts of France, including Paris. Meanwhile, 3 Troop set about selecting and training recruits to make up for the losses in Normandy, while 4th Special Service Brigade, attached to I Corps, crossed the Seine at Duclair and advanced through France and Belgium.

Among those released from Fresnes Prison when Paris was liberated were three survivors of Operation Hardtack 11 – Sergeant Caron and Corporals Madec and Meunier. Still missing were Navrault and Pourcelet. Madec had tried swimming to the MTB in the darkness but, exhausted and cold, he had returned to the beach and, joining 'Jones' and Chapman, guided them across the minefield to join the rest of the patrol. However, the raid had alerted the Germans and 'Jones' and Chapman were both captured. Pourcelet, Navrault and Madec were sheltered in a barn by a farmer before they made their way to St Omer where they split up. Navrault and Pourcelet reached Paris where Navrault's mother put them in touch with the Resistance, but attempts to pass them along an escape line proved fruitless and so they joined Pourcelt's family in Amiens. Navrault joined the Raphanel Resistance in the Puy de Dôme and was in a battle with German security forces that practically wiped out his unit. He then took charge of a sabotage group and rejoined 5 (French) Troop after liberation. Madec, wearing his battledress jacket stripped of insignia, also reached Paris by hitch-hiking bicycles and train. Sheltered by his sister, a mayor gave him papers suggesting that he was a farmer just released from forced labour in Germany. Sergeant Major Wallerand had given him an address of a bar in Agen in the South of France but when the owners were unable to help he was unsuccessful in finding an escape line to England, and then travelled to the village of Kerneval, where Lieutenant Mazeas, the French Administration Officer, had a farm. Madec joined the Resistance and, forming a sabotage group, took part in several clashes with German forces. Helping to liberate Rosporden, his group harassed enemy convoys until Madoc heard that Lieutenant Mazeas, who was badly wounded on D-Day, was recuperating at his farm and later rejoined 6 Troop.

Caron and Meunier had rested in a hut near the beach and reached St Omer four days later. Sheltered by a widow, who then put them on a train to Fresnot-le-Grand, they reached Meunier's home where his family contacted the Resistance, however both were separated during a Gestapo raid. Caron reached Paris and remained until the capital was liberated. Meunier also reached Paris but was arrested on his way to Spain. Admitting to be a commando, he was beaten up and half-drowned in Fresnes by Gestapo interrogators suspicious of him and condemned to death.

Meanwhile on 3 June, 4 (Belgian) Troop of seven officers and seventy-seven men had arrived in Eastbourne from Vis and, after some leave, a month later they were sent to the Cliff Climbing School at St Ives. On the 17th, the Norwegians, after several frustrating months of inactivity in Lerwick, also arrived in Eastbourne and were sent on parachute training at Ringway and cliff climbing at St Ives. When Commander-in-Chief, Plymouth asked No. 10 (Inter-Allied) Commando to supply a detachment to raid the Isle de Yeu, in the Bay of Biscay, in Operation Rumford, and gather information on harbours, beaches and the extent of German occupation, Lieutenant Dauppe and five other ranks from the Belgian Troop were selected; they were joined by Corporal Harvey from the Special Service Group Signals Company. The raid commander was Lieutenant Colonel Laycock.

The raiding party left Plymouth on the Hunt class destroyer HMS *Albrighton* at 5.00pm on 25 August in good weather, and by 1.15am next morning were one and half miles from the island. After the dory was lowered, the destroyer withdrew out to sea for 5 miles as it was believed that a 75mm battery on the north-west point might be manned. With Lance Corporal Legrand at the helm, as a strong swell pushed the dory toward Port Joinville, Dauppe instructed Legrand to edge west. At 2.05am, Dauppe, Corporal Delener and Legrand, and Privates van der Bosche and Van den Daeje landed by rubber dinghy. Harvey remained on the dory with the S-Phone anchored about 50 yards offshore. The patrol crept past a large low building about 70 yards inland and, finding nothing, then followed a track leading to Port Joinville, but again found nothing of interest, and returned to a structure about 600 yards to the north-west which they thought was a building but was actually a haystack. By 3.00am time was short, nevertheless they followed another track that led to a large white farmhouse and two outbuildings. Snoring was heard and a recently used bucket was outside a door. When Dauppe and Deleneer opened the shutters, a man who arose from a bed to shut them turned out to be a widower living with his six children. Agreeing to return to England in exchange for a reward, and provided that he was returned within three days, he told the eldest child, a girl aged thirteen, to look after the family. He said that the Germans had left the previous night taking their equipment and stores. The Belgians linked up with the dory at 3.45am and within the hour, after a thorough soaking and motoring against a stronger swell, Legrand brought it alongside the destroyer where Dauppe was debriefed by Laycock.

While returning to Plymouth, Commander-in-Chief, Plymouth ordered the destroyer to intercept two trawlers sighted by an RAF Beaufighter 60 miles west of Brest. Two hours later, she closed to within half a mile of them and fired two shells across their bows which induced the trawlers to run up white flags. Fresh from their Adriatic experience, the Belgians boarded one trawler and the Royal Navy seized the second, capturing twenty-two German sailors who admitted that they had 'done in' their officers and were making for Spain. The trawlers were sunk and at 12.45am on 27 August, the destroyer disembarked the commandos at Mill Bay Docks, Plymouth at 8.00am. Even at this late stage of the war, Lieutenant Colonel Laycock noted in his operational report that although communications between destroyer and dory were good, the Royal Navy should note that the silhouette of the destroyer was considerably larger than a MTB. Operation Rumford was the last small-scale raid carried by No. 10 (Inter-Allied) Commando on the Atlantic coast.

Chapter 14

Operation Market Garden

By the end of August, the rapid advance of 21st Army through Northern France and Belgium had stretched the 300-mile supply line from Arromanches to near breaking point. General Eisenhower, stressing the importance of Antwerp as a logistic pivot for the advance into Germany, instructed that the defences covering the seaward approaches must be cleared, in particular the German fortress on the island of Walcheren guarding the River Scheldt. On 27 August, General Montgomery suggested the island be seized by the 1st Allied Airborne Army, however this was vetoed by General Lewis Brereton, its commander, who believed that an airborne assault on a flooded, heavily-defended island in the middle of an estuary was, to say the least, impractical.

With British commanders firmly focused on striking deep into the Ruhr, 11th Armoured Division, in a brilliant coup, occupied Antwerp on 4 September as far as the Albert Canal, thereby saving the sluice gates and port facilities from demolition, and then stopped, as did the rest of XXX (British) Corps. A strategic error later admitted by Lieutenant General Horrocks, the Corps commander, it allowed the German Fifteenth Army to avoid encirclement by crossing to Walcheren and making for the Rhine via North and South Beveland and east to Arnhem. On 5 September, which became known as *Dolle Dinsdag* (Mad Tuesday), the Arnhem Resistance reported that intermingled in columns of civilians retreating across the bridges into Germany were military units. When Field Marshal Walter Model, who commanded Army Group B, established his headquarters in Oosterbeek at the Tafelberg Hotel, Resistance activist Wouter van der Kraats bluffed his way into the courtyard and noted the insignia of German staff cars. By mid-September, about 100,000 Germans had escaped the net.

Operation Market Garden was designed by General Montgomery to shorten the war by laying an airborne carpet (Market) and seizing key bridges so that 21st Army Group could advance at speed (Garden) the 60 miles from Neerpelt on the Belgian/Dutch border and over the Rhine at Arnhem with:

- 101st (US) Division capturing the Wilhelmina and Willems Canal Bridges at Son and Veghel respectively.
- 82nd (US) Airborne Divisions seizing the bridges over the River Maas at Grave and Waal at Nijmegen.
- 1st (British) Airborne Division capturing the road and rail bridges at Arnhem.

At a planning conference, when Lieutenant General Frederick Browning, who commanded the 1st Allied Airborne Corps and was in overall command of the assault, was told that XXX Corps should be at Arnhem within forty-eight hours, he said he could hold on for four days but, prophetically, added that he felt that the operation was one bridge too far. The story of Operation Market Garden has been told many times, however we must briefly review the role of the Dutch Resistance.

SHAEF valued Resistance movements and while plans changed to meet strategic situations, mobilizing the Resistance did not. In its two-page Daily Summary, one page was usually devoted to summarizing Resistance activities – for instance, No. 97, dated 11.0800 September 1944, states that 'railway sabotage is being carried out in accordance with orders received by the Resistance Groups'. Although the Resistance had reliable information on German locations, routines, strengths and personalities useful to Operation Market Garden, according to Cornelius Ryan, General Montgomery told Prince Bernhard that he doubted the accuracy of the reports: 'I don't think your resistance forces can be of any help to us.' It seems that he was also vague in telling Bernhard about the operation.

Although occupation inevitably led to disillusionment, the Dutch Nazi Party was not widely supported, nevertheless, some young men enlisted into either the Wehrmacht or the motorized 5th SS Panzergrenadier Wiking Division of non-German volunteers, or the Dutch 4th SS Volunteer Panzergrenadier Brigade. 'Englandspiel' had shattered some Resistance factions, and although the lack of mountains and forests to hide men and supplies and a flat terrain sliced by waterways confined movement to railways and roads, some groups had survived German counter-intelligence operations. However, politics and the dysfunctional nature of resistance meant there was no central headquarters and operations were conducted with little co-ordination.

As the two exhausted French Troops were returning from Normandy, 2 (Dutch) Troop was mobilized. On 5 September, the South African Second Lieutenant Ruysch van Dugteren left Eastbourne with three commandos to be bodyguards to Prince Bernhard. Corporal van Woerden was later sent to the Princess Irene Brigade in Europe, where he ferried members of the Eindhoven Resistance to and from Brigade HQ in Grave and joined recce patrols. Next day, Lieutenant Knottenbelt, Sergeant van der Veer,

Corporals Michels and Westerling and Privates Bendien, Blatt, de Koning and van Lienden left to train for Bureau voor Byzondere Opdrachten (BBO) support to the Resistance. The balance of the Troop was initially assigned to 52nd (Lowland) Division, which was earmarked to reinforce 1st Airborne Division, as the Dutch Liaison Mission tasked to liaise with the Resistance and vet loyal Dutch. As the order of battle took shape, Captain Linzel and four men joined 52nd (Lowland) Division on 8 September, while Sergeants van Gelderen and Kruit and Private Baggermans were sent to HQ 1st (British) Airborne Corps. Two days later, fifteen men were attached to 1st Airborne Division and were joined on the 13th by Lieutenant Knottenbelt when Linzel realized that the detachment had no officers. Most of the Troop was distributed with the 1st Airlanding Brigade, and also with Commander Royal Engineers (Lieutenant Colonel Sam Myers) at Divisional HQ or with the 1st Airborne Divisional Signals Squadron. On 12 September, Troop Sergeant Major van der Bergh and fourteen commandos joined 82nd (US) Airborne Division. Corporal Persoon was attached to the US Signal Corps. Three days later, the 101st (US) Airborne Division was reinforced by Sergeant van der Wal and four men, including Private Bothe attached to the US Signal Corps. (See Appendix 6 for the Dutch Order of Battle.)

As Operation Market Garden took shape, Colonel Thorne-Thorne and Colonel Boddington, of the Royal Dutch Army, running Civil Affairs at Corps HQ finalized plans to administer liberated areas. Captain Jack Bryden at Corps Rear in UK had overall responsibility for counter-intelligence managing the 'black listed' personalities and contact with friendly 'white list' persons. A Jedburgh team attached to each Division was tasked to co-ordinate the military activities of Resistance. Typically consisting of two officers and a wireless operator, with British ones usually selected from the Royal Armoured Corps, missions had proven useful supporting Allied operations in France by co-ordinating the Resistance. Differences between the British and Americans led to the latter forming the Office of Strategic Services (OSS) and the formation of the Special Forces HQ (SFHQ). HQ 1st Airborne Corps Jedburgh 'Edward' had overall command of operations from England controlling 'Clarence' (82nd (US) Airborne Division), 'Daniel II' (101st (US) Airborne Division) and 'Claude' with the British. This team consisted of Dutch Army Reserve Captain (Intelligence) Jacobus Groenewoud, US Lieutenant Harvey Todd and Technical Sergeant Carl Alden Scott.

SHAEF did not want insurrection in Holland while liberation was in doubt and in preparation for Operation Market Garden, on 13 September, General Eisenhower instructed SFHQ:

Consider most important that resistance movement in HOLLAND be instructed to remain underground except in southern districts which will be affected by the operation concerned. Subsequent instructions will be issued for raising the other districts of HOLLAND as the advance inland progresses.

On 16 September, 1st Allied Airborne Army instructed that only Resistance directly affected by the landings should be mobilized and other groups were to induce a railway strike to delay German reinforcements threatening the operation.

Landing astride the road from Eindhoven to Nijmegen near St Oedenrode at about 1.00pm on 17 September, the 101st (Airborne) Division encountered stiff anti-aircraft fire and although the jump was successful, it was unable to prevent German engineers blowing up the Wilhelmina Canal Bridge at Son. Dutch civilians and parachute engineers were soon constructing a wooden footbridge. Sergeant Visser served as second pilot in a Waco glider carrying HQ 501st Parachute Infantry Regiment. Since the fighting took up most of the Division's time, General Maxwell Taylor left the management of the civilians to his Dutch Liaison Mission, and although there was some difficulty establishing the credibility of volunteers, about 200 Dutch civilians, including known Resistance, were cleared.

The 82nd Airborne Division landed about 5 miles south-east of Nijmegen on the Heights of Groesbeck, on the German border, and within six hours had seized a route for XXX Corps, except that the massive Waal Bridge over the Maas-Waal Canal was in German hands. Privates Bloemink and van der Linde both jumped; Troop Sergeant Major van der Bergh's glider landing was rough and an American warrant officer was impaled on some metal. On his way to Divisional HQ in woods near in Groesbeck, van der Bergh sent a patrol to capture Germans reported by some civilians to be in the church. Sergeant van Dulleman, a former military policeman, landed in a Waco glider as part of Divisional Intelligence and Security. When Corporal Kniff saw a jeep and men falling into the sea, he was told the frame of the gliders weakened after loading. Emigrating with his parents to Canada in 1926, he had reached England in 1942 with his friend August 'Buck' Bakhuys-Roozeboom, who was with 1st Airborne Division. Landing at Groesbeck, under shellfire, when the pilot hit a deep ditch around a large pond, the jeep inside shot forward and killed him. The rest reached some woods under fire but were pinned down until nightfall. He later contacted the Mayor of Groesbeck and Resistance groups along part of the road from Eindhoven that became known as 'Hell's Highway'.

Corporal Kokhuis was attached to the HQ 504th Parachute Infantry Regiment and landed by glider north of Overasselt. Coming under fire as he scrambled out, he returned enemy fire with his Thompson and believes he killed the German sniper. Freeing the jeep from the wreckage, the driver and Kokhuis drove to Regimental HQ at Overssaelt where he began work detaining several alleged collaborators. On one occasion, after persuading the daughter of the mayor of Wychen, who was accused of collaboration, to tell him where he was, he led a patrol of six soldiers to the town hall and arrested the mayor, who brandished a pistol, and escorted him to the interrogation centre in the town castle.

HQ 1st Allied Airborne Corps also landed on the Heights of Groesbeck. The Waco carrying Sergeant van Gelderen hit a cow and upended as its nose dug into sand, causing several casualties inside. Sergeant van Gelderen, a South African who had enlisted in the Dutch Army in Pretoria, was attached to Civil Affairs. During 18 and 19 September, assisted by local labour, under heavy fire and frequently attacked by German aircraft, he built a small forward landing strip. After capturing three prisoners and detaining two Dutch collaborators, Sergeant Kruit went on a recce and came across two merry British soldiers guarding Mook Bridge, and later met several Allied tanks. While communications with the two American divisions were good, nothing was heard from the British. Lieutenant General Browning was losing control of the operation.

When on 20 September, the 3rd Battalion, 504th Parachute Infantry Regiment crossed the Maas-Waal Canal under intense fire and outflanked the Germans defending the Waal Bridge; Corporal Kokhuis survived the fighting. Sergeant Kruit had been detached from Corps HQ to the Division and crossed the bridge with two Americans to help evacuate the village of Slijk-Ewijk but was ambushed on an open road. Although the jeep was damaged, the driver skilfully turned it around and reached Lent, where they decided there was no way of getting through. Kruit tried again with a motorcycle that he found in a glider but was again forced to turn back. On the same day, Sergeant Major van der Bergh rescued a German pilot who had bailed out, landed on a roof and had been seized by some civilians. Kokhuis later entered a convent that housed a SS stores dump and joined several patrols to Cleve in Germany, on one occasion dealing with a niece of Herman Goering who was complaining about the theft of silver.

The employment of the Nijmegen Resistance was a fine example of prompt execution because Brigadier General James Gavin trusted his Dutch Liaison Mission and Jedburgh Clarence to exploit its value. Guides and interpreters accompanied patrols, their lack of knowledge of command and control and field discipline solved by distributing them throughout the Division, and giving them uniforms. The overall result was that there was no widespread refugee problem clogging up vital roads. Private Donald Pearsall of 2/508th Parachute Infantry Regiment, later wrote: 'Those brave civilians with orange bands on their arms, they were everywhere ... they informed us of German movements time and again. Many of us are alive today, because of these brave men ... Those fighting

Dutchmen in Orange I will never forget, they were some of the bravest men I had ever met.'

Major General Robert Urqhuart, who commanded 1st Airborne Division, barely had a week to plan the seizure of the Arnhem bridges and when his staff calculated loading tables, the lack of aircraft forced him to spread the landings over three days:

17 September
- 1st Parachute Brigade to seize the Arnhem bridges for twenty-four hours.
- 1st Air Landing Brigade to develop a perimeter in the western suburbs of Oosterbeek to defend the approaches to Arnhem.
- Divisional HQ to land.

18 September
- 4th Parachute Brigade to seize the high ground north of Arnhem.

19 September
- 1st Polish Independent Parachute Brigade to land south of the Rhine, cross and form a perimeter to the east.
- 52nd (Lowland) Division to be flown in when the airhead was secure.

German deployments around Arnhem meant that the DZs and LZs were 7 miles west of the bridges in open ground east of Oosterbeek. In spite of Resistance reports that strong German forces, including the 9th 'Hohenstauff' SS Panzer Division, were in the area being passed to Dutch liaison officers back in England, these were rejected as unreliable and enemy strength was assessed as low. Second Army Intelligence had also noted that 10th 'Frundsberg' SS Panzer Division was in the town. Part of General Wilhelm Bittrich's II SS Panzer Corps, both of these divisions were battle-hardened, but were tired. Although the Germans knew a major attack was likely and had stiffened their defences close to the border, their planners believed that Arnhem had little strategic value and had moved the two divisions to rest areas near Oosterbeek. When Queen Wilhelmina then broadcast that liberation was imminent, a senior Arnhem regional Resistance leader, Reserve Captain G.C. Wunderink, unsuccessfully tried to convince the various groups to co-operate under his leadership, but was rejected on the grounds that his group would reap the rewards at their expense.

1st Airborne Division began landing at 12.00pm on 17 September with Divisional HQ, Jedburgh Claude and 1st Airlanding Brigade all on LZ 'S' and 1st Parachute Brigade on DZ 'X'. Claude ran into trouble when Technical Sergeant Scott was unable to find the glider carrying his radio in a container. Captain Groenewoud and Lieutenant Todd then followed 1st

142

Parachute Brigade on their 7-mile advance to Arnhem and recovered documents of intelligence from a captured German HQ at Rijnpaviljoen. Several patients and their nurses from a nearby lunatic asylum fled into woods.

En route to Arnhem were the twenty-eight jeeps of 1st Airlanding Brigade Recce Squadron and Corporal Tom Italiaander from the Dutch Liaison Mission. Italiaander was employed as a geophysicist in Bogota, Columbia when in 1941 he reached England from Canada. His Horsa containing a jeep and two British soldiers had an uneventful landing at LZ 'S' at about 2.00pm, but it was not until 3.35pm that the column set off for Arnhem along a lane towards the railway line. They were soon ambushed, probably by the teenagers and convalescent veterans of the 16th Waffen-SS Training and Replacement Battalion who had reacted to the landings by establishing a blocking position at Wolfsheze. Their presence was a considerable shock to the lightly armed paras and within hours the fighting was heavy and confused. Wireless communications were difficult.

Lieutenant Knottenbelt and Private Bakhuys-Roozeboom landed with Divisional HQ. Joining 3rd Parachute Battalion advancing to Arnhem, Knottenbelt was approaching Oosterbeek when the leading platoon shot up a German Army Citroen and killed its four occupants, the lifeless Major General Kussin falling from his seat, clutching a cigarette. As the Arnhem town commander, he had been advised not to use the main road. Knottenbelt searched the body and car for documents, cut Kussin's epaulettes from his leather overcoat and pocketed them. Also in the column was Captain John Killick, Intelligence Corps, who commanded 89 Parachute Field Security Section and ran counter-intelligence operations. He was intending to join the FS Sub-Section attached to 1st Parachute Brigade, and was soon interrogating prisoners and making intelligence assessments for Divisional HQ until all hands were required in the battle for the bridge.

Landing with the Intelligence Section, HQ 1st Air Landing Brigade on LZ 'S' at about 1.00pm was Private Jan van der Meer. Crossing the railway towards the mental hospital, Brigadier Higgs established his HQ near Wolfsheze to defend the approaches to Arnhem from the south and south-west. Van der Meer met Lieutenant Commander Arnoldus Wolters, Royal Dutch Navy, who, as the 'official representative of Dutch government with full powers' was assisting Colonel Hilaro Barlow, Civil Affairs, 1st Airborne Division. He was an intelligence officer and the only sailor at Arnhem. Private Beekmeyer also landed on LZ 'S' with the Intelligence Section, 7th KOSB at about 1.30pm. Clambering from the Horsa to the Battalion piper playing the Regimental March 'Blue Bonnets Over the Border', he questioned several bewildered Dutch people on German dispositions and twenty Germans held in a temporary prisoner-of-war cage in a glider guarded by the military police near Divisional HQ.

Sergeant de Waard was in the same Horsa as Major General Urquhart. Attached to Major Oliver Newton-Dunn, who was part of the Divisional Operations staff, after the glider landed in a large potato field, de Waard met some nervous Dutch churchgoers. After explaining what was happening, they took him to a house where the National Anthem was sung in expectation of liberation, an experience that he found intensely moving. As Divisional HQ was established in the Hartenstein Hotel in Oosterbeek, it was slowly dawning on the Division that there was a problem with communications. Food had been left on the dining-room tables by Sunday diners. De Waard, who had passed the body of Kussin, was soon interrogating prisoners and Dutch civilians freed from Arnhem Prison. He also met a refugee from Ijmuiden and asked him to greet his parents, which the refugee did.

During the night, 1st Air Landing Brigade had a tough time defending the DZs. Next day, Private Beekmeyer took part in a 7th KOSB bayonet charge against the low-grade 3rd SS Home Guard Battalion of Dutch volunteers threatening the drop by 4th Parachute Brigade on DZ 'Y'. Four hours late, because of fog in England, the Brigade lost six Dakotas and two gliders to flak en route from the coast, and supplies had gone astray. During the night, the Battalion became embroiled in heavy fighting around the Polish DZ 'L' at Johanna Hove Farm. Beekmeyer was accompanied for most of the day by an Arnhem police officer, who evacuated the occupants of the farm. Several Dutchmen seeking arms and equipment, including a forester and others escaping from forced labour at the Luftwaffe airfield at Delen, also arrived to help.

Next morning, Oosterbeek began to fill up with British soldiers battling to create a perimeter around Arnhem Bridge. At 4.00am, unknown to 3rd Parachute Battalion struggling to reach Arnhem, and with Major General Urquhart missing, 1st and 11th Parachute Battalions and 2nd South Staffords advanced through Oosterbeek in a co-ordinated move but encountered determined opposition at first light. At about 7.30am, Urquhart returned to Divisional HQ and, learning that his Division was being compressed into two contracting perimeters, with 2nd Parachute Battalion cut off from 1st Parachute Brigade, sent Colonel Barlow to organize the drive of 2nd South Staffords and the 1st and 11th Parachute Battalions to the bridge. When Barlow was killed by mortar fire, the 3rd Parachute Battalion pushed forward to help the 1st Parachute Battalion. The South Staffords and 11th Parachute Battalion, meanwhile, were fought to a standstill and about fifty soldiers were trapped in Arnhem Museum, among them Private Hubertus Gubbels, who was attached to the South Staffords. He used a museum telephone to call his parents at Ede apologizing that he would not be able to see them as quickly as he hoped, and was captured.

At Divisional HQ, the 1st Air Landing and 4th Parachute Brigades Field Security Sections were assembled into a single unit and worked with Dutch commandos hunting collaborators, and searching houses previously occupied by the Germans for documents of intelligence value. The Resistance leader Pieter Kruijk contacted Wolters and suggested the British use the telephone network; however Divisional HQ felt, with good reason, that it was insecure. In spite of the British reservations, Wolters and Sergeant de Waard passed messages to Arnhem using an Oosterbeek dentist telephoning a friend. It is ironic that even as the British paras occupying their homes were having communications problems, the Dutch were telephoning friends and relatives. Two German women manned the Arnhem exchange throughout the battle.

Knottenbelt had returned to Divisional HQ and soon discovered that the Resistance was inactive after some of its members had been arrested during the summer and the remainder were in hiding. He had been told:

> The principle as laid down in the briefing that the Mission Claude was to act in only an advisory capacity to the Divisional Staff with regard to the recruitment of civilians was not applied in practice as, understandably enough, the British Staff Officers preferred to place the whole responsibility for the vetting and the organization onto the Dutch personnel available.

He successfully recruited fifty Dutch, including a group hiding in woods led by the Dutch naval officer, Charles van der Krap, and assembled them into the Orange Battalion. Supplied with House of Orange armbands, they helped the Dutch Liaison Mission and 89 Parachute Field Security Section round up collaborators, collect supplies, serve as guides, particularly in urban areas, guard prisoners and act as stretcher-bearers.

Late on 18 September, when the fighting around Arnhem Bridge intensified with the shelling of the town, Lieutenant Todd was wounded in the face by splinters when a sniper shot at him. Two Dutch police officers, Constables van Kuick and Hogenboom, remained at the former Military Police Station. Its telephone was twice used by Captain Killick during the day reporting the situation at the bridge to Divisional HQ, on the second occasion to Lieutenant Knottenbelt.

After a civilian had reported to Captain Groenewoud that a strong column of German armour was approaching Arnhem from Amsterdam, a determined attack developed across the bridge and the situation for 2nd Parachute Battalion became progressively bleak – shortage of ammunition, mounting casualties, little food, very short of water and cut off. When Groenewoud and Todd offered to contact a local doctor and arrange for medical supplies to be sent from St Elisabeth Hospital at Oosterbeek, they had covered only a few yards when Groenewoud was shot dead by a sniper. Todd then learnt from the doctor that the hospital authorities had been warned by the Germans not to send any help. For his gallantry since landing, Groenewoud, the short-sighted Dutch volunteer reject who had enlisted in South Africa, was awarded the Military Cross of William 4th Class, the equivalent of the VC.

During the day, Sergeant de Waard met Private Bakhuys-Roozeboom sitting in a jeep and about to depart in an attempt to reach 2nd Parachute Battalion. Accompanied by two members of the Resistance dressed in uniforms, Jan Diepenbrock and Hendrik Beekhuisen, under fire, the jeep, driven by a major, sped from the Hartenstein Hotel and made for the railway bridge near the station. About 400 yards after joining the road to Arnhem, they intercepted a German ambulance full of ammunition and were returning to Oosterbeek with this much-needed prize when they were ambushed near the bridge. As the major accelerated, Bakhuys-Roozeboom was throwing grenades when he was shot in the head and, slumped into the front between the major and Beekhuisen, was taken to the Hartenstein Hotel where he died, the only Dutch commando to be killed in the battle at Arnhem. Private August Bakhuys-Roozeboom was later buried in the St Elizabeth Hospital field cemetery, however, when the bodies from it were being transferred to the military cemetery in the town, his data were lost. Years later, a Mr Hey identified his grave and with the approval of the Commonwealth War Graves Commission, Bakhuys-Roozeboom was re-interred in a ceremony attended by family and veterans of 2 (Dutch) Troop on 5 May 1997.

Private Helleman spent the first days with 1st Borders near the Heveadorp Ferry. After the Battalion withdrew to the western outskirts of Oosterbeek, he and another soldier were escorting a member of the Dutch Nazi Party and five prisoners when, near the railway bridge, a sniper wounded one of the prisoners and the Nazi. Sheltering in some houses for several hours, he learnt that earlier in the day a soldier had been wounded in a jeep and believed it to be Bakhuys-Roozeboom. Beekmeyer joined a 7th KOSB patrol hunting a sniper but when he was separated by the shelling and fighting, he joined about 100 paras crossing the railway, who convinced him to remain with them because it was too dangerous to rejoin the KOSBs. Next day, the group broke up an infantry and tank attack, but were eventually forced to surrender.

Lieutenant Leo Heaps, a Canadian seconded to the British Army, had jumped, for the first time in his life, from a Dakota during the afternoon of 17 September. Commanding the 1st Parachute Battalion Transport Platoon, he had become separated from his Battalion and attached himself to Divisional HQ where he carried out tasks others could not, or preferred not to do. During the night of the 20th, General Urquhart asked him to take supplies to 2nd Parachute Battalion, which they needed desperately. He suggested his best chance was to use the Heveadorp ferry, which was still being operated by its skipper. Heap knew Lieutenant Knottenbelt from his work with the Dutch and that he was quietly playing an important role collecting intelligence. Having persuaded him, he then invited Lieutenant Johnny Johnson, a 8th (US) Army Air Force liaison officer, to join the attempt, together with two sleepy glider pilots who were woken from a trench. Departing at midnight with two relatively undamaged jeeps loaded with food and ammunition, Knottenbelt, in the leading jeep with Heaps, was suspicious of the entire escapade and used his knowledge of Germans dispositions to reject every suggestion except the ferry. On reaching the Rhine, Heap sent the two glider pilots to investigate some noises from the undergrowth but they never returned. Heaps then switched on the headlights, and in the misty beam, saw that the listing ferry was about 50 feet from the bank. The officers were puzzled by several abandoned defensive positions, but then a dazed Royal Engineer stumbled out of the night and mentioned that the ferry had recently been scuttled by its crew, and that he was searching for his wounded. When the officers boarded the ferry and discovered that its gears had been smashed, they returned to the Hartenstein Hotel.

Early on 21 September, the men at Arnhem Bridge broke into small groups and, leaving the wounded behind, tried to evade capture. Few did. After several days of rain and fog in England, the 1st Polish Independent Parachute Brigade landed on an insecure DZ east of Driel suffering a few casualties but, without boats, were unable to cross the river. Although told not to trust the Dutch Underground, Lieutenant Wladsylow Brzeg, the Brigade Field Security officer, weeded out collaborators and German agents at Driel, and the village soon became a magnet for Resistance cells.

With despondency at the hopelessness of the situation evident in Divisional HQ, Heap suggested to Colonel Charles Mackenzie, the Chief of Staff, that he cross the Rhine and contact XXX Corps; no one raised any objections. During the evening, Heaps and Lieutenant Johnson left for Oosterbeek and, stopping near some trenches, possibly 1st Borders, they met Private Gobetz, who Heaps knew to be part of the Dutch Liaison Mission. Herman Gobetz was the youngest of the Arnhem commandos and had joined the Dutch Army in Pretoria. Inviting him to join as an interpreter, the trio reached the Rhine where Gobetz was providing cover. As Johnson and Heap put on life preservers several silent, grey shapes materialized out of the river mist. These turned out to be dinghies paddled by about twenty-three Poles. Heaps told the senior officer to contact Gobetz, who would then guide them to Oosterbeek, however in the confusion of the darkness, as Heap later learnt from Gobetz when they met in Stroe prison camp, the Poles never linked up with Gobetz and the entire group was either wounded or taken prisoner. Gobetz waited by the river for most of the night but was wounded and captured by a German patrol, which, because he was wearing Dutch insignia and was a commando, treated him as a partisan. Kept in solitary confinement and threatened with execution, he was later sent to a prison camp.

By 22 September, the 43rd (Wessex) Division had linked up with the Poles. Across the Rhine, the hungry and thirsty remnants of the 1st Airborne Division were being squeezed in Oosterbeek by exhausting street fighting. Around Divisional HQ, relentless mortaring and snipers from woods confined the soldiers to their trenches throughout the day. As soon as one sniper was dealt with, he was replaced. They watched Dakotas drop supplies, only to see the parachutes float into German hands. Air support was nowhere to be seen. The 1st Recce Squadron had consolidated north of the Hartenstein Hotel with Corporal Italiaander dug in on the edge of an open field. As German pressure forced 1st Airlanding Brigade to retire to Oosterbeek, he briefly met Private van der Meer plodding past the Blind Institution as Brigade HQ moved to near a pond south of the Hartenstein Hotel. Van der Meer had escaped injury when the Brigade Intelligence Section took a direct hit on 20 September. After landing, he had accompanied several recce patrols and found documents of intelligence value, until casualties and the scale of the fighting led him to defend the HQ and interrogate prisoners. Private van Barnfeld saved the life of a British soldier when he amputated the remains of his shattered leg with a penknife, for which he was awarded the Dutch Bronze Cross. Not only had he swum the Rhine to contact the Poles, he had been involved in some of the fiercest fighting in Oosterbeek, and had taken part in an attack on a mortar position. Lieutenant Commander Wolters also interrogated prisoners held in the tennis courts at the rear of the hotel, and debriefed civilians. On 24 September, as 'Johnson', Wolters translated for Colonel Graeme Warwick, the senior Divisional medical officer, negotiating a truce with General Bittrich for the evacuation of the wounded from both sides inside the British perimeter. Later that night, 4th Dorsets made a valiant but forlorn attempt to cross the river when reinforcements should have been at least a brigade.

It was now apparent that there was no alternative but evacuate 1st Airborne Division and Operation Berlin was activated in which the wounded and selected units would cover the withdrawal of the survivors across the Rhine opposite Driel. During the evening, Sergeant de Waard, now almost deaf from the shelling, was told that the situation was bad. On one occasion, he was reading about the situation in a *Daily Express* dropped with supplies when a mortar bomb landed nearby, wounding him in the head. At 9.00pm on 25 September, Lieutenant Knottenbelt and Private Helleman received the order to withdraw and, in a night of downpours, reached an assembly point overlooking a collection of assault boats and

DUKWS ferrying men across the river under German shelling. Knottenbelt had no wish to wait in an exposed meadow and joined the swimmers, but was wounded. When his smock was searched in hospital and the epaulettes of General Kussin were found, this led to speculation that he had shot the general. Corporal Italiaander was ferried across in a stormboat and reached Nijmegen, while Private van Barnfeld, who could not swim, clung to the side of an assault boat. Helleman crossed safely as did van der Meer, who continued to help in the rescue.

Next morning, the Hartenstein Hotel was very quiet. Sergeant de Waard left his trench containing a glider pilot and two paras, and was told by the prisoners in the tennis court and a sleepy doctor that Divisional HQ had pulled out during the night, leaving the wounded. The quartet was furious and although de Waard considered changing into civilian clothes, they decided to make their way to the Rhine, with his rifle the only one between them, but they clashed with a German patrol and one of the paras was shot in the back. Near the river, when they ran into another patrol and de Waard was shot in the foot, the quartet surrendered to Germans who were more interested in cigarettes. During the afternoon, the prisoners were taken in wood-burning lorries to Apeldoorn and placed in cattle trucks marked with Red Crosses that took them to the huge prison camp at Fallingbostel. Beekmeyer was also captured and linked up with Privates Gobetz and Gubbels.

Two members of 2 (Dutch) Troop failed to reach Arnhem. Sergeant Luitweiler was in a Horsa that made an emergency landing near Biezenmortel. Unloading its two jeeps, the Polish officer, two glider pilots and two RASC drivers decided to drive to Arnhem and fought their way past a German patrol at Helvoirt. They hid near Esch, which is near Haaren, until some Dutch warned them of a bigger force. One of the drivers fell out the jeep in the pursuit and was captured. Concealed in a wood for several days, after being given a tent and some food stolen from the Germans, they were guided to Campina Heath and joined about 100 British and American paratroopers near the village of Boxel until liberated on 24 October. Private de Leeuw was in a glider that landed on Schouwen Island. He and its two Glider Pilot Regiment pilots remained hidden until 6 December when they joined twelve members of the Resistance escaping to Walcheren after they had stolen a large number of ration cards from the Germans three days earlier. On the way to meet a British MTB, they ran into a German patrol; ten of the Dutch were captured and hung in Renesse four days later. De Leeuw, the two pilots and a female student escaped. The three soldiers were later betrayed and ended up as prisoners of war in Amsterdam.

Of the about 10,200 troops who landed at Arnhem, 1,440 were killed or died of wounds and 3,000 wounded were captured, as were 2,500 uninjured. About 2,400, including Poles and 4th Dorsets reached safety. Of greater significance was the contribution the Resistance made in smuggling more men to safety – 145 of the 350 airborne soldiers hiding around Arnhem were smuggled to safety in Operations Pegasus 1 and 2. Although 2 (Dutch) Troop had suffered only one fatality during the battle, it lost another commando on 5 October when Private Hagelaars was shot trying to visit his parents in Den Bosch. The news that Private Gubbels was a prisoner was passed to his wife Sybil in a German-English Radio Service broadcast on 14 October.

On his return to England, Major General Urqhuart praised the 'wonderful support we had been given by the Resistance men and women' collecting information, especially about the disposition of tanks. His report also notes the actions of Lieutenant Commander Wolters and Lieutenant Knottenbelt's commandos as 'First class'. In relation to 2 (Dutch) Troop, the Divisional post-operation intelligence assessment noted:

> Information from friendly civilians was generally found to be fairly reliable after allowance had been made for the personality of the bearer, and after he had been vetted by the Dutch liaison party. The population was co-operative. Initially a large number of young men rallied to the cause, but disappeared in proportion as the shelling and mortaring grew. Several rendered excellent service, and the highest praise is due to those few who helped our wounded throughout and stayed with us to the last.

Knottenbelt, in his after-action report, noted that his greatest difficulty was a lack of information regarding the Arnhem Resistance because he lacked details of loyal Dutchmen, and relied on his instinct to verify individual reliability. The 1st Allied Airborne Army credits the Nijmegen and Arnhem Resistance with maintaining communications and providing information via telephone.

Arnhem was a strategic disaster and a heroic defeat. As recriminations emerged, General Browning, the Guards, Establishment and husband of the acclaimed author Daphne du Maurier, was quick to blame the defeat on Major General Sosabowski for not crossing the Rhine – he had no boats. And yet it was Browning who had deprived the airborne assault of thirty-eight aircraft because he wanted to lead his Corps into action, and who had identified Arnhem Bridge to be a bridge too far, but failed to stand his ground. While he departed for higher appointments, the Polish general ended up as a factory storeman.

Chapter 15

Operation Infatuate – Walcheren

The failure to open up the port of Antwerp condemned British and Canadian troops to eighty-five days of heavy fighting in the flooded low-lands of the Battle of the Scheldt in the misery of a cold autumn. Arnhem had given the Germans confidence that they could prevent invasion, indeed Allied operations in Holland were at a standstill because the long logistic chain from Normandy was at full stretch.

Guarding the Scheldt was Walcheren. Lying about 60 miles west of Antwerp and carved by the Dutch during their battles with the sea, the island is saucer-shaped with dykes and sand dunes protecting the interior. The only connection to the mainland was the 1,200-feet-long, 40-feet wide causeway to South Beveland, no more than 4 feet above the surrounding tidal flats, consisting of a cycle path and a single-line railway. The small town of Westkapelle was perched on one of the oldest sea defences in Holland, Westkapelle Dyke, which stretched for about 3 miles and ranged from 200 to 330 feet in width at its base, rising to 30 feet in height. Flushing was a port and dockyard.

In 1944, Walcheren was defended by the 70th Infantry Division and elements of Naval Commander, Southern Island commanded by Lieu-tenant General Wilhelm Daser from his HQ at Middelburg. 1/1019th Grenadier Regiment defended Flushing with the 2nd Battalion defending south-east Walcheren. The town was a honeycomb of strongpoints and anti-tank defences. 1020th Grenadier Regiment defended north-west Walcheren. The Division was known as 'The Stomach' or 'White Bread' because it was formed from Russian Front veterans whose stomach wounds and illnesses necessitated special dairy diets. Naval Commander, Southern Holland was an independent naval formation with under com-mand 202nd Naval Artillery Regiment manning twenty coastal artillery batteries using a mix of German and captured artillery. Each was prefixed with the letter 'W' by Allied planners – for instance, W-15 north of Westkapelle, manned by 6 Battery, was equipped with four British 3.7-inch anti-aircraft guns captured at Dunkirk and two 3-inch anti-aircraft guns in the open. The 810th Naval Flak Regiment manned batteries at Flushing and along the coast to Zoutelande.

On 27 September, the balance of No. 10 (Inter-Allied) Commando, namely the HQ and Belgian and Norwegian Troops, was ordered to join the British Liberation Army, and embarked on a ship at Snaresbrook Dock. Five days later, they disembarked at Arromanches and moved into No. 60 Transit Camp. On 10 October, Lieutenant Colonel Laycock was ordered by Combined Operations to join 4th Special Service Brigade for the assault on Walcheren.

Meanwhile, the Dutch commandos attached to 52nd (Lowland) Division joined HQ 1st British Airborne Corps at Nijmegen on 4 October and then on the 11th, those attached to the US airborne divisions rejoined the Troop assembling in the residence of the former Dutch burgomeister in Eindhoven. When Captain Linzel offered them the choice of returning to England or taking part in future operations, the decision was unanimous – two days later the Dutch joined the Commando arriving by road in Bruges and were billeted in St Andreaas. When a few 4 (Belgian) Troop visited family and friends for the first time since 1940, one commando found that his father had been imprisoned for collaboration and another that his wife had left him for Luftwaffe pilot. Training in the sand dunes around Den Haan was concentrated on attacking coastal artillery emplacements.

Operation Infatuate opened on 2 October with the civil population being warned by leaflets of air raids. Next day, at about 2.15pm, the twenty-six Lancasters of 103 and 576 Squadrons took advantage of minimal cloud to approach from the south and breach the dykes in four places – at a cost of 172 Dutch killed. At Westkapelle, a 35-yard crater had spread to 70 yards by 3.00pm and expanded to 380 yards as the sea chipped at the sand. On 7 October, Flushing and the batteries near Domburg were raided. Two days later, the 1st (Canadian) Army began clearing the Scheldt defences, while the 3rd (Canadian) Division fought a grim battle in the soaking flatlands around Breskens against the experienced 64th Infantry Division, and isolated Walcheren by seizing South and North Beveland. From 16 to 31 October, the 2nd (Canadian) Division made several bloody attempts to cross the causeway, all of which failed.

Meanwhile, plans were finalized to land on Walcheren. The Commando Mountain Warfare Training School provided Keepforce to mount Operation Tarbrush recces of the Westkapelle beaches. In the first, on 15/16 October by eight men, four radar-directed searchlights challenged MTB 621 (from 55th MTB Flotilla (Eastern Task Force)) and prevented the dory being lowered. A few nights later, Captain Saunders and Sergeant Joe Berry were in a dinghy that was swept south past the breach. After having trouble linking up with the dory and then being unable to raise the MTB on the S-Phone, Saunders decided to use the wind and current to reach Ostend after hitting the German-occupied Zeebrugge pier after 35 miles and seven hours at sea. A third recce three nights later in mist was abandoned because the Germans were alert. After some debate over sea conditions, the landings were planned for 1 November in a three-pronged assault. 156 and 157 Infantry Brigades of 52nd (Lowland) Division were to attack the causeway. In Operation Infatuate One, No. 4 Commando was to land at Flushing, followed by 155 Infantry Brigade (4th and 5th King's Own Scottish Borderers (KOSB) and 7/9th Royal Scots) and advance to Zoutelande. In Operation Infatuate Two, 4th Special Service Brigade was to land at Westkapelle.

Operation Infatuate was the only time that No. 10 (Inter-Allied) Commando fought as a unit. The Dutch Troop was split with Captain Linzel and thirteen commandos attached to No. 47 (Royal Marines) Commando, including Corporal Italiaander, who had landed at Arnhem. The eleven attached to No. 4 Commando were commanded by Lieutenant de Ruiter and included several commandos who had also been on Operation Market Garden. Their role was to provide interpreters and guides, particularly in Flushing, where the Resistance was known to be active. The 3 (British) Troop detachments were still attached to their D-Day units.

In support was 1st Lothian and Border Yeomanry, from 30 Armoured Brigade, 79th Armoured Division, providing Sherman flail mine-clearing tanks. The 5th and 6th Assault Regiments of 1 Assault Brigade RE provided Churchill AVREs armed with 12-inch spigot guns firing 25lb explosive charges packed into canisters, four tank-launched bridges and four with ditch-clearing fascines. The 2nd (Canadian) Division Artillery Group, 9th Army Group, Royal Artillery and 76th Anti-Aircraft Brigade near Breskens provided 314 guns. Naval Force T consisted of the Bombardment Squadron, including the battleship HMS *Warspite* and the monitors HMS *Erebus* and HMS *Roberts*, the Support Squadron Eastern Flank, a mix of twenty-seven landing craft providing flak, guns and rockets for inshore direct artillery support and L (LCA) Squadron landing craft. 11 Royal Tank Regiment provided drivers for the Buffalo Amtracs and Weasel snocats landing from N (LCT) Squadron.

For Infantuate One, the planners accepted recommendations by Captain P.H. van Nahuis that No. 4 Commando should land at a promontory of rubble and rubbish dumped in between two long piers almost in the centre of Flushing, nicknamed Uncle Beach. A month before, Nahuis had been a police inspector and a leading member of the Resistance; he was now a Dutch Army captain. Uncle Beach was defended by beach and underwater obstacles covered by bunkers. With Flushing divided into the docks and shipyards separated from a residential area by a neck of land about 400 yards wide, Lieutenant Colonel Dawson divided the town into several sectors named after towns in which the Commando had been billeted and planned a four-phase operation:

Phase One
- Keepforce to mark the assault beach.
- A Section of 1 Troop accompanied by the Dutch Troop Corporal Bill de Liefde, who spoke German, to form the beachhead.

Phase Two
- The rest of 1 Troop and 2 Troop to exploit inland.
- Naval Beach Parties of J and part of L Commando to act as beachmasters.

Phase Three
- Royal Engineers and the naval Landing Craft Obstruction Clearance Unit to clear underwater obstacles.

Phase Four
- The rest of the Commando under the command of Major Kieffer to wait offshore until summoned to land.

When, on 31 October, a MTB checking the sea state off Walcheren signalled that it was suitable for a landing, Admiral Ramsay and Lieutenant General Symonds, who commanded 1st (Canadian) Army, instructed Operation Infatuate to get underway. Late in the afternoon, 4th Special Service Brigade embarked on the landing craft tied up in the damaged port of Ostend. At Breskens, hopes of surprise disappeared when German observers shelled, through a smokescreen, twenty Weasels making their way upstream from Terneuzen and the port causing several casualties. The Keepforce dory hung on the back of their MTB was wrecked. They decided to use a Landing Craft Personnel (Survey) (LCP (Svy)).

Soon after midnight, the landing craft squadrons cleared Ostend and by 3.15am had joined a convoy of 182 vessels protected by Naval Force T heading north into improving sea conditions, although the cloud base remained low. At 3.00am, No. 4 Commando and 155 Infantry Brigade paraded at Breskens in drizzle. At 4.00am, the two LCPs (Svy) and single LCA now allocated to Keepforce slipped into the darkness; then forty-five minutes later, the artillery opened fire and started fires that illuminated the distinctive windmill marking Uncle Beach. Low cloud had prevented Lancasters taking off, nevertheless Mosquitoes bombed Flushing. At 5.20am, Keepforce, under fire from German mortars and machine guns, strayed from Uncle Beach. Ten minutes later, 30 yards from the beach, when the LCA carrying Captain Rowcastle and No. 1 Section snagged on underwater defences, the commandos dropped into the freezing sea and swam or waded to the low wooden jetty at the base of Orange Mole. Scrambling up the stonework, cutting barbed wire and laying white tape for the following troops to follow, they approached a bunker housing a 75mm gun where the Dutch Corporal Bill de Liefde, who was carrying a green signal lamp marker, ordered the occupants to surrender. When several German sailors filed out, the last man was seen to be carrying two primed stick grenades and was shot.

Meanwhile, a Keepforce LCP (Svy), embarrassingly, first went to the wrong jetty and was greeted at Orange Mole, as recalled by Sergeant Berry, by 'a horrible Army commando sergeant who scornfully told us "We've been here for ten minutes!"' The Royal Navy beach parties laid navigation beacons and then the Beachmaster, Lieutenant Harry Hargreaves, who had guided No. 4 Commando ashore at Dieppe, used his signal lamp for No. 4 Commando to commence Phase Two. The rest of 1 Troop landed and destroyed two machine-gun posts firing on landing craft approaching Uncle Beach. 2 Troop passed Troon, captured a bunker housing a 50mm gun in a rehearsed attack, and advanced towards Falmouth, systematically attacking pillboxes covering the approaches to Flushing. They even used a captured 75mm gun against their former owners. Nevertheless, by the time the third wave was approaching Uncle Beach at 6.30am, the German defences elsewhere were fully alert and when the LCA carrying 4 (Heavy Weapons) Troop was sunk, the commandos dragged a 3-inch mortar ashore. They then recovered the second one and some ammunition. When a LCA carrying Royal Engineers snagged an underwater obstacle, the sappers struggled ashore with their equipment, including mine detectors. 3 Troop, joined by 4 Troop, set off to seize Bellamy Park amid increasing German resistance.

At 6.40am, when Phase Four was ordered, 5 (French) Troop approached Uncle Beach in two LCAs under command of Captain Lofi. The landing craft with No. 2 Section (Lieutenant Chausse) spun out of control, smashed into the jetty when the coxswain was wounded by machine-gun fire and sank; the Frenchmen scrambled ashore. The second LCA was also abandoned, forcing 2 Section (Sergeant Major Messanot) and a (Dutch) Troop detachment to wade shoulder high to the beach. Several Frenchmen and two Dutch were wounded. After regrouping, 5 Troop followed 3 Troop to the town square near Bellamey Park. When Kieffer landed with his HQ and 6 (French) Troop, under the command of Lieutenant Guy Vourc'h, and saw that his proposed command post at Orange Windmill was still occupied by the Germans, he sent Lieutenant Guy Hattu and his HQ Section Bren gun team to eject them. The Troop lost two men wounded. At about 7.30am, with most of No. 4 Commando ashore, 4th KOSB landed largely at full strength.

5 Troop found their progress impeded by narrow streets stubbornly defended by aggressive, well-sited German machine-gun nests and snipers, quite apart from stick grenades. For the next five hours, street fighting in Flushing was aggressive and confusing. During the interrogation of two prisoners, one who spoke French said that the Germans had been instructed to withdraw into the Army bomb-proof barracks. Corporal de Liefde took a message to the French that a church was being defended and it was attacked by No. 1 Section; another prisoner was captured. At the Main Market crossroads, No. 2 Section went firm on Bree Street under heavy fire which killed Lance Corporal Jean Montean and the two prisoners. Lieutenant Chausse, Sergeant Major Messanot and Sergeant Paillet were ambushed while recceing the barracks and Chausse was slightly wounded by a grenade. When Captain Lofi reported to Major Kieffer that he was held up, Lieutenant Colonel Dawson gave him his reserve, D Company, 4th KOSB, to take over the fighting around the barracks.

Meanwhile, 6 Troop, guided by Captain van Nahuis, set off to seize the post office at the northern end of Wilhelmina Street. Initially encountering light sniper fire, they found the heavily defended Post Office was being reinforced by Germans withdrawing from other parts of Flushing, nevertheless No. 1 Section (Lieutenant Senee) stormed the building and took fifty prisoners. A small group led by a German officer held out on the first floor until silenced by five Frenchmen who climbed on to the roof and tossed grenades through windows. Vourc'h then led 6 Troop to the big crossroads in the 'Bexhill' sector outside the dockyards and established a defensive line from the dockyard gates at Betje Wolf Plein to Binnenboezim Lake. It was about 7.45am. Second Lieutenant Ruiter left with a French half-section from 6 Troop to contact the Resistance said to be near Dover but was cut off. Several men managed to escape while others sheltered with Dutch families and trickled back over the next few days.

6 Troop soon came under close-range fire from the school in Goosje Besken Street to their rear, in particular, from a pillbox. Part of Troop HQ succeeded in crossing the street but heavy fire dispersed the remainder into three houses on the corner of Badhuis Street. At about 8.00am, concentrated fire forced a German company advancing down Badhuis Street to withdraw and for the next two hours Lieutenant Senee's section, in the building at the corner of Badhuis Street and Glacis Street, drove off several German attacks at the cost of three killed, but took seven prisoners. At about 8.15am, the French were reinforced when a British 4 (Heavy Weapons) Troop managed to get a Vickers machine gun across the street into Vourc'h's HQ, but lost a man killed when they tried with the second gun. A 4th KOSB platoon then joined the beleaguered Frenchmen and Vourc'h despatched them to reinforce Senee, who was under severe

pressure as another German attack was dispersed by the steady thud-thud of the Vickers before it jammed. Unknown to the French, in a house across Betje Wolf Plein, the Poppe Resistance group sniped at the Germans, until, about 10.00pm, they were forced to abandon their position, but not before they captured Kapitanleutenant Blissinger, the Port Second-in-Command. He had orders from General Daser in his pocket to demolish the docks and cranes. By 9.00am, Old Town was generally in the hands of No. 4 Commando and 4th KOSB, although there was still resistance from the bomb-proof barracks, some pillboxes and Merchant's Hotel. Commando HQ was using a captured 75mm to shell the hotel.

Corporal de Liefde was with a British and a French commando taking a message to the French when a sniper forced them to take cover near the barracks. Ducking into a room, the trio were surprised to find it full of Germans sorting out equipment and cleaning weapons, and quickly captured them. With artillery and air support beginning to break up counterattacks, two Dutch Troop sergeants dissuaded the police and the Resistance from joining the fighting. Lieutenant de Ruiter, who spoke excellent German, escorted officer prisoners to the cage on the beach. One was mortified to learn his escort was junior in rank until he learnt his surname and then brightened up, assuming that he was related to Admiral de Ruyter whose statue was on the seafront.

By midday, Hove and Worthing were in British hands. With 5 (French) Troop still being prevented from advancing along the narrow neck of land between the lake and the sea, Lieutenant Colonel Dawson and Kieffer agreed that the Troop must press the defence and would be withdrawn after dark so that the position could be shelled. Throughout the morning, 810 Marine Flak Battalion had made life extremely difficult on the beach and had prevented 5th KOSB from landing until 2.00pm, when the Battalion rushed ashore in waves of five landing craft, followed by 7/9th Royal Scots, bringing most of 155 (Lowland) Infantry Brigade ashore. Prisoners were pressed into service helping 144th Pioneer Company unload supplies from landing craft. During the night, Brigadier McLaren took over responsibility for the fighting from Lieutenant Colonel Dawson.

When Corporal de Liefde told Lieutenant de Ruiter that he had learnt from civilians that the Germans intended to blow up the Scheldt Shipyards, he took some factory workers and fourteen members of the Resistance, but found nothing of significance. When an informant then reported that fourteen German engineers working on a ship had mined it with explosives but wanted to surrender, at 10.00pm, de Ruiter and Corporal Bothe reached the shipyards, with the informant leading, in case it was a ploy to ambush British troops. After getting lost in the yards for a short time, Ruiter captured the Germans while Dutch shipyard workers defused the explosives. After a German sentry insisted on being taken

157

prisoner, the column reached the Verboon Bridge later then expected to find that the recognition signals arranged with No. 4 Commando had not been passed to the Scottish platoon now guarding it. De Ruiter was crossing to discuss who 'owned' the prisoners with an officer, when everyone scattered as mortar bombs landed. Agreement was then reached and the column crossed the bridge. De Liefde later went to the docks after reports of Germans firing from the portholes of the ship *Willem Ruys*, killed one German and captured another, who told that him there were more in a small hut.

By 7.00am the next morning, as mopping up in Flushing began, 5 (French) Troop came under heavy fire from a quadruple 20mm flak cannon in a bunker at the southern end of Goosje Busken Street in Dover. While preparing for the assault, they withdrew when six Typhoons carried out a low-level attack on the bunker, although this did not silence the cannon. Captain Lofi sent No. 2 Section and a PIAT to occupy the roof of a cinema to cover No. 1 Section. With the 20mm commanding the street, in some of the most intense fighting in the battle, the Frenchmen 'mouseholed' their way towards the bunker by blowing holes in house walls, clearing each house and its garden, and moving to the next. By the afternoon, the Troop had reached a corner overlooking the bunker and a house defended by the Germans. Here they came across evidence of German ruthlessness: a Dutch family shot for sheltering one of the commandos who had been with de Ruiter when he had been ambushed. At about 4.30am, some Germans running from the house were cut down. Reaching an anti-tank wall across the end of the street, the Troop was sufficiently close for a PIAT to fire through the blockhouse embrasures, but there was still no sign of surrender. Corporal Michel Lavezzi and Sergeant Paillet were preparing to unseat the door hinges with explosives when the door opened and a white cloth on a long stick was waved, followed by three Kriegsmarine officers and about sixty dusty and tired gunners. After thirty-six hours of tough fighting, Lofi was down to three officers and forty-seven commandos. No. 4 Commando then went firm as 155 Infantry Brigade took over the advance.

About 5 miles east of Westkapelle, at 5.45am on 1 November, the start of the fighting in Flushing could be heard in the distance. At 6.00am, Captain Pugsley received a signal that heavy mist over the Dutch and Belgian airfields would jeopardize air support and naval air observation, nevertheless he and Brigadier Leicester agreed that since the sea was calm, the landings should be made. Leicester's plan was:

- Nos 41 (Royal Marines) and 10 (Inter-Allied) Commandos to land on Red Beach, north of the gap and clear the approaches to Westkapelle.

- No. 48 (Royal Marines) Commando to land on White Beach and advance to Zoutelande.
- No. 47 (Royal Marines) Commando to land behind No. 48 (Royal Marines) Commando and link up with 155 Infantry Brigade at Flushing.
- Green Beach to the right of White Beach was the logistic beach.

The landing order of No. 10 (Inter-Allied) Commando was as follows:

- LCT carrying Commando HQ, 4 (Belgian) Troop of ninety all ranks, minus A Section and an officer and fourteen Norwegians. Four Buffalos and four Weasels.
- LCT with 5 (Norwegian) Troop minus the detachment. The Troop numbered ninety-seven all ranks.
- LCT carrying a Belgian Sub-Section and part of 1st Lothian and Border Yeomanry.
- LCT carrying the A Sub-Section commanded by Lieutenant Meny and part of 1st Lothian and Border Yeomanry.

Ashore, Coast Battery W-17 was firing at Breskens and as ML 902 moved inshore to mark navigation beacons, W-13 and W-15 flanking Westkapelle opened fire. At 8.20am, the Bombardment Squadron opened fire on pre-planned targets, although HMS *Erebus* reported turret failure. This was followed ten minutes later by twelve rocket-firing 183 Squadron Typhoons attacking German positions and the artillery opening fire. As the landing force approached, the Support Squadron Eastern Flank moved in to give direct support, but quickly came under accurate punishment from Coastal Battery W-13 and the anti-aircraft guns of 810th Naval Flak Battalion. Battery W-11 to the south of the gap also traversed its guns. Nine support landing craft were sunk and eight damaged costing 172 men killed and over 125 wounded, nevertheless the Squadron had drawn fire from the landing craft and had forced the Germans to expend substantial amounts of ammunition. By 10.17am, Battery W-13 had fired all 200 rounds.

No. 41 (Royal Marines) Commando landed at 9.58am relatively un-scathed and advanced towards Westkapelle. Behind them, ten minutes later, as No. 10 (Inter-Allied) Commando approached, the burning LCT 513 carrying tanks passed close to the Commando HQ LCT, which then experienced several near misses until, 150 yards from White Beach, its bow jammed hard against beach defence stakes. For the next ten minutes, the LCT was a sitting duck. The Dutch Troop Buffalo was set on fire, Corporal 'Hamilton' was killed and Captain Emmet, the Adjutant, wounded. Morale rose when the LCT carrying the cheering 5 (Norwegian) Troop powered past. On the beach, Lieutenant Gudmundseth exchanged his soaking battledress trousers with a prisoner. On board, it was getting dangerous and after the burning Buffalo was pushed overboard, the commandos dropped into the chilly sea and swift current. The wounded Private 'Watson' supported Emmett until both were rescued and taken to 105th (Canadian) Hospital in Ostend where Emmet lost three fingers. By 10.50am, Laycock had established Commando HQ near a bunker, and within half an hour was joined by his three Buffalos and four Weasels carrying the radios and equipment.

LCT 513 was hit six times, setting the Shermans and AVRE on fire, and wounding two Belgians and a liaison officer. When LCT 650 carrying Second Lieutenant Dauppe lodged on underwater obstacles and was hit in the stern, the Captain followed the damaged LCT 513 from the beach until he was ordered to join a second pair of LCTs on White Beach. On landing, Private Stichnot was seriously wounded and the Bren gunner Private Burggraeve was hit in the foot by an exploding shell while engaging the German defences. He was later awarded the Belgian Croix de Guerre.

Meanwhile, A Troop, No. 41 (Royal Marines) Commando (Captain Paddy Stevens), came under fire from the lofty, brick Westkapelle Tower being used as an artillery observation post at the northern end of the main street. Debussing from their Buffaloes, the Royal Marines and a Sherman overran a few defenders. When the staircase was seen to be blocked with barbed wire, Stevens asked Sergeant 'Gray' and Corporal 'Latimer' to invite the Germans to surrender. 'Gray', a Czech socialist, gave his Thompson to 'Latimer' and with Stevens stepped into the middle of the road and translated the invitation to surrender. This resulted in a German sergeant coming out to discuss terms, meanwhile, 'Latimer' had entered the tower by another door and when 'Gray' saw him leading out several Germans, he told the sergeant that it was pointless discussing anything – his men were surrendering. The Sherman was one of just two 1st Lothian and Border Yeomanry command tanks to survive the landings.

By 11.15am, 4 (Belgian) Troop, minus eight casualties, and the Royal Marines were mopping up western Westkapelle. The Norwegians were passing through when mortaring from Battery W-15 killed Privates Sverre Rosland and Lief Larsen, and wounded seven others. In the middle of the market square, a Norwegian wounded by splinters in the stomach was tended by the Belgian Father Corbisier who left shelter to inject him with morphine. Commando HQ took over a coffin-maker's shop in Westkapelle. Advancing to Battery W-15, Captain Hauge noticed that Y (Royal Marines) Troop was advancing across open ground and positioned his Troop to give covering fire. When the battery and its 120 gunners were captured, the Norwegians raised their flag at 1.30pm before linking up with the Belgians and a Churchill AVRE half a mile north-east of Westkapelle to prevent counter-attacks. The AVRE had set fire to the lighthouse. By 4.15pm, Commando HQ had advanced to Battery W-15 along with several forward observation and unit liaison officers formed into an infantry section after they had become separated from their units by the gap at the beaches. The Norwegian stores dump took a direct hit in the afternoon. Locally, the night was largely uneventful except for intermittent sniper and machine-gun fire. Ahead, the Royal Marines captured Battery W-17 about half a mile west of Domberg and entered the town after dark, but were subjected to heavy and accurate mortar fire from a strong defensive position centred around a water tower perched on a hill. Nevertheless by dawn, large numbers of Germans were surrendering.

Meanwhile, No. 48 (Royal Marines) Commandos had landed, but their attack on Battery W-13 was initially repulsed. The landing of No. 47 (Royal Marines) Commando was reminiscent of D-Day with landing craft beached astride the gap after being diverted by heavy fire. On board the LCT carrying Commando HQ and B Troop, a shell streaked through a Royal Engineer Buffalo and exploded underneath a Weasel carrying a flame-thrower, causing such an inferno that only twenty-eight men from the sixty-strong Troop landed. The Dutch Troop landed north of the gap and ferried across in Buffaloes. Meant to have been assembled by 2.00pm, it was not until 7.00pm that the Commando had done so. Next morning it passed through No. 48 (Royal Marines) Commando and advanced toward Battery W-11, which was the last major position between Zoutelande and Flushing. At about midday next day, Brigadier Leicester was pressurized by II (Canadian) Corps to silence the German batteries covering the Scheldt and link up with 155 Infantry Brigade. Since this strategy took precedence over operations to the north, at 1.00pm he instructed No. 41 (Royal Marines) Commando, less two Troops, to join Nos 47 and 48 (Royal Marines) Commandos, and for Lieutenant Colonel Laycock to continue operations with B and X Troops under command.

During the afternoon, the Belgians followed by the Norwegians entered Domburg, which was still half occupied by the Germans, and were joined shortly after dark by three Buffaloes carrying much-needed ammunition. At 6.00pm, half an hour after Laycock had sent Lieutenant Pierre Roman and a small Belgian B Section patrol to recce the water tower, Major Pocock, who commanded A Squadron, 1st Lothian and Border Yeomanry, arrived with two Shermans and two AVREs. The ground was above sea level and a track ran along the top of the dyke toward Batteries W-5 and W-17. To the east of Domburg and south of the dyke was a 2-mile strip of thick woods running to Fort de Haak. The formidable Battery W-18 was cunningly located in a small dip on the western edges of the woods. Multi-barrelled mortars were a nuisance.

When Roman reported that the water tower defences were supplemented by barbed-wire entanglements and mines, Laycock instructed Captain Hauge to attack the position next day. At 7.30am on 3 November, a

Canadian 5.5-inch battery and the Shermans propped on steep dunes shelled the German positions until their bellies became vulnerable to anti-tank fire, and they withdrew. At 1.15pm, as the Belgians advanced through Domburg and entered the woods on the right, with the two Royal Marines Troops in reserve on the dyke on the left, covered by a rolling barrage; the Norwegian attack faltered when a gap could not be found in the defences, and Private Lars Holstad was killed. Soon after a ladder had been thrown across the entanglements, Captain Hauge was badly wounded in the right arm when a mine exploded. Laycock had intended the attack be three phased, controlled by Commando HQ, however when the Troop 3-inch mortars blew holes in the barbed wire, Lieutenant Olav Gausland, who had taken over from Hauge, instructed Second Lieutenant Skutle to take over his No. 1 Section and then led the Norwegians in an 800-yard advance towards the water tower, assaulting trenches and attacking a bunker by lobbing two grenades through the embrasures. The Troop mortars scored a direct hit on a house full of Germans near the water tower which pre-cipitated the surrender of 211 Germans, who were handed over to 3 (British) Troop. Gausland reported to Commando HQ that all three phases were complete but at the cost of one killed and two wounded. The Belgians lost seven wounded. Landing craft were still finding it difficult to beach at Westkapelle, and for two days the Troops endured captured German rations until a parachute drop near Zoutelande relieved the situation. Lieutenant Colonel Laycock sent the Weasels to Domburg and Westkapelle to requisition food.

The next objective was Battery W-18 manned by 2/202nd Naval Artillery Battalion. At 12.45pm next day, after Typhoons had put in a 'rather useless attack', according to Laycock, the Belgians advanced through the woods thick with undergrowth and ideal for defence to the south. With B Troop, the Shermans and AVREs in close support, the Belgians, battle-hardened after Italy, quickly advanced 1,000 yards but at the cost of an officer and six men wounded from snipers and mines. The Royal Marines were slower. At 6.30am on 5 November in appalling weather, the Norwegians relieved them and were hindered by snipers and mortar fire. When the Troop ran into a minefield in open dunes and Sherman shells bounced off the battery emplacement, No. 10 (Inter-Allied) Commando withdrew half a mile to allow the stronger two Royal Marines Troops to attack W-18. Gausland withdrew to the shelter of the woods and when Second Lieutenant Rommetvedt was wounded by a sniper, reducing the Troop to three officers, Second Lieutenant Gummendstedt took over his Section. During the night, enemy anti-tank gunners shouted that they wanted to surrender but were ignored by the suspicious Norwegians who told them to approach with their hands raised. None materialized.

Meanwhile, No. 47 (Royal Marines) Commando had been repulsed from its first attack on Battery W-11. Brigadier Leicester was again reminded by II (Canadian) Corps of the urgency of linking up with 155 Infantry Brigade. Reinforced by A Troop, No. 48 (Royal Marines) Commando and the 2 (Dutch) Troop detachment attached to the weakened B Troop, the Commando finally broke into the German position and then linked up with No. 4 Commando who had been embarked in Buffaloes to attack Batteries W-3 and W-4. During the attack, three grenades landed among the Dutch wounding nine, including Corporal Ubels with a severed artery, Corporal Kokhuis in the thigh and Bloemink. An attempt by Ubbels to make a tourniquet with his commando knife cord failed and he became weaker until Troop Sergeant Major van der Bergh and Sergeant Dulleman arrived and stopped the flow of blood. They also arranged for the wounded to be carried to the landing craft by prisoners, who the Dutch noticed were elderly.

With the Scheldt open, minesweepers began to sweep the channel to Antwerp. Brigadier Leicester sent No. 41 (Royal Marines) Commando and the two other Heavy Weapons Troops north across the Westkapelle gap to join No. 10 (Inter-Allied) Commando.

On 6 November, at 8.30am, after a day in reserve, the Belgians relieved 5 Troop and sent a fighting patrol to collect the anti-tank gunners, however they were ambushed by interlocking fire from four Spandaus and Captain Danloy radioed that speed and determination were critical. A Section on the right and B Section attacked the German position. Lance Corporal Legrand manning an A Section 2-inch mortar was wounded in the back by mortar shrapnel but refused evacuation. The attack faltered when A Section was forced inland by a minefield, Lieutenant Meny was mortally wounded in the chest and Private Dive was killed. With two bullets in his shoulder, Sergeant Artemieff led the Section in a bayonet charge, personally overrunning a Spandau, until pinned down by a machine gunner in a house. When Sergeant de Leener and Lance Corporal Legrand attempted to advance by taking command of the Sub-Sections and drew heavy fire, Captain Danloy instructed Roman to attack the house from the left covered by A Section. Legrand was then severely wounded in the shoulder, and although treated by the Commando Medical Officer, still refused to be evacuated. With the Belgians outgunned, Laycock ordered the Royal Marines Heavy Weapons Troops Vickers to support them and B Section surged forward to overrun the German position. The next objectives were the dunes to the north of the woods and, with A Section giving covering fire, B Section seized them against limited opposition with the two Shermans providing valuable support by pumping shells into the German positions. When no counter-attack developed, Roman led a patrol to recce German activity in an adjoining wood. For their leadership and gallantry during the fighting, Lieutenant Roman was awarded the MC, Legrand the MM and Sergeant Artemieff a second Croix de Guerre to the one that he had won in Italy.

Meanwhile, Brigadier Leicester sent Nos 4 and 48 (Royal Marines) Commandos across the Westkapelle gap to reinforce the No. 10 (Inter-Allied) Commando battle group, which had now been fighting non-stop for a week in an element of the battle for Walcheren that goes largely unrecognized today.

At 7.30am on 7 November, the Norwegians relieved the Belgians and protected the right flank of No. 41 (Royal Marines) Commando and the two Heavy Weapons Troops as they attacked the Black Hut, which lay between Battery W-18 and Battery W-19. The position was commanded by an experienced German major with Russian Front veterans from the 1012th Infantry Regiment, determined to make the Allies fight every yard through a position studded with machine-gun nests covering minefields, booby traps and field defences. At his disposal, he had several radio-controlled mini tanks filled with explosive known as 'Goliaths'. At 10.00am, Typhoons beat up the Black Hut and then Royal Engineers swept for mines with the tanks following, although the leading AVRE bottomed on a mine, killing three of the crew. Accompanied by Tactical HQ No. 10 (Inter-Allied) Commando, for three hours the Royal Marines advanced through the position capturing over 300 Germans. When the Royal Marines were about to cross an anti-tank ditch and came under heavy fire from the right, a prisoner said that the majority of the W-19 garrison had moved into the woods; a Typhoon strike plastered the area, nevertheless the two leading Troops were forced to withdraw several hundred yards for the night. Meanwhile, the Norwegians fought through the woods before overrunning a farm at Oostkapelle and several small positions before settling down for the night about 1,500 yards short of Battery W-19.

At 3.00am on 8 November, Sergeant 'Gray' and Corporal 'Latimer' left the No. 41 (Royal Marines) Commando lines and crossing a minefield, placed themselves near the German positions and captured a small patrol carrying a container of coffee. Under interrogation by 'Gray', the Germans refused to divulge the name of their commanding officer, meanwhile 'Latimer' had drifted off into the night. 'Gray' then saw a burly figure emerge from the bunker and ask for his coffee – clearly the battery commander – and just as 'Gray' was about to capture him, 'Latimer' leapt from the top of the bunker and rugby tackled the German. Returning to No. 41 (Royal Marines) Commando, with 'Gray' translating, the officer agreed to encourage his men to surrender. Another officer captured later in the day reported orders were circulating to surrender.

At 5.45am, Gausland and his two officers were planning to attack Battery W-19 by direct frontal assault across open ground when they were unexpectedly relieved by No. 4 Commando. Leaving No. 10 (Inter-Allied) Commando to hold the line and placing No. 41 (Royal Marines) Commando in reserve, Brigadier Leicester launched a Brigade attack on the battery, which surrendered with barely a shot fired. Patrols rounded up the naval gunners in the woods. No. 4 Commando then pushed through Overduin Woods and met the two 52nd (Lowland) Division brigades within a mile of Vrouwenpolder, after they had crossed the causeway. With No. 48 (Royal Marines) Commando the Brigade reserve, Nos 41 (Royal Marines) and 10 (Inter-Allied) Commandos then moved into defensive positions about a mile south of Vrouwenpolder.

At about 8.15am, Regimental Sergeant Major Morris was with Tactical HQ in a small copse when four armed Germans arrived with a note from Captain Vourc'h in a forward position giving them safe passage. The Germans were taken to Commando HQ where Sergeant 'Gray' interpreted for Lieutenant Colonel Dawson, who negotiated a formal ceasefire at the German HQ at Vrouwenpolder at 1.00pm, and the eventual surrender of about 1,400 Germans. 4th Special Service Brigade had lost 103 killed, 325 wounded and sixty-eight missing during the eight days of fighting. No. 10 (Inter-Allied) had lost two officers at Commando HQ wounded and eight Dutch wounded. 3 (British) Troop had one private killed during the landings. Between them, the Belgians and Norwegians took the heaviest casualties with the Belgians losing an officer and a private killed and sixteen other ranks wounded, while the Norwegians lost one killed with two others dying of wounds, and two officers and twelve other ranks wounded. There is no doubt that the 200 Inter Allied commandos had the toughest time at Walcheren. Its exploits in preventing a German force from interfering with 4th Special Service Brigade south of the gap are largely unrecognized.

On 11 November, No. 10 (Inter-Allied) Commando, including the Dutch, embarked on a LCT at Flushing and returned to Bruges where they thought a Remembrance Day parade was a welcome back. On the 20th, when they returned to Eastbourne, the Dutch strength was down to two officers and seventeen other ranks. It would take over 100 minesweepers sixteen passages up and down the 70-mile channel before the River Scheldt was deemed clear on 26 November, and the first coasters were able to unload their cargoes at Antwerp.

Chapter 16

Belgium and Holland

The four members of 2 (Dutch) Troop selected for a mission before Arnhem were trained for a BBO mission conceived by Prince Bernhard to assist the Netherlands Binnenelandsche Strijdrachten (NBS; Netherlands Forces of the Interior) in the expectation that Operation Market Garden would help in an Allied breakthrough. Attached to the SAS Brigade, they attended a short course at Uxbridge followed by sabotage training near Oxford. Private van Lienden unfortunately broke his foot parachuting from a tethered balloon at Ringway and returned to Eastbourne.

During the night 25/26 September, in Operation Gobbo-Potia, Sergeant Blatt, a practising Jew who had lived in Germany, jumped 200 miles north of Arnhem near Orvelte in the province of Drenthe with five Belgian SAS. His role was to contact Sergeant Peter Tazalaar, also of the Dutch Troop, who had parachuted in several weeks earlier with a radio operator to gather intelligence on German deployments in the expectation of the Allied advance. However, on the same night that 1st (Airborne) Division was evacuated, the operation was aborted. In spite of objections from the Belgian SAS Lieutenant Debefve, Blatt was permitted to stay in Holland to co-ordinate the intelligence flowing from the Resistance, which was in danger of decreasing after Arnhem.

After several delays from poor weather, on 11 October, a Halifax took off with Sergeant Major van der Veer, Corporal Bob Michels and Private Nick de Koning bound for northern Holland. Van der Veer was a former police officer who, in 1940, had cycled to Nantes with several Dutch police officers, including Ubels, and reached England via Brest. In 1942, he trained with SOE until he was injured. The rest of the course were executed in Englandspiel. Koning was living on an Argentine ranch 1,200 miles from Buenos Aries when a German neighbour told him, on the day that his country attacked Holland, that they were now enemies. Deciding to fight for his country, he caught a ship to Bristol and eventually joined the Dutch Troop. Also on board was the Belgian SAS Warrant Officer Groenewart.

166

By the time the aircraft arrived over the designated DZ near Veenhuizen, German activity had forced the reception committee to move the DZ 4 miles away. The pilot released them too late and when the agents and the containers plunged through a wood in one stick, Koning injured his knee. Met by the North Drenthe Knock Plug Resistance, the commandos were given police uniforms; van der Veer went to Drenthe and Michels to Groningen.

De Koning and Groenewart travelled to Friesland in a car with German military plates. From the town of Swichum, de Koning, masquerading as a farmer known as Arie Prins, trading in young bulls, began to instruct the Resistance in weapon training and sabotage. When a letter from a captured member of the Resistance was found by German interrogators in February 1945, he posed as a midwife and adopted the name Albertus Werkman. The Greidegeuzen Resistance quickly came to admire his courage and brazen attitude towards the Germans, and by early April he had formed the 3,000-strong Provinciale Resistance Army which was supplied with 2,000 weapons parachuted in and 2,000 seized from prisoners. He organised the capture of three bridges but not before the Germans had made a thorough search of Swichum for him. He was briefly detained until a member of the Resistance dressed as a police officer 'arrested' him as a black marketeer.

Sergeant Major van der Veer was taken to a farm near Garminge, a hamlet about 2 miles from Westerbork, but was betrayed by a Dutch female courier engaged to a member of the Gestapo. On 26 October, he avoided capture, hiding in deep hay in the stable, when a German patrol searched the farm. The patrol then marched cross-country on a compass bearing towards the farm where Sergeant Blatt and the Belgian SAS were staying, 3 miles from Garminge, and again burrowed into the hay. The German intention to spend all night searching was diverted by drink and weapons deliberately left by the Dutch Resistance for them to find, which gave Blatt and the Belgians the opportunity to escape. Removing the insignia from their uniforms and pretending to be German parachute troops on special duty, they stayed at isolated farms and houses, and marched south bluffing their way over bridges and through checkpoints. After six anxious and hungry days, a farmer put them in touch with the Resistance through which the Belgians reached Allied lines. Blatt remained in Drenthe.

After the German patrol had left Garminge, van der Veer remained hidden in a bolthole in a potato pit because most young men had left the area for various reasons and he could not risk being seen. On the third night, the farmer told him he must leave the farm and when van der Veer climbed out of the bolthole, he was confronted by a police officer, Dirk Stoel, who had been a friend at the pre-war police training school. When

Stoel proposed to take van der Veer to his home at Westerbork police station, he mentioned that it was also the HQ of the local Feldgendarmarie. Van der Veer thought the suggestion crazy until he realized he would be safe, right under the noses of the Germans. Also based in the police station was Major General Botcher, the German area commander. For three months van der Veer remained inside Stoel's married quarter and soon recognized every German arriving at the police station. The walls were thin enough for him to overhear conversations between Botcher and his staff, and their telephone conversations. Eventually 'Constable' van der Veer accompanied Stoel 'on patrol' to train Resistance groups in weapon handling, demolition and minor guerrilla tactics.

Meanwhile the SAS Brigade, which was formed prior to D-Day by assembling the Belgian, British and French squadrons under a single HQ for large-scale operations, was attached to II (Canadian) Corps during their advance through north-east Holland. In Operation Amherst, the French were tasked with preventing the Germans from adopting fixed defensive positions and also to cause alarm throughout the enemy rear. Most of the defending troops were from the Dutch 4th SS Volunteer Panzergrenadier Brigade. The strategy plan was to seize three German air bases, including the large one at Steenwijk, and eighteen bridges over canals, including seven over the Appledoorn Canal. The operation was commanded from Belgium by Brigadier Michael Calvert, who had distinguished himself in Burma as a Chindit commander. On 8 April, 684 men from the 3rd and 4th (French) Parachute Battalions, the French element of the Brigade, dropped from C-47 Dakotas in sticks of about fifteen onto forty-six DZs, spread across northern Holland. Heavy cloud led to some DZs not being properly identified, some sticks landed miles from their targets and did not link up with the ground forces for a fortnight. Lieutenant Knottenbelt, after several delays, parachuted in near Barneveld on 3 April to support NBS operations.

In late March, thirty members of the Resistance had assembled about 30 miles from Westerbork in woods near Appelscha for training by van der Veer. During the night of 8 April, the group, most dressed in German military uniforms, split into about five patrols for a navigation exercise when an aircraft passing low overhead was assumed to be a damaged bomber. At the end of the exercise, when explosions were thought to be the Germans blowing up ammunition dumps before withdrawing, van der Veer thought the noise would shield the Resistance practising grenade throwing. When he and their leader, Mr Kees, went into the woods to look for suitable place, they heard people in a deep gully. Creeping close and seeing soldiers, the Resistance surrounded them and as dawn broke, van der Veer leapt into the middle and invited them to surrender. The first man who stirred was wearing a red beret. Realizing that the 'bomber' was probably an aircraft dropping paratroopers, he shouted, 'Don't shoot! We are from the Dutch Underground!' and then realized, to his horror, that forty paras were pointing their weapons at him as they did not understand what he was saying. To his relief, when an officer introduced himself as Major Sicaud of the French Parachute Regiment, van der Veer explained that Dutchmen wearing German uniforms had surrounded the gully.

The paras and the Dutch returned to the Resistance hideout where Sicaud explained that his company should have been dropped 10 miles to the north in order to seize a bridge. When he then mentioned that two sections commanded by Lieutenant Samson had been dropped near Graminge with orders to attack the German HQ at Westerbork, van der Veer cycled from the woods at about 6.00am to warn Dirk Stoel. Whilst giving a young girl hitch-hiking, with blisters but without papers, a lift on the crossbar, three Dutch SS stopped them on a canal towpath and instructed them to repeat 'Scheveningen' in Dutch. When van der Veer asked why, they said that paratroopers had dropped in the night and that the British could not pronounce 'Scheveningen'. Halfway to Westerbork, a tyre punctured and, to make matters worse, they saw Dutch SS with a machine gun guarding a canal bridge. Explaining that he wanted to escape the fighting and felt safer among the Germans, van der Veer said he had no idea who the girl was except that she had told him her farm had been rocketed by British aircraft pursuing a German truck and she had escaped with nothing except the clothes she was wearing. To his surprise, one of the SS soldiers asked if they were hungry and advised them to go to his HQ for some food; he then instructed several Dutch Home Guard to repair the tyre. As they made their way to the HQ and were crossing a railway line, van der Veer was again asked by a soldier to say 'Scheveningen'. The man checked van der Veer's identity card, saw there was no photograph and was just saying that he must be properly questioned when three Spitfires strafed a nearby goods train. Amid a hail of flying wood, stones and metal, the SS dived for cover while van der Veer and the girl escaped in the chaos.

After about 2 miles, the bicycle had another puncture and van der Veer boldly told three farmers in a wood, 'I can't tell you who I am but, in the name of the Queen, lend me a bicycle and I promise you it will be returned within forty-eight hours.' One of them replied, 'I trust you,' and hauled his bicycle from a haystack. The pair reached Westerbork without further incident and van der Veer guided Stoel, his wife and their baby to the woods near Applesche. When he met Lieutenant Samson in woods nearby preparing to attack Westerbork, he offered to guide him to the German HQ. The Frenchmen first arrested a Dutch collaborator and then, taking the Germans completely by surprise, killed about forty of them at the cost of just three dead, and captured General Botcher who was badly wounded. By the time Operation Amherst finished on 16 April, the French had killed about 270 Germans, wounded 220 and captured 187 at the expense of twenty-five killed, thirty-five wounded and twenty-nine missing. Most of them had ignored the Geneva Convention following the massacre at Oradour-sur-Glane, a village in France destroyed by the 2nd SS Panzer Division on 10 June 1944.

After the Germans had withdrawn from Westerbork, van der Veer was staying at another farm when, at about 4.00am on 11 April, the farmer woke him saying that he could hear strange noises, which van der Veer recognized to be tanks. Reaching the Town Hall at 6.00am, he arrested the burgomaster and, told him that he was a commando sent by Prince Bernhard; the man realized that the occupation was over and offered him a cup of coffee. Van der Veer insisted that the Dutch tricolour must first be raised so that when the Allies arrived they could see that the town had been liberated. As van der Veer was drinking his coffee, he took a telephone call from the Commandant of the Westerbork concentration camp asking about the situation. Van der Veer replied that it could not be better and, telling him that tanks were in the main street, put the receiver outside the window. The Commandant shrieked down the phone insisting to know who he was, so van der Veer replied in English, 'Why not speak in English? If you can't speak English, it's time you learnt!' The line then went dead.

The camp had been opened by the Dutch authorities during the summer of 1939 to house Jewish refugees from Germany. In July 1942, the Germans converted it into a transit camp for forced labour and then for extermination. The prisoners were able to buy goods impossible to find elsewhere in Holland, a ploy used by the SS to avoid problems during transfers to such camps as Auschwitz. The tragedy was that the SS had little to do with the transfers because they were made by a Jewish security service fearful of being deported, often under the control of Dutch policemen. Among those who passed through its gates was Anne Frank, the young Dutch diarist. Nothing remains today of the camp except a piece of twisted railway track pointing to the sky.

After Walcheren, 4 (Belgian) and 5 (Norwegian) Troops returned to Belgium for rest and refitting. No. 10 (Inter-Allied) Commando returned to Eastbourne with Lieutenant Colonel Laycock leaving a Tactical HQ under Major Franks to administer 2 (Dutch) and 3 (British) Troops, who were still attached to HQ 4th Special Service Brigade at Middleburg. Nos 4 and 48 (Royal Marines) Commandos were on North and South Beveland respectively, while No. 41 (Royal Marines) Commando remained deployed throughout Walcheren. No. 47 (Royal Marines) Commando held the mainland north of the Scheldt. Generally, there was little evidence of German activity. The Army Commando stayed until 12 November 1944 and then moved to Goes, which is near Breskens, for rest, refitting and training.

At the end of November, the Norwegians were sent to Bergen-op-Zoom to prepare for an attack on North Beveland, but when this did not materialize, the Troop was sent to Breda. Meanwhile, Major Franks and Major de Jonghe were attached to HQ Special Service Group where de Jonghe was ticked off by Brigadier Mills-Roberts for wearing corduroy trousers as opposed to battledress. By May, corduroys were worn by most officers in 1st Commando Brigade.

So far, only the French had previously had the foresight to establish a Troop to replace battle casualties. On 8 November, Major de Jonghe was instructed to recruit 327 men for additional Belgian Troops, and by the New Year had trained sufficient men to form the Flemish-speaking 9 Troop in Polegate and the French-speaking 10 Troop in Seaford. Captain Danloy, promoted to major, created a Battalion HQ within the Commando order of battle. The Norwegians recruited an officer and fifteen men from the Norwegian Brigade. On 17 November, Lieutenant Knottenbelt and Corporal van Creveld held recruiting drives in liberated Holland and, of the mainly 700 former members of the Resistance who attended selection battle school at Nunspeet, the privations of occupation resulted in just seventy passing the commando course. No. 10 (Inter-Allied) Commando was the now the largest unit in the Special Service Group.

Back in England, the Belgians carried out several exercises. On 21 February 1945, in the Holywell area, 10 Troop landed to join 4 Troop, which had jumped by a simulated parachute drop, to attack a 'jet-propelled research station' held by a British 'mobile troop' represented by 9 Troop. On 17 April, 10 Troop experienced near disaster when a Sub-Section making its way along the beach, from the Birling Gap firing ranges to Beachy Head, were cut off below the white cliffs by a combination of the spring tide, a south-westerly wind and a fierce undercurrent, and huddled on the rocks. When a wave carried Private Somerville out to sea, Lance Corporal Jean Terundon and Private Herve van der Werve, with considerable difficulty, rescued him and applied artificial respiration. As the tide ebbed, Terundon sent two men to alert Canadian anti-tank gunners exercising at Birling Gap. They in turn informed a Royal Canadian Army Medical Corps doctor and two orderlies, who treated Somerville and whisked him to the Princess Alice Hospital in Eastbourne.

On the wintery morning of 16 December, the 5th Panzer, 6th SS Panzer and 7th Armies attacked the US 1st and 3rd Armies in the Ardennes. When it appeared that Antwerp was threatened, I (British) Corps, defending a 60-mile front along the River Maas, was reinforced by 4th Commando Brigade amid intelligence reports that the Germans intended to land airborne troops behind Allied lines and launch attacks across the River Maas. Both had been renamed from Special Service Brigades on 6 December, much to the relief of the commandos, delighted to be rid of the shortened title 'SS'.

When the offensive was repulsed in January 1945, 4th Commando Brigade moved eastwards to Oosterhout where No. 47 (Royal Marines), which was joined by the Norwegians on 23 December, and part of 48 (Royal Marines) Commando defended a sector of the Maas. The rest of the Commando remained on South Beveland to react to German airborne forces still thought likely to attack or raid Antwerp. There were several clashes with the enemy in the snowy cold of winter across the bleak landscape.

Still attached to No. 4 Commando, the 1st Marine Fusilier Commando Battalion was reinforced by 7 (French) Troop, and in January 1945, after some leave, it was instructed to dominate the islands of Schouwen, Overflakkee and Tiengemten north of North and South Beveland to prevent enemy infiltration and sabotage. The 5,000 reasonable quality enemy soldiers backed up by artillery on Schouwen, an island the size of the Isle of Wight, were calculated to be a counter-attack threat from the north-west and to be in a position to raid the docks at Antwerp.

After dark on 17 January, sixty-three men, mostly from 7 (French) Troop commanded by Captain Willers, landed on Schouwen from three LCAs covered by two armed motor boats to attack two artillery bunkers. Landing undetected in rough seas at 3.30am next morning, Willers split the patrol into two; while he breached two dense networks of barbed wire and seized the bunker only to find it empty, Sergeant Major Delmont's patrol approached the second bunker. When they and the landing craft were spotted, flares soared into the night and, coming under fire from 20mm cannon and machine guns, the French withdrew taking six Dutch civilians found in a farm, but then stumbled into another German position. In the confusion, a commando was wounded. Willers retired when he heard the outbreak of firing. By now, it was 5.00am and low tide; in spite of the surf, the landing craft withdrew, covered by the motor boats.

The next major raid on Schouwen took place when Captain Lofi and a 5 Troop patrol left Colinjsplat and landed from three LCAs on 14 February at about 7.00pm. After a difficult approach through sand dunes, part of the force was held up by thick barbed wire and came under accurate fire, so Lofi ordered the entire force to withdraw, taking with them ten civilians thought to be of intelligence value. Under interrogation by 2 (Dutch) Troop next morning at Commando HQ, they proved ill-informed about German activities. The final raid was a month later when Captain Guy Vourc'h and 6 (French) Troop landed from three LCAs to attack an enemy position during the night of 11/12 March, backed up by artillery support. Leaving Colinjsplat at 10.00pm on a still, clear night, they had returned within four hours. Flooding and the need for the commandos to avoid the dykes and paths, in case they were seen, confined them to wading through icy streams flanked by water-soaked bullrushes and reeds. As the Troop neared the German position, they encountered thick barbed-wire entanglements in the freezing water. Alert German sentries spotted the French attempting to cut the wire, and opened heavy and accurate fire with machine guns and rifle fire, wounding four commandos. The raids had shown that the Germans were well positioned in heavily defended bunkers surrounded by dense field defences and barbed wire. Next day, No. 4 Commando returned to Middleburg where for three days it provided escorts for Queen Wilhelmina visiting Walcheren.

On 25 March, No. 48 (Royal Marines) Commando, under command of 116 Brigade, Royal Marines, moved north of s'Hertogenbosch on the banks of the River Maas with orders to harass the Germans on a 10,000-yard front. Although the front was static, there were frequent clashes. On 7 April, the Commando took over the stretch of the Maas around Kapelsche Veer from a Polish battalion for a week, and then returned to 4th Commando Brigade to take over defending a 35,000-yard stretch of the Maas between Willemstad and Geertruidenberg. Under command were the partly trained 1st Belgian Fusilier Battalion and 600 Dutch volunteers holding the front line, while the Commando was in reserve and advised on raids. The reinforced 2 (Dutch) Troop was attached to the Commando to help train the irregulars, and also for liaison duties.

When irregulars reported that the Germans were evacuating the Biesbosch, on 20 April, X Troop sent a patrol under the command of Major Wall to test the reports, in Operation Bograt. Accompanying it was the German Second Lieutenant Peter 'Kingsley', badged Royal Fusiliers and one of six former 3 (British) Troop commissioned after D-Day, and posted to other Commandos. The patrol motored across the Maas in two dories both towing a three-man canoe, the plan being to land on Steenen Muur to check several houses and then withdraw, leaving 'Kingsley' and two Royal Marines in an observation post. Wall landed with his patrol and at 2.10am, 'Kingsley', having found that the houses were empty, called forward the dories, but in the darkness of a moonless night, they missed the rendezvous. The Germans were alerted when the Royal Marines ambushed a cycle patrol, and for the rest of the day there were several clashes as the commandos struggled to avoid capture. Communications were lost when a Royal Navy wireless operator, threatened with drowning from the weight of his radio, ditched it in deep water. About twenty enemy prisoners were killed in a short action when a German force attacked shortly before dusk. After dark, Major Wall instructed 'Kingsley' and his patrol to return to the original landing place and lie up while he island-hopped back to the Maas. Failing to find a boat, Wall, his batman and a Dutch interpreter tried to swim across the main channel, but, cold and tired, they found refuge in a farmhouse on the German-held western bank. Meanwhile, Lieutenant Colonel Price, the commanding officer, with the Germans near to defeat and concerned about the disappearance of the patrol, mobilized the entire Commando to find them. At about 4.14pm on 21 April, while the Troops searched the Biesbosch, Y Troop crossed from Pauluszand to Steenen Muur and found 'Kingsley' and his observation post, cold, wet and hungry; they eventually located Major Wall and his patrol in a barn. The other Troops clashed with several German patrols.

The last operation in the Biesbosch took place on 22 April but when little of consequence was found, both sides settled down to defensive operations, except for battery and counter-battery fire on specific targets. On 1 May, the commandos watched aircraft parachuting food to starving Dutch communities in Operation Manna.

Chapter 17

The Advance into Germany

After the Germans launched their Ardennes offensive, Captain 'Griffith' and fifteen experienced 3 (British) Troop NCOs joined 1st Commando Brigade as a Troop when it sailed in the second week of January 1945, as reinforcement from Tilbury to Ostend. Sergeant Major 'Howarth' had taken over from O'Neill' as Troop Sergeant Major. Transported by train to Helmond in snow-covered Holland, the Brigade joined VIII Corps and deployed along the banks of the River Maas near Asten with No. 45 (Royal Marines) Commando in reserve. No. 46 (Royal Marines) Commando had replaced No. 4 Commando which was with 4th Special Service Brigade.

No. 47 (Royal Marines) Commando, from 4th Commando Brigade, re-inforced by 5 (Norwegian) Troop on 23 December, was already in the line. After recovering from wounds sustained at Walcheren, Captain Hauge returned bringing eighteen replacements commanded by Lieutenant Gabriel Smith. They included Private Olav Bjorndalen, a former farmer and whaler who had married in 1939 and had then escaped to England where he transferred to the Troop and took part in several MTB raids. When the Troop moved into the front line at Geertrudenburg, they joined the Royal Marines on several raids. No. 47 (Royal Marines) Commando was then ordered to attack Kapelsche Veer Island during the night of 13/14 January.

Kapelsche Veer Island, low lying, bleak and measuring about 5 miles long, and one and a half miles wide, was about 20 miles north of Breda. On the north side, between the Maas and a tributary known as 'Old Little Maas' was a small harbour. Along the northern rim ran a 5-foot-high dyke; 300 yards to the south, running parallel, was the 15-foot high 'Winter' dyke. Both broadened out to a reasonably firm plateau in the middle of which stood a small cottage. Frequent snowfalls and falling temperatures had frozen the surrounding flooded fields. Elements of the German 6th Parachute Division reinforced by Army Group 'H', which was com-manded by General Student, defended the island. Needing to convince Allied commanders that he was prepared to threaten the lines of communication from Normandy, his men had converted the island into networks of trenches and bunkers burrowed into the dykes almost impervious to shelling. They were short of machine guns, and supplies were ferried across the river. Under command of the Canadians, a 1st (Polish) Armoured Division platoon had failed to seize the island on the last day of 1944 and a week later a Polish battalion captured the harbour but, unable to overcome the Germans dug in along the dyke, was forced to withdraw. No. 47 (Royal Marines) Commando was then instructed to attack the island. The plan was for Q (Royal Marines) and 5 (Norwegian) Troops to provide a diversionary attack from the right targeting the cottage, with the rest of the Commando assaulting on the left. Hauge was unsure that Lieutenant Smith and his replacements were ready for the operation but eventually agreed that they could take part.

A bitterly cold, heavy frost carpeted the ground and Canadian artillery was shelling the island as the troops left their positions on 13 January. The main force crossed the Maas but was driven back by alert defenders, who then concentrated on the diversion and their infantry bridge laid by Polish engineers. The Norwegians were channelled by the ground and field defences into advancing on a narrow front, and a Bren gunner was killed by a machine gun firing on fixed lines. No. 1 Section advanced to within about 100 yards of the enemy but was then pinned in the middle of Canadian artillery fire from one bank and German mortars and artillery firing from the other. Briefly held up by the shelling, No. 2 Section covered No. 1 Section battling a further 75 yards until stopped by ferocious fire and grenades bouncing down the dyke slopes and exploding on the frozen ground. Soon after Lieutenant Smith was killed when he stood to throw a grenade, No. 1 Section withdrew, but both Sections were then pinned down close to the German positions, a tactic that the Norwegians were comfortable with because, at Walcheren, they had learnt that the safest place from mortar fire is close to the enemy. Captain Hauge and his Tactical HQ were mortared, and a commando killed and another wounded. Q Troop also ran into trouble, nevertheless, with the Norwegians giving covering fire they twice launched attacks and on the third attempt, broke in to the cottage before being driven back. Although both Troops had taken heavy losses and were low on ammunition, Commando HQ ordered another attack, however, with 50 per cent casualties of five killed and seventeen wounded, seven seriously, and Lieutenant Gausland about to advance with the surviving twenty-four, Hauge instructed the Troop to withdraw. It was their last action of the war. An estimated 140 Germans were thought to have been killed during the night. On 16 January, the battered Norwegian Troop and No. 47 (Royal Marines) Commando was withdrawn to Walcheren. Kapelsche Veer was seized a fortnight later by the 10th (Canadian) Infantry Brigade supported by tanks at a cost of 350 casualties.

As part of the Allied strategy to line up on the western banks of the River Rhine, Second (British) Army advanced to the western borders of Germany, where vigorous opposition was expected. Freezing winds whipped across the flat terrain and snow lay in deep drifts among the fields and ice-covered ponds, streams and canals. By now the patrolling skills of 3 Troop were much in demand. In preparation for a recce patrol crossing the Maas, Corporal 'Masters' led a small patrol to find a position to cover the crossing and, stumbling on several barges tied up on the towpath, spent six hours lying motionless in the snow watching them. The recce was aborted until a week later when Sergeant 'Drew' used his native German on a prisoner snatch to capture two sentries guarding a shed.

On 22 January, 1st Commando Brigade was ordered by 7th Armoured Brigade to eject the enemy from a sector between the Maas and Roer near Sittard. During the night of 22/23 January, Brigade HQ sent No. 6 Commando across the Juliana Canal on the ice to seize Maasbracht and go firm as No. 45 (Royal Marines) Commando passed through. Supported by a 1st Royal Tank Regiment squadron and advancing toward Brachtenbeck railway station south-east of the village, the Commando was held up by the aggressive Huebner Battle Group, a well-led mix of parachute troops and· ex-Luftwaffe personnel, including flying crews, lining the Montefortebeck Canal. During the fighting, Lance Corporal Harden RAMC was posthumously awarded the Victoria Cross for rescuing wounded under heavy fire. No. 6 Commando then rolled up the enemy by advancing from the north and both Commandos, supported by Cromwell tanks of the 8th Hussars, crossed the canal. No. 45 (Royal Marines) Commando went into reserve leaving Nos 3 and 6 Commandos to capture Linne, just in front of the Siegfried Line. To keep the pressure on the Germans, Brigadier Mills-Roberts sent out strong combined tank/infantry patrols with the commando Troops dismounting to search woods and built-up areas. 3 Troop did not like this type of patrolling because the tanks feared anti-tank attacks, and naturally kept moving, which usually meant a lengthy walk to rejoin them. Nevertheless, when a patrol dislodged several Germans from the edge of a stream, one man hid in a windmill to avoid detection by a 3 Troop detachment searching the three levels, but he surrendered the next day, hungry and cold. Later, a body provided not only confirmation of German unit identification, but also several thousand guilders split between the Troop.

On another patrol, Captain 'Griffith' and his batman, the British Private Henderson, ran into withering German machine-gun fire at a farm called Spielmanshof. Needing to establish if the farm had been converted into a strong position, an E Troop, No. 45 (Royal Marines) Commando fighting patrol, and six members of 3 (British) Troop, commanded by Captain Ian Beadle MC, were sent to investigate on a night lit by searchlights bouncing beams off clouds earthwards. Leaving the Royal Marines near the farm, the six from 3 Troop found the farmyard deserted except for an abundance of domesticated chickens and rabbits, possibly being fed by Germans. Stealthily approaching the farmhouse, the patrol heard the distinctive sound of a machine-gun barrel knocked against a tree. Rejoining the Royal Marines with the report, and shortly after Corporal 'Spencer' had returned with several dead rabbits, the patrol commander ordered everyone to open fire for two minutes and then retire. The Germans replied with six machine guns and mortared the vacated marine position. A few days later, a mounted group of Dutch partisans, including a striking young woman, arrived at Brigade HQ and accused the Troop of going to Spielmanshof, pointing at the skin of a rabbit on a fence. 'Masters' hurriedly changed the conversation and arranged for the group to be given weapons, blankets and food. The search for food was endless and 3 Troop was utterly ruthless in persuading farmers and shopkeepers across the border in Germany to hand over chickens and rabbits. 'Masters' was told by Lieutenant Colonel Nicol Gray to ensure that every Troop in the Commando had a goose, so when a farmer objected to the requisitioning, he snarled that at least he was safe and not threatened with torture and death.

When HQ 7th Armoured Division required information about Merum, a village north of Linne near Roermond, the task was given to the Royal Marines. Between Linne and Merum, the River Maas made a large loop, a lock at the north-west effectively turning the area into an island some 2,500 yards from west to east, and about 1,000 yards from north to south. Because of its shape, this was initially referred to as 'Bell Island' but when No. 45 (Royal Marines) Commando remembered the Royal Marines assault on Belle Isle, off the Brittany coast, in 1761, the Operation Order issued on 27 January was headed 'Belle Isle'. E Troop was to form a bridgehead through which D Troop would pass to examine the lock facing British troops holding the west bank of the Maas. B Troop would then drag boats on sledges across the island, recross the Maas and raid Merum. The crossing point was about 100 yards wide and with the current fast flowing, No. 1 Troop, Royal Marines Engineer Commando established a ferry service. H-Hour was fixed for 9.30pm on 27 January. The night was cold and a full moon reflected onto the snow-covered fields, a godsend for defenders. A breakdown in artillery communications delayed H-Hour until 10.00pm. With some men in snow suits, D Troop, accompanied by Captain 'Griffith' and Private 'Mason', advanced across the white landscape but were stalled in a violent battle in woods to the east of the lock; when it was in danger of being overrun, the B Troop raid on Merum was cancelled, the Troop was instructed to reinforce the beachhead and help rig

178

a line across the river for the ferry service. The Germans then attacked the beachhead, just as survivors from D Troop trickled into the perimeter, and were ferried across the river with the wounded in the Goatleys and others clinging to the side. 'Mason' swam across.

Next night, Captain Beadle led a small E Troop patrol, which included Captain 'Griffith', to the beachhead where five dead Germans were found. On the body of a captain, 'Griffith' found a map detailing the positions of the Huebner Battle Group and the Mueller Parachute Regiment to the south-west of Roermond. The patrol also found a thoroughly confused German, who under interrogation at Commando HQ said the German force on the island consisted of fifty men from the Mueller Regiment, and the Captain had been their commander. When the Germans broadcasted their success by naming the eleven dead and six prisoners, Sergeant Major 'Howarth' met with the Germans to collect the dead. Although nonplussed to meet a British soldier speaking perfect German, the German Sergeant Major returned the bodies but refused to be taken prisoner, even though he admitted that the war was lost, and appealed to 'Howarth' not to make his life difficult. 3 Troop later learnt that the Sergeant Major and his men had been censored for their negotiations and were replaced by two sergeants and twenty-two men, who promptly surrendered. When a third group arrived, the commandos floated a boat filled with explosive down-river to blow up their supply boat, the resulting explosion blowing out the windows of nearby houses. Soon afterwards 'Howarth' was sent to an OCTU.

VIII Corps was always pressing for enemy identification, which meant prisoners. During a thaw in February, fresh from visiting 2nd Commando Brigade in Yugoslavia, Lieutenant Colonel Vaughan, smart in his Service Dress among the commando smocks, arrived at Brigade HQ and reminded Brigadier Mills-Roberts of an earlier promise of a patrol. Crammed into a Goatley behind a scheduled No. 6 Commando fighting patrol, in Mills-Robert's patrol was Major de Jonghe, whose poor paddling technique was rectified by the Brigadier. Landing on a mudbank, the patrol burrowed into mud as it came under heavy fire, nevertheless four prisoners were captured. Vaughan's smart uniform, covered in mud, was cleaned and pressed before he left.

1st Commando Brigade remained in the line until 6 March when it concentrated at Venray and trained for Operation Plunder, the crossing of the Rhine, its particular task being the capture of Wesel. A frontal assault out of the question, Brigadier Mills-Roberts decided to land about 4,000 yards west of Wesel at a muddy inlet known as Grav Inlet, approach from the north and 'disappear' into the town before the defenders realized it. 3 (British) Troop was divided in pairs among the Commandos, Sergeant 'Masters' and Corporal 'Harris' joining No. 45 (Royal Marines) Commando. When Lieutenant Colonel Gray asked 'Masters' to acquire a shotgun so he could hunt, 'Masters' exchanged three double-barrelled 12-bore shotguns for six cartons of cigarettes from a forester.

1st Cheshires were assigned to reinforce the Brigade and link up with 17th (US) Airborne Division, scheduled to drop north of Wesel. Artillery was available from the 1st Mountain Regiment 4.5-inch howitzers with sapper and assault boat support provided by 84th Field Company, Royal Engineers. The Brigade travelled by train to its assembly areas on 23 March and watched Lancasters bomb Wesel. At 9.30pm, No. 46 (Royal Marines) Commando and Brigade HQ, covered by the 25-pounders of 6th Field Regiment shelling the eastern bank, crossed the 300-yard Rhine in Buffaloes and overran several German positions. No. 6 Commando, crossing in Stormboats and Buffaloes, took several casualties,

'Masters' escorted an artillery forward observation officer and his signaller. Lurching to the Rhine in a Buffalo just as Wesel was bombed and the artillery opened fire, the amtrac waddled across the river. Midstream, 'Masters' saw a Buffalo burning and later learnt that it contained Sergeant 'Villiers' and Corporal 'Seymour' crossing with No. 46 (Royal Marines) Commando. Both were killed. As his Buffalo reached the bank, it was too steep to use the rear door and everyone clambered over the side, except for the signaller, weighed down with a heavy wireless, who was unceremoniously hauled out and rolled onto the ground. When the lieutenant later realized that he had left his map and its artillery information in the Buffalo, the situation was resolved when he met his counterpart with No. 46 (Royal Marines) Commando. By the time 'Masters' reached Wesel, he had returned to Commando HQ and was talking with Brigadier Mills-Roberts and Lieutenant Colonel Gray when they were all blown off their feet by a Panzerfaust weapon fired at short range. Gray was badly wounded. 'Masters' and Corporal 'Harris' were soon interrogating prisoners, including Home Guard, in a cellar at a small table covered by a blanket. Three were of unusually high rank, but two refused to talk. The third, considered to be arrogant, was fooled into admitting that he belonged to a Special Use Unit reporting direct to Army HQ. Studying his map, 'Masters' and 'Harris' then convinced him that they knew everything about him and that they were artillery observers for a counter-attack force that had assembled in a village. On his way to report his findings to Commando HQ, 'Masters' arranged for the village to be shelled.

At 10.30am next day, a 1st Cheshires patrol contacted the US paras. Meanwhile, Brigadier Mills-Roberts had found that his HQ was located about 100 yards from that of General Deutsch, who commanded the Wesel garrison. When he refused to surrender, Regimental Sergeant Major Woodcock and a No. 6 Commando attack killed Deutsch. Later in the day, when 'Masters' sent two prisoners with a message for a group of determined Germans near a wire factory and they failed to convince them to surrender, he watched an American airborne infantry company and a British tank troop attack the position, which eventually fell, after they had inflicted a number of casualties. 'Harris' was so furious about the losses that he hit a German corporal, an act he regretted. With the number of prisoners mounting, 3 Troop were also hard pressed searching houses and German positions for items of intelligence interest. By the 25th, Wesel was firmly in British hands.

On 3 April, Regimental Sergeant Major Howarth was returning in a lorry to rejoin 3 Troop with other British reinforcements, after successfully completing OCTU, when it was hit by a shell, killing both him and the driver. Howarth's body could only be identified by the silver Buffs cap badge he habitually wore in his beret.

Next day, amid frequent spring downpours, 1st Commando Brigade, now under command of 6th Airborne Division, and still in VIII Corps, was approaching Osnabruck in a pincer movement with 11th Armoured Division. The Brigade Major, Major Maxwell Harper-Gow, was in a Brigade HQ jeep driven by Marine Keith Thompson when its windscreen disappeared in a hail of glass slivers and they both dived into a ditch as it was ambushed. In the second jeep, Captain de Jonghe was cut by flying glass and a corporal was wounded in the face. Behind the jeeps, on motorcycle, was the German-speaking Corporal K.E. Clarke. He grabbed a bicycle belonging to a German civilian taking cover during the crossfire, cycled up the road and not only arranged for a medical team to go to the site of the ambush, but also persuaded an artillery battery to shell the German position. Meanwhile, a Military Government major and his driver drove into the middle of the crossfire and also joined de Jonghe in the ditch when his Hillman Utility Vehicle windscreen was shattered. Harper-Gow was astonished when Clarke, dressed in civilian clothes, rode past with a cheery wave, disappeared into Osnabruck and later rejoined Brigade HQ, having learnt from several townspeople the disposition of German military deployments. For this brazen act of courage, Clarke was only awarded Mentioned in Despatches. Although he was a member of No. 10 (Inter-Allied) Commando, he is not listed as part of 3 Troop.

Before entering Osnabruck, Brigadier Mills-Roberts instructed Major de Jonghe that he was to detain the Gestapo Area Commander. Next morning in Osnabruck, de Jonghe – who had been pursued by the Gestapo in Occupied Belgium – and his patrol returned to Brigade HQ carrying the body of the German in a blanket, who he claimed had attempted to escape. HQ VIII Corps were unhappy that a valuable prisoner was dead. Corporal 'Harris', the sole surviving member of 3 Troop, who had been attached to No. 45 (Royal Marines) Commando since D-Day and had become particularly valuable to the Commanding Officer, Lieutenant Colonel Blake, persuaded a contingent of Hungarians conscripted into the German Army to surrender, against the wishes of their officers.

During the crossing of the River Weser on 6 April, 1st Commando Brigade, still under command 11th Armoured Division, was opposed by the aggressive 12th SS Training Battalion in well-concealed positions covering the east bank and the town of Leese. When a weak beachhead was established by the 1st Rifle Brigade near Stolzenau, No. 45 (Royal Marines) Commando crossed as reinforcement and became involved in close-quarter fighting in woods with snipers who proved particularly trouble-some. Using the cover of the riverbanks and narrow beaches, Commando HQ was pinned down from three German trenches only a few yards above them, protected on their right by a hedge and on the left by the river. When Blake nodded to 'Harris', 'Harris' scrambled onto the towpath and sprayed the area with his Thompson, killing two SS and kicking one prisoner over to Blake. Running out of ammunition, he persuaded a corporal in charge of a Bren gun team to give him their gun and opened fire on other enemy positions. Unluckily for him, a Spandau bullet peeled the magazine back into his face, blinding him in the left eye. 'Harris' had also been wounded in Normandy and was later awarded the Military Medal.

With the Royal Marines confined to the beachhead, the remainder of 1st Commando Brigade entered the bridgehead, turned south, advanced through a marsh and attacked Leese from the east, capturing a V2 missile factory in the process. The Brigade then advanced to Helsdorf near the River Alert and the HQ was placed in a large farmhouse. That night there was a commotion in the kitchen and the handsome, blonde daughter of the farmer hysterically burst into the sitting room, accusing a member of 3 Troop of wanting her *'flesh'*. Going into the kitchen, the Trooper indicated to Brigadier Mills-Roberts that he actually wanted a meat sandwich that she was making on the table, not the girl.

The Germans then held up 11th Armoured Division at the River Aller, although the road and rail bridge at Essel had not been demolished. Although the Aller was not wide, if the Germans blew the bridges, it would still take a major operation to cross it. Needing to know if the road bridge was wired with explosives, Brigadier Mills-Roberts asked Captain 'Griffith' and another commando officer to inspect it; they donned life-jackets and floated downstream, but as they reached it, the German engineers blew it up, showering them with debris. The pair swam to the western bank and rejoined the Brigade now moving south towards the rail bridge, which was captured during the night of 10/11 April by the men of No. 3 Commando who removed their boots so they could cross silently. With Brigade HQ established on the eastern banks of the river, as the commandos advanced north along the eastern bank and seized the damaged road bridge, intelligence from a prisoner suggested the 2nd Marine Fusilier Battalion south of Essel was preparing to counter-attack.

As 1st Commando Brigade dug in, Captain 'Griffith' persuaded a German farmer to dig his trench. Then at 8.00am on the 11th, several well-executed attacks by the Germans, across the heavily wooded countryside dispersed with sand dunes, got to within about 50 yards of the bridgehead, where snipers were causing problems. Early in the fighting, 'Griffith' was talking to Major Beattie – he had formerly been the 10 (Inter-Allied) Commando Signals Officer and was now the Brigade Signals Officer – in his trench when someone yelled at 'Griffith' to take cover, to which he replied, 'Don't you know I'm bulletproof.' A few minutes later he was shot in the kidneys and died almost instantly. The fighting around the beach-head raged all day and was so severe that, during a lull, the bodies of the German Commanding Officer, his Adjutant, Regimental Sergeant Major and two company commanders were found close to Brigade HQ. With 1st Mountain Regiment playing a critical role, No. 6 Commando charged across the damaged road bridge and seized it from another Marine Fusilier company, forcing the Germans to withdraw and for No. 3 Commando to link up with the commandos at Essel. Of Captain 'Griffith', Brigadier Mills-Roberts later wrote:

> After this, at dusk, we buried James Griffiths. This German – who had allied himself to our cause – was a great favourite with everyone and we were very sad to lose him. We lifted James into his grave at the same time as the Medium Regiment fired for the last time – it was a real soldier's funeral.

A few words that epitomized No. 10 (Inter-allied) Commando. Captain Monahan, who, in August, had been detached to SOE for a Jedburgh mission in France, replaced 'Griffith'.

1st Commando Brigade advanced north-east and, fighting its last battle on the banks of the Elbe–Trave Canal, captured Lauenberg on 30 April. On 8 May, it had reached Neustadt, in what became East Germany, where it was joined by the three Belgian Troops.

On 11 April, the whole of No. 10 (Inter-Allied) Commando, now commanded by Lieutenant Colonel Franks, joined the advance after arriving at Ostend in a long convoy of thirty-two vehicles carrying Tactical HQ of 3 officers and 5 other ranks, 9 officers and 88 men of the Dutch troop, 3 officers and 26 men of No. 3 (British) Troop, and 11 officers and 240 Belgians – a total of 26 officers and 375 commandos divided into an advance party and main body. When the Commando joined 4th Commando Brigade at Middleburg, the Belgians, ordered to link up with 1st Commando Brigade, caught up in the village of Emsdetten. On 5 May, the Troop was sent to Lübeck where it guarded the 28th 'Walloon' SS

Volunteer Grenadier Division, which had surrendered to the British in late April. The Division had been formed as the 5th 'Walloon' Assault Brigade in 1941 and was initially employed on anti-partisan duties in the Soviet Union until it took part in the fighting on the Russian Front. Swept aside on 20 April, when its Divisional Commander fled to Spain via Denmark, the Division surrendered to the British, three days before the German surrender.

Chapter 18

Disbandment

Hostilities over, the prisoners began reappearing. Corporal 'Jones' of 3 (British) Troop was released on 30 April, as was Corporal Gaston Pourcelet after the disastrous Operation Hardtack 11. After joining his family in Amiens, Pourcelet joined the Resistance in Besançon until arrested on a minor charge and sent to Buchenwald concentration camp in 1944. In 1945, he was marched from one camp to another until liberated, a skeleton weighing just 44kg.

Investigations into the disappearance of Trepel's patrol led to SS and Gestapo officers being questioned by Second Lieutenant Hulot in Rotterdam Prison without success. An investigation by Captain Miles Bellville, a Royal Marine drafted to Combined Operations, found their graves, but they were named as Allied airmen, and he initially concluded that five died from drowning and one from exposure, until a local cemetery keeper claimed that they had not all died at the same time. Bellville unearthed a German Army report from one of the bunkers, Widerstandsnest 37, which reported that at 2.30am on 29 January, a day after the raid, when the occupants had been alerted by shouts from the sea, a patrol found a rubber dinghy with three bodies in it; a fourth body was found in the sea. The following week, Trepel was found and two months later, the sixth man. The report concluded that the men were French-Canadian commandos, but this does not explain why they were buried as airmen.

Left on Houlgate beach on 17 May 1944 in Operation Tarbrush 10, Lieutenants 'Lane' and Wooldridge had overshot their rendezvous and were sandwiched between two German patrols firing at the dory as it left with the NCOs. When the patrols eventually left, 'Lane' flashed signals out to sea but there was no response, so they walked along the beach until they found the dinghy and launched it, with sunrise only thirty minutes over the horizon. By dawn, when they were a mile offshore, a motorboat full of German soldiers approached from Cayeaux, both officers realized that resistance was pointless and dramatically threw their pistols and equipment overboard. At Cayeaux, interrogated by Wehrmacht officers with the usual threats of being handed over to the Gestapo, 'Lane' convinced the Germans that his thick Hungarian accent was Welsh. Moved to another barracks, 'Lane' picked the cell lock but they bumped into a German guard, who mentioned that there was no point escaping because, around the corner, was another sentry. Eventually both officers were driven, blindfolded, to a château, which turned out to be HQ Army Group B. Taken one at a time into a long room, at the end of which were Field Marshal Rommel and his Adjutant, Captain Lang, both officers parried Rommel's questions about their activities and the expected Allied invasion. Transferred to Fresnes Prison in Paris, the Gestapo interrogations were not as brutal as expected because Rommel had ordered they be treated as prisoners of war. At Oflag IXH/AH, 'Lane' divulged his identity to the Senior British Officer, Colonel Euan Miller, who used the MI9 intelligence and communication links to pass on the information that 'Lane' had gathered, including the location of Rommel's HQ.

Captured on 10 June, Private 'Saunders' also concealed his identity and after a fruitless attempt to escape from a train taking him to Paris, ended up in a prison camp near Sagan on the River Oder. In 1945, he escaped from a prisoner-of-war column and, picked up by the Soviets after swimming across the river, was employed to drive carts for officers. Sent to a labour camp helping Soviet Army engineers build a bridge across a river, he decided that he did not want to be a slave, escaped and jumped trains to Odessa where he persuaded a British merchant ship captain to take him to England. By then, 3 (British) Troop had been disbanded. Taken prisoner during the night of 19/20 June 1944 on patrol with Lieutenant Littlejohn, Lance Sergeant 'Thompson' also concealed his true identity until liberation.

After being captured during at Arnhem, Privates Beekmeyer, Gobetz and Gubbels of 2 (Dutch) Troop were sent to a prison camp near Dresden. In February 1945, following the confusion after the controversial bombing, Gobetz and Gubbels escaped but were captured near the Czech border. In April, they again escaped, reached American lines near Chemnitz and returned to Eastbourne on 15 May along with Sergeant de Leeuw. In Stalag XIB/357 at Fallingbostel, when Sergeant de Waard was admitted to the camp hospital when his foot became seriously infected; a Yugoslav doctor persuaded a German medical officer that there was no need for amputation and treated it with sulpha antibiotics. De Waard was released on 16 April and arrived in Eastbourne two days later.

On the cessation of hostilities, the French Troops spent a short time with No. 4 Commando guarding 91 Civilian Internment Camp at Recklinghausen, which contained Nazis without identification, those who had served with the SS or had been involved in concentration camps. After the victory parade in Paris, the three French Troops were absorbed into the

French Armed Forces as Naval Commandos. Several men were killed in Indo-China and Algeria. The French Troops were not the only French commando units. The First French Army in the Mediterranean formed the Battalion d'Afrique, the Battalion de Choc and the Battalion de France, although none were trained at Achnacarry.

2 (Dutch) Troop also guarded the Recklinghausen Camp, before returning to the United Kingdom on 7 August. A month later, the Troop went back to Holland and, with the Korps Insulinde, was absorbed in The Netherlands Army as the Commando Korps. The Dutch Marine Corps has close links with 3rd Commando Brigade. Linzel helped a former member of 2 Troop, Raymond Westerling, form Detachment Special Troops in Indonesia. Westerling later led a coup of young officers in Indonesia; Linzel was wounded in Korea, left for dead and retired as a brigadier. There is a thriving Dutch No. 10 (Inter-Allied) Commando re-enactment group which since 2004 has organized the 7-mile commemorative march from Spean Bridge to Achnacarry House.

3 (British) Troop was spread across Germany with detachments posted to the BAOR Pool of Interrogators and Commando Interrogation Team, subordinated to the General Staff (Intelligence), I (British) Corps), screening over 250,000 prisoners of war held in camps at Rheinburg and Wickwrath. The Troop also played a full part in the de-Nazification strategy and helped in screening the staff at the Krupp headquarters and several other major companies. Those detached to 287 (with 9th Durham Light Infantry), 318, 347 and 348 Field Security Sections in Schleswig-Holstein were summarily transferred to Intelligence Corps units that were self-sufficient in finding accommodation, rations and transport. While hunting war criminals, Private 'Jackson' was involved in the interrogation of Colonel Rudolf Hoess, the Commandant of Auschwitz, after he had been arrested by 92 Field Security Section near Flensburg. 'Jackson's mother had been murdered at Auschwitz. Others were involved in covert operations. When in late 1945, the Wehrwolf Resistance group activated Operation Edelweiss to assassinate British soldiers by using a cache of weapons hidden near Hildesheim, they did not realize that they had been penetrated by Field Security, which included Corporal 'Gilbert'. Believing him to be sympathetic, the group persuaded him to supply a military vehicle so that they could move their weapons more safely. In the meantime, a counter-intelligence operation established key points along the intended route. When the Wehrwolf group ran into a road block, probably sensing double-cross, the leader held a revolver to 'Gilbert's' head and ordered him to drive, however 'Gilbert' managed to slip the clutch, which slowed the vehicle down enough for soldiers to surround it. Some members of the Troop were attached to the Town Majors of the Military Government, such as at Unna. Others were attached to Public Safety

Branches, whose role was to vet, retrain and work with the German police and maintain order. Some found pursuing Jews making money on the black market a difficult task. In many respects, the fact that the German police do not have a reputation for corruption and brutality is down to the fairness shared by the Public Safety Branches. Others were attached to 36 Broadcasting Control Unit and 30 Information Control Press Unit. Staff Sergeant 'Marshall' was in Coleshill, Birmingham with 39 German Working Camp. Bizarrely, Lieutenant 'Masters' was sent to train the Gold Coast Regiment in West Africa. When Lieutenant 'Gray' heard that his parents might be in the Theresienstadt concentration camp, he drove the 450 miles from Walcheren to Czechoslovakia and persuaded the Soviet authorities to allow them and several other Jews to be taken to England.

On 28 May, the 2nd Commando Brigade Half Troop arrived in England. For some of those recruited in 1944, it was the first time. After a test for interpreter training in mid-July, they joined the Control Commission in Germany in August. Sergeant 'Anson' worked with the Field Intelligence Agency (Technical) obtaining information on Nazi scientific and medical activity. Three joined the Public Safety Branch in Hamburg and worked with the German police to maintain order. Private 'White' visited his sister, Martha, in Berlin, the only survivor of his family.

By March 1946, Commando Field Security had been disbanded and when 117 Intelligence Team was formed on 1 July, 3 Troop were offered postings with the Intelligence Corps. Most turned the invitation down, preferring to retain their wartime experiences through the Commando Association. 'Gilbert' and 'Nelson' both accepted the offer, with 'Gilbert' eventually becoming Head of Station for the British Security Service Organisation in Düsseldorf.

In a changing world in which the emerging threat was the Soviet Union, the disposal of 3 Troop was fraught with difficulty. As early as November 1943, the Home Office suggested there was no reason to give the Troop preference over equally deserving cases. At the request of his men, on 19 April 1944, Captain Hilton-Jones began the naturalization process by assembling the names for Major General Sturges, who supported the request in a Top Secret letter, in which he summarized that 3 Troop had been 'trained for and employed on work of a highly combatant nature and are volunteers ... their behaviour and work has always been most satisfactory ... this is a good sub group, well able to look after itself, and has done excellent work'. However, the Home Secretary decided there was no reason to make an exception for those serving in the Forces. On 20 December, the Army Council instructed that naturalization should not be assumed, except for those married to British women. In a Top Secret letter to the Commando Group dated 2 May 1945, Lieutenant 'Langley' wrote that the Troop had several issues. Completing vetting questionnaires would risk compromising them, indeed MI5 had a dossier for each man recruited in England except for those recruited in the Mediterranean, whose applications were held by the Central Mediterranean Force. No records were held by the Commando of the period when the men were interned. About twenty had married British women, had British-born children and had homes in the UK. All had UK-based next of kin, however a high percentage of the Troop had real next of kin either living in enemy territory or whose whereabouts were not known, particularly those who had lost relations in concentration camps or were imprisoned in them. In September, shortly before No. 10 (Inter-Allied) Commando was disbanded, Lieutenant Colonel Laycock wrote a letter to Major General A.J.K. Pigot, Director of Recruiting and Demobilisation, listing those seeking naturalization, including serving soldiers listing their parent units, former members of the Troop serving as officers in other units and those discharged after being wounded. But it was not until 15 November that the Home Secretary announced that applications could be submitted by those serving in the Armed Forces, which numbered about 4,000 Army, 5,000 in the RAF and about 200 in the Royal Navy. A meeting held on 7 December between the Home Office and the War Office, which was represented by Pigot, agreed that those who had enlisted in the United Kingdom would be given a high priority. There was a meeting in March 1946 between Demobilisation Depot 4 and Combined Operations, to discuss the disbandment of '10 Commando' – this was actually a cover for 3 Troop because the other Troops had returned to their national Governments. Lieutenant 'Langley', who was now commanding the Troop, contacted present members, including the wounded, and advised those applying that they would be supported by testimonials from Combined Operations and the Troop. Then in May, the War Office decided all applicants would be interviewed. This effectively delayed the Troop serving with the Control Commissions from applying for vacancies in the Commission as civilians because they were 'still enemy aliens'. While the Home Office remained prepared to give priority to the commandos, Pigot objected strongly on the grounds that they had no better claim than anyone else. Combined Operations accepted the delays until August when another attempt was made to persuade the War Office to change its mind. Pigot flatly refused to do so and thus each commando was processed individually with priority based on length of service. In the meantime, those who had been discharged were instructed to report monthly to a police station as 'enemy aliens'. As has so often happened, the British Army was slow, and remains so, to show its gratitude to those who help it in times of need.

In a letter to the Commando Group in May 1945, Lieutenant Langley lists one officer and thirteen other ranks killed in action and two missing believed killed, but does not include the one Czech known to have been killed and two missing believed killed at Dieppe, and the officer cadet who died in a road accident in Normandy. This means that twenty members of 3 Troop were killed between 1942 and 1945. Several Jews were buried in Commonwealth War Graves cemeteries with Christian crosses on their gravestones until their true identities emerged and the crosses were replaced with Jewish stars. Of the twenty wounded, according to Langley, seven were serious enough to be discharged, but that does not include the one Czech, Private 'Platt', wounded at Dieppe. At Ashton Wold House in Northamptonshire, the Hon. Miriam Rothschild, wife of Captain 'Lane', planted a grove of trees in memory of those killed serving with the Troop. The brainchild of 'Brian Groves' and designed by John Neilson, a stone plinth erected on 15 May 1999 in Penhelig Park, Aberdyfi, commemorates the affiliation of the Troop to the town. In total, the Troop was awarded one MC, one MM, one Croix de Guerre, one MBE, one BEM, one Certificate of Commendation and three Mentioned in Despatches. This relative lack of recognition is explained by the fact that the Troop never fought as a unit and was detached to use their special skills as linguists and interrogators. Commanding officers were sometimes disinclined to recommend awards for men who did not belong to their units.

The Belgian Battalion joined 146th Heavy Anti-Aircraft Regiment, part of 80th Anti-Aircraft Brigade which was used for occupation duties in Eutin district of the British enclave of Neustadt, in an area that later became part of East Germany. The Regiment had responsibility for Military Government of preserving law and order and assisting the British Town Major in organizing the repair of essential services. HQ Troop was at Niendorf. 4 Troop was with 716 Heavy Anti-Aircraft Battery at Gluschen-dorf, while 9 Troop at Bad Schwartau was with 465 Heavy Anti-Aircraft Battery. 10 Troop was attached to 414 Heavy Anti-Aircraft Battery at Ahrensbok and liberated Neustadt concentration camp, which was almost as unpleasant as Belsen. They also found emaciated survivors and some dead victims of Buchenwald concentration camp with their SS guards. The Belgians forced the guards to dig their graves and then shot them. Major de Jonghe and a patrol found a prison camp of Belgian and Serbian other ranks. Unlike many other camps, it was spotlessly clean and had a small band. De Jonghe led round-ups of Nazi sympathizers, some from information obtained by the Field Security Sections and others denounced by Germans ready to ingratiate themselves with the Allies. The Belgians escorted the 28th 'Walloon' SS Volunteer Grenadier Division to Brussels. On 15 May, 4 (Belgian) Troop was renamed the Commando Regiment under Belgian command, and returned to Belgium in September. In 1951, Lieutenant Colonel Danloy formed the Para-Commando Regiment. A Museum to Belgian commandos was opened on 4 July 1980 on the initiative of Lieutenant General Pierre Roman, who had served with the Troop, in the presence of Major General (Retired) Danloy. As part of the Para-Commando Regiment, 2nd Commando Battalion is a direct descendant of 4 (Belgian) Troop. In a room dedicated to the Troop Chaplain, Father Corbisier, are the names of those who died while serving with the Troop.

After the costly attack on Kapelsche Veer, 5 (Norwegian) Troop was withdrawn to Flushing and then sent to Bergen-op-Zoom to train for the crossing of the Rhine. However, the Norwegian High Command needed the Troop for the liberation of Norway and, after returning to Eastbourne on 9 February, it returned to Norwegian command on 30 April and, next day, was flown in penny packets, as 'civilians', to Sweden where they joined the Norwegian Brigade poised to cross the border should the Germans refuse to surrender. Despite receiving orders that the Troop was not to wear their Green Berets and were to remove commando insignia, Captain Hauge ignored the instruction and 5 (Norwegian) Troop crossed the border on 9 May. Four days later, the Troop provided the Guard of Honour in Oslo when Crown Prince Olav returned to Norway. Of the four Western nationalities in No. 10 (Inter-Allied) Commando, only the Norwegians did not develop the Commando tradition. The Troop was broken up and the men distributed to district commands throughout Norway.

The Polish Troop was disbanded along with the Polish formations that had served with the Allies. Every commando who served with the Troop was given a certificate of appreciation signed by Major General Laycock and was an honorary member of the Commando Association. In 1962, on the 21st anniversary of its formation, Lord Mountbatten sent a letter to the reunion:

> It was my privilege to make the decision in 1942 to form the Polish troop on No. 10 (Inter-Allied) Commando. The splendid Commando unit was set up later that year under command of Captain Smrokowski. The Polish Commando troops proceeded on active service operations in 1943. Their morale was always of the highest order and I was very proud to have them under my command, and send them my sincere greetings on the occasion of their 21st Anniversary Celebrations.
>
> Mountbatten of Burma, Admiral of the Fleet

No. 10 (Inter-Allied) Commando held its farewell dinner at the Drive Hotel, Eastbourne and then, in September, moved its HQ to 19 Hatfield Square when 33 St Leonard's was requisitioned.

The Commando was disbanded shortly after the move and faded into history, its legacy largely forgotten and mentioned only in passing.

Appendix 1

Known Details of Members of 3 (British) Troop

Adopted Name	Real Name	Nationality	Unit	Comments
Andrews, Pte Harry	Hans/Richard Arnstein		Royal Sussex	Killed, Orne Bridgehead, 19 August 1944
Anson, Cpl Colin	Claus Leopold Octavio Ascher	German	Royal Sussex	
Arlen, Pte Richard	Richard Abramovicz	German	Royal Sussex	Killed, Orne Bridgehead, 7 June 1944
Barnes, Pte Robert	Gotthard Baumwollspinner	German	Buffs	Wounded three times, Italy
Bartlett, Capt Kenneth	Karl Walter Billman	German	Buffs	OC CMF Half Troop
Bate, Pte		Czech		Missing, Dieppe – PoW?
Bentley, Sgt Fred	Frederic Bierer		Intelligence Corps	
Broadman, Sgt Geoffrey	Gottfried Sruh		Buffs	
Carson, Pte Peter	Peter Carlebach	German	Buffs	Discharged, climbing accident, March 1944
Clark, Cpl K.E.	Eugen Litvak	Stateless	Royal Hampshires	
Dale, Sgt Leslie	Einar Reska	Danish	Royal Sussex	
Davies, Pte	Max Dobriner	German	Royal West Kents	
Dickson, Geoffrey	K. Dungler/Dandler	Austrian	Buffs	
Douglas, Sgt K.	Harry Nomberg	German	Buffs	
Drew, Sgt Harry	Wener Goldschmidt	German	Royal West Kents	
Dwelly, Capt Vernon		British	RAF and Royal Tank Regiment	
Emmett, Lt 'Bunny'				
Envers, LCpl H.G.	Hans Feder	German		Wounded, Orne Bridgehead, 19 August 1944

Adopted Name	Real Name	Nationality	Unit	Comments
Farr, Cpl Tommy	Ernst Freytag	German	Buffs	Killed, Orne Bridgehead, 11 June 1944
Fletcher, Fred	F. Fleischedr		Royal Worcesters	Killed, D-Day
Franklyn, Cpl George	Max Gunther Frank			Killed, Orne Bridgehead, 13 June 1944
Fuller, Sgt Eugene	Eugen von Kagerer-Stein	Austrian	Royal Hampshires	
Gilbert, Ronnie, MBE	Hans Guttman	German	Royal West Kents	
Groves, Sgt Brian	Konrad Goldschmidt	German	Royal West Kents	Discharged after wounded, Italy, 5 January 1944
Gordon, Sgt Maj Henry	Kurt Geiser	German	Royal Hampshires	
Gray, 2Lt Freddy	Manfred Gans	German	Royal West Kents	
Griffith, Lt Keith	Kurt Glaser	German	Royal West Kents	OC 3 Troop. Killed, Germany, 11 April 1945
Harris, LCpl Ian, MM	Hans Hajosch	German	Royal West Kents	Wounded Orne, Bridgehead and Germany
Henderson, Pte		British	Royal West Kents (?)	Batman to Capt Griffith
Hepworth, Pte Walter	Fritz Herschthal	German	Royal Hampshires	
Hepworth, Pte F.	Herschthal	German	Royal Hampshires	
Hilton-Jones, Maj Bryan		British	Royal Artillery	OC. Captured, Orne Bridgehead
Howarth, RSM Eric	Erich Wolfgang	German	Buffs	Killed, Germany, 3 April 1945
Pte Jackson, Fred	Peter Jacobus	German	Royal Hampshires	
Jones, Cpl	Vladamir Kottka	Russian	Royal Hampshires	Captured, Op Hardtack
Kendal, Lt Harold	Guenther Hans Knobloch		Intelligence Corps	
Kingsley, 2Lt		German	Royal Fusiliers	Commissioned
Laddy, Max	Max Lewinsky		Royal West Kents	Killed, D-Day
Langley, Lt Ernest	Ernst Landau	Austrian		Commissioned
Latimer, Maurice	Mortiz Levy/Max Loewy	Czech	Royal Sussex	Wounded Dieppe
Lawrence, Ernest	Ernst Lenel	German	Royal West Kents	Missing, Orne Bridgehead, 22/23 June 1944
Mason, Gary	K. Weinberg	German	Royal West Kents	

Adopted Name	Real Name	Nationality	Unit	Comments
Masters, Lt Peter	Peter Arany	Austrian	Ox and Bucks LI	
McGregor, Jack	Kurt Manfred	German	Royal West Kents	
Merton, Michael	Ludwig George Blumenfeld		Royal Fusiliers	Attached SOE
Miles, Lt Patrick	Hubertus Levin		Buffs	Killed, Orne Bridgehead, 13 June 1944
Monahan, Capt		British	Royal Fusiliers	
Moody, LCpl Peter	Kurt Meyer		Royal Hampshires	Commissioned
Nelson, 2Lt Vernon	Werner Zweig	German	Royal Sussex	Killed, Orne Bridgehead, 13 June 1944
Nichols, Lt Gerald	Heinz Nell	German	Buffs	Wounded, Normandy
Norton, Ernest	Eli Nathan	German	Royal West Kents	Wounded, Dieppe
O'Neill, Sgt Maj Oscar	Oswald Henschel	Czech		Missing, Dieppe – PoW?
Platt, Pte	B. Platek	Czech		
Rice, Pte		German	Royal Hampshires	Discharged, Orne Bridgehead, 14 June 1944
Ross, Cpl Steven	Stephan Rosskamm	German	Royal Sussex	Killed, Rhine Crossing, 23 March 1945
Saunders, Sgt George, MM	Georg Salinger/Saloschin	Hungarian		Commissioned
Sayer, LCpl	Gyula Szauer		Buffs	Missing, Dieppe – PoW?
Seymour, Pte Herbert	Herbert Sachs			Commissioned
Shelley, Lt Percy	Alfred Samson	German	Royal Marines	Discharged after wounded, Italy, July 1943
Smith, Pte		Czech		Wounded, Normandy
Spencer, LCpl Tom		German		Discharged after wounded, Orne Bridgehead, 23 July 1944
Stewart, Lt David	David Strauss	German	Royal Marines	Captured, Orne Bridgehead, 20 June 1944
Streeten, Paul	Paul Hornig	Austrian		
Swinton, Tommy	Gyorgy Schwitzer/Schweizer	Hungarian	Royal Sussex	
Terry, LCpl Peter, MM	Peter Tischler	Austria	Royal Sussex	
Thompson, Sgt Walter	Walter Gabriel Zadik	German	Royal Hampshires	

Adopted Name	Real Name	Nationality	Unit	Comments
Trevor, Charles	Hans Baum			Wounded, Orne Bridgehead, 8 June 1944
Turner	Oscar Pollaschek	Austrian	Royal Sussex	
Villiers, Sgt Ernest	Egon Vogel			Killed, Rhine Crossing, 24 March 1945
Warwick, Pte R.		Stateless	Essex	
Watson, Pte William	Oscar Wasserman	German	Royal Hampshires	Wounded, Walcheren
Webster, Pte Ernest	Ernst Weinberger			Killed, D-Day
Wells, LCpl Peter	Werner Averhahn	German	Royal Hampshires	Killed, Italy, 19 January 1944
Wilmers, Capt John	Hans Wilmersdoerffer	German	Special Air Service	Commissioned

Sources:
List compiled by Martin Sugarman.
Naturalization Letter signed by Lieutenant Langley, dated 2 May 1945.
Nominal Role accompanying QT878/44 dated 13 September 1946 signed by Lieutenant Colonel Laycock.

Appendix 2

Order of Battle
No. 10 (Inter-Allied) Commando
1942–1945

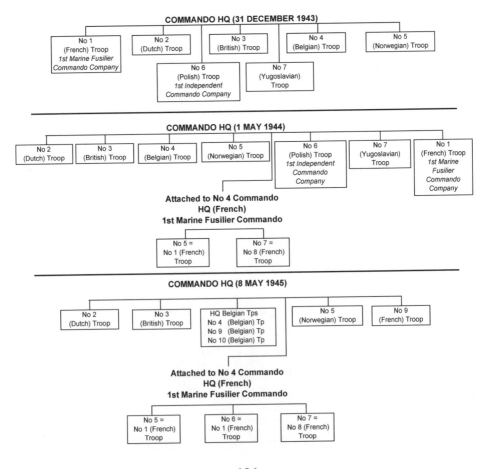

COMMANDO HQ (31 DECEMBER 1943)

| No 1 (French) Troop *1st Marine Fusilier Commando Company* | No 2 (Dutch) Troop | No 3 (British) Troop | No 4 (Belgian) Troop | No 5 (Norwegian) Troop |

| No 6 (Polish) Troop *1st Independent Commando Company* | No 7 (Yugoslavian) Troop |

COMMANDO HQ (1 MAY 1944)

| No 2 (Dutch) Troop | No 3 (British) Troop | No 4 (Belgian) Troop | No 5 (Norwegian) Troop | No 6 (Polish) Troop *1st Independent Commando Company* | No 7 (Yugoslavian) Troop | No 1 (French) Troop *1st Marine Fusilier Commando Company* |

**Attached to No 4 Commando
HQ (French)
1st Marine Fusilier Commando**

| No 5 = No 1 (French) Troop | No 7 = No 8 (French) Troop |

COMMANDO HQ (8 MAY 1945)

| No 2 (Dutch) Troop | No 3 (British) Troop | HQ Belgian Tps No 4 (Belgian) Tp No 9 (Belgian) Tp No 10 (Belgian) Tp | No 5 (Norwegian) Troop | No 9 (French) Troop |

**Attached to No 4 Commando
HQ (French)
1st Marine Fusilier Commando**

| No 5 = No 1 (French) Troop | No 6 = No 1 (French) Troop | No 7 = No 8 (French) Troop |

Appendix 3

Basic Organization of
No. 6 (Polish) Troop – Italy 1944

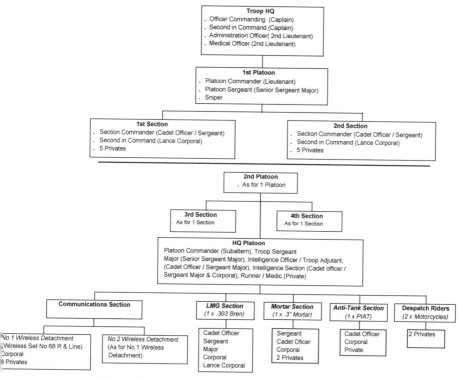

Troop HQ
- Officer Commanding (Captain)
- Second in Command (Captain)
- Administration Officer(2nd Lieutenant)
- Medical Officer (2nd Lieutenant)

1st Platoon
- Platoon Commander (Lieutenant)
- Platoon Sergeant (Senior Sergeant Major)
- Sniper

1st Section
- Section Commander (Cadet Officer / Sergeant)
- Second in Command (Lance Corporal)
- 5 Privates

2nd Section
- Section Commander (Cadet Officer / Sergeant)
- Second in Command (Lance Corporal)
- 5 Privates

2nd Platoon
- As for 1 Platoon

3rd Section
- As for 1 Section

4th Section
- As for 1 Section

HQ Platoon
Platoon Commander (Subaltern), Troop Sergeant Major (Senior Sergeant Major), Intelligence Officer / Troop Adjutant, (Cadet Officer / Sergeant Major), Intelligence Section (Cadet officer / Sergeant Major & Corporal), Runner / Medic (Private)

Communications Section

No 1 Wireless Detachment (Wireless Set No 68 R & Line) Corporal, 8 Privates

No 2 Wireless Detachment (As for No 1 Wireless Detachment)

LMG Section *(1 x .303 Bren)*
Cadet Officer
Sergeant
Major
Corporal
Lance Corporal

Mortar Section *(1 x .3" Mortar)*
Sergeant
Cadet Oficer
Corporal
2 Privates

Anti-Tank Section *(1 x PIAT)*
Cadet Officer
Corporal
Private

Despatch Riders *(2 x Motorcycles)*
2 Privates

Note: There were variations of ranks in Platoons.

Appendix 4

No. 10 (Inter-Allied) Commando Raiding Table

Occupied Norway, France and the Channel Islands

Date	Operation	Target	Situation Report
22 November 1942	From Lerwick	Bergen area	Four of No. 5 (Norwegian) Troop aboard three MTBs. Aborted when the vessels were spotted by a German aircraft.
27/29 November 1942	From Lerwick	Bergen area	Four of No. 5 (Norwegian) Troop aboard one MTB. Anchored in a fjord and gathered information from fishermen.
27 December 1942	From Lerwick	Bergen area	Five of No. 5 (Norwegian) Troop aboard one MTB. Aborted due to poor weather.
23/24 January 1943	Cartoon from Lerwick	Island of Stord	Ten of No. 5 (Norwegian) Troop joined fifty-three of No. 12 Commando and attacked a pyrite mine.
23 February/3 March 1943	Crackers From Lerwick	Stokkevaag/Gjeteroy	Three of No. 5 (Norwegian) Troop and detachments from Nos 12 and 30 Commandos. Poor weather prevented a landing and an observation post to overlook Sognefjord port. Substantial amount of information gathered, including from local newspapers.
14/16 March 1943	Brandy from Lerwick	Floroe harbour	Seven of Norwegian Troop and a No. 12 (Army) Commando detachment on two Norwegian MTBs attacked two German ships and laid mines. One MTB abandoned after grounding.
18/21 March 1943	From Lerwick	Stadt	Two No. 5 (Norwegian) Troop and No. 12 Commando detachment clashed with a German patrol. Raid abandoned.

Date	Operation	Target	Situation Report
9 April 1943	From Lerwick	Stadt	Nine of No. 5 (Norwegian) Troop and seventy of No. 12 Commando attack on Rugsundoy anchorage and a coast battery abandoned. Locals report increase in German reprisals after raids.
1/4 September 1943	Forfar Beer	Eletot	No. 12 Commando detachment and one from No. 1 (French) Troop. Beach Recce.
	Forfar Item	St Valery-en-Caux	Six of E Section, No. 3 Para Troop, 10 Commando and two of No. 12 Commando parachuted to gather information on a searchlight. Recovered by MTB.
24/25 December 1943	Hardtack 11 from Dover	Gravelines	Beach recce by No. 1 Troop. MTBs diverted to attack German convoy.
24/25 December 1943	Hardtack 11 from Dover	Gravelines	Beach recce by six No. 1 (French) Troop. Dory swamped. One presumed drowned and five survivors joined Resistance.
25/26 December 1943	Hardtack 7 from Dartmouth	Sark	Recce. One 12 Commando and four of No. 8 (French) Troop.
	Hardtack 28 from Dartmouth	Jersey	Recce. One 12 Commando officer and five of No. 8 Troop. British officer killed.
26/27 December 1943	Hardtack 4 from Newhaven		Cliff recce. Eight of 12 Commando and one of No. 8 (French) Troop. Forced to withdraw by German patrol.
	Hardtack 13 from Newhaven	Benouville	Cliff recce. 2 SBS and eight of No. 1 (French) Troop climb aborted – no way up.
	Hardtack 21 from Newhaven	Quineville	Area recce. Six of No. 1 (French) Troop. Returned with details of Element C anti-tank obstacles.
27/28 December 1943	Hardtack 23 from Dover	Bray near Ostend	Area Recce. Six of No 1 (French) Troop. Aborted when MTB ran aground.
	Hardtack 7	Sark	Five of No. 1 (French) Troop.
10 February 1944	From Lerwick	Norwegian coast	Six of No. 5 (Norwegian) Troop on Timberforce duties.

Date	Operation	Target	Situation Report
11 February 1944	From Lerwick	Norwegian coast	Seven of No. 5 (Norwegian) Troop on Timberforce duties with Norwegian Navy MTB and patrol ship.
14 February 1944	From Lerwick	Norwegian coast	Seven of No. 5 (Norwegian) Troop with Norwegian MTBs as Timberforce. Two Norwegian ships torpedoed off Kristiansand.
17 February 1944	From Lerwick	Norwegian coast	Two of No. 5 (Norwegian) Troop as Timberforce.
23 February 1944	From Lerwick	Norwegian coast	Ten of No. 5 (Norwegian) Troop as Timberforce.
24/25 February 1944	Premium (Hardtack 36) from Dover	Wassenaar near Scheveningen	Area Recce. Six of No 8 (French) Troop. All six died.
19 March 1944	From Lerwick	Norwegian coast	Six of No. 5 (Norwegian) Troop.
14/15 May 1944	Tarbrush 3 from Dover	Bray Dunes	Sea too rough for landing.
	Tarbrush 5 from Dover	Les Hemmes	Landing prevented by German naval activity in the Channel.
15/16 May	Tarbrush 8 from Dover	Quend Plage	Anti-tank Teller mine 42 brought back.
	Tarbrush 10 from Dover.	Onival	MTB navigational error led to landing in wrong place.
16/17 May	Tarbrush 3	Bray Dunes	German sentry seen. Royal Engineers identified Teller mines.
	Tarbrush 8	Quend Plage	Patrol ashore for twenty minutes when a firefight broke out. Reported no mines attached to beach defence posts.
17/18 May	Tarbrush 10	Onival	Poor weather prevented landing.
	Tarbrush 10	Onival	Infrared camera taken to photograph Element C known to be inland. Captain Wooldridge RE and Lieutenant 'Lane' of 3 Troop captured and interviewed by Field Marshal Rommel.
25/26 August	Romford	Isle de Yeu	Five of No. 4 (Belgian) Troop. Brought back a Frenchman for debriefing.

Appendix 5

Assessed 3 Troop
Order of Battle – D-Day

HQ Second Army	Pte 'Tennant'. Driver to Major General Sturgis.
HQ 1st Special Service Brigade	Maj Hilton-Jones and Pte 'Trevor'.
No. 3 Commando	Cpls 'Turner', 'Seymour', 'Bartlett', 'Lawrence', Ptes 'Hepworth' and 'Spencer'.
No. 4 Commando	Sgt 'Howarth', Cpl 'Howarth' (WIA), LCpl 'Sayer', Ptes 'Graham', 'Franklyn' (KIA) and 'Thompson'.
No. 6 Commando	Cpls 'Nicholls' and Drew, LCpl 'Masters', Ptes 'McGregor' and 'Mason'.
No. 45 (Royal Marines) Commando	Sgt 'Stewart', Cpl 'Shelley', LCpl 'Saunders' and Pte 'Arlen'.
HQ 4th Special Service Brigade	Cpls 'Envers' and 'Moody'.
No. 41 (Royal Marines) Commando	Sgt Maj 'O'Neill', Sgt 'Gray' (WIA), Cpls 'Swinton' and 'Latimer'.
No. 46 (Royal Marines) Commando	Sgt 'Gordon', Cpl 'Gilbert', Pte 'Walker'.
No. 47 (Royal Marines) Commando	Sgt 'Fuller' (PoW – escaped), LCpls 'Terry' (WIA) and 'Webster' (KIA), Ptes 'Laddy' (KIA), 'Davis' and 'Andrews' (WIA).
No. 48 (Royal Marines) Commando	Cpl 'Douglas', LCpls 'Boardman' and 'Norton'.

Sources:
Dear, *10 Commando*.
Masters, *Striking Back*.
Sugarman, *No. 3 Jewish Troop*.

Appendix 6

Operation Market Garden – 2 (Dutch) Troop Order of Battle

5 September
Prince Bernhard HQ

Lt Ruysch van Dugteren, Cpls van Woerden and Steengracht, Pte van Creveld.

6 September
BBO Training

Lt Knottenbelt, Sgt van der Veer, Cpls Michels and Westerling, Ptes Bendien, Blatt, de Koning and van Lienden.

52nd Lowland Division

2 Troop joins as Dutch Liaison Mission.

8 September
1st Airborne Division

Sergeants van Gelderen and Kruit, Private Baggermans.

HQ 52nd Lowland Division

Capt Linzel, Lt de Ruiter, Cpl de Liefde, Ptes Boelema and P.A. Visser.

10 September
1st Airborne Division

Sergeant de Waard (PoW), Corporal Italiaander, Privates Beekmeyer (PoW), Bakhuis-Roozeboom (KIA), Baggerman, de Leeuw, Gobetz (PoW), Gubbels (PW), Helleman, Juliard, van Barneveld and van der Meer.

12 September
82nd (US) Airborne Division

Troop Sergeant Major van der Bergh, Sgts Dullemen, van der Wal, Ubels and Visser, Cpls Elshof, Kloezeman, Kokhuis and van der Steen, Ptes Bloemink, Cramer, van der Gender, Knijff, Peetom and van der Linde.

52nd Lowland Division

Cpl de Liefde and Private Boelema transferred to 82nd (US) Airborne Division.

13 September
1st Airborne Division

Lt Knottenbelt (WIA) arrived as Officer Commanding Dutch Liaison Mission

15 September
101st (US) Airborne Division

Sgts van der Wal and R.B. Visser and Corporal van der Steen. Cpl Elshof and Pte Bothe joined from 82nd (US) Airborne Division.

HQ No. 10 Commando

Ptes Juliard (1st Airborne Division) and Peetom (82nd (US) Airborne Division) returned to Eastbourne – did not speak Dutch.

Appendix 7

No. 10 (Inter-Allied) Commando Recipients of British Gallantry Awards

Rank and Name	Troop	Location	Award
Captain Kieffer	French Troop	Normandy	MC
Lieutenant F. Vourc'h	French Troop	Hardtack 21	MC
Sergeant Balloche	French Troop	Dieppe	MM
Sergeant Messanot	French Troop	Walcheren	MM
Private Boccador	French Troop	Hardtack 7	Mentioned in Despatches
Major Hilton-Jones	3 Troop	Normandy	MC
Lieutenant 'Lane'	3 Troop	Tarbrush 10	MC
Sergeant 'Nelson'	3 Troop	River Maas	C-in-C Recommendation
Corporal Clarke	3 Troop	Germany	Mentioned in Despatches
Corporal 'Harris'	3 Troop	Germany	MM
Lieutenant 'Kingsley'	3 Troop	River Maas	Mentioned in Despatches
Lance Corporal 'Saunders'	3 Troop	Normandy	MM
Private 'Davies'	3 Troop	Tarbrush 10	Mentioned in Despatches
Lieutenant Roman	Belgian Troop	Walcheren	MC
Lance Corporal Legrand	Belgian Troop	Walcheren	MM
Captain Hauge	Norwegian Troop	Walcheren	MC
Lieutenant Gausland	Norwegian Troop	Walcheren	MC
Private Sigvaldsen	Norwegian Troop	Walcheren	MM
Captain Smrokowski	Polish Troop	Italy	MC
Lance Corporal Rosen	Polish Troop	Italy	MM

Bibliography

Ambrose, Steven, *Pegasus Bridge*, Pocket Books, London, 1985.

Austen, Lieutenant Colonel A.F., 'British Army Manpack Radios 1939–45', *Military Illustrated Past and Present*, No. 50, July 1992.

Belschem, Major General David, *Victory in Normandy*, Chatto & Windus, London, 1981.

Brayley, Martin, 'Le Brodequin Britannique 1939–45', *Militaria*, No. 206, 2002.

Brayley, Martin and Ingram, Richard, *The World War II Tommy: British Army Uniforms, European Theatre 1939–45 in Colour Photographs*, Crowood Press, 1998.

——, *Khaki Drill & Jungle Green: British Tropical Uniforms 1939–45 in Colour Photographs*, Crowood Press, 2000.

Brown, Arthur, *The Jedburghs. A Short History*, www2/The Jedburghs, November 1999.

Carman, W.H., 'The Distinction of Army Commandos 1940–45', *Military Illustrated Past and Present*, Nos 10 and 11, December/January and February/March 1990.

Carver, Field Marshal Lord, *The War in Italy 1943–45*, Pan Books in association with the Imperial War Museum, London, 2001.

Chappell, Mike, *Army Commandos 1940–45*, Osprey Elite 64, 1996.

Cholewczynski, Geroge, *Poles Apart*, Sarpedon, New York, 1993.

Churchill, Major General Tom, *Commando Crusade*, William Kimber, London, 1987.

Clark, Lloyd, *Battle Zone Normandy – Orne Bridgehead*, Sutton Publishing, Stroud, 2004.

Dear, Ian, *10 Commando 1942–45*, Grafton Books, London, 1989.

Deeley, Graeme, *Worst Fears Confirmed*, Barny Books, Grantham, 2005.

Dunning, James, *It Had to be Tough*, Pentland Press, 2000.

——, *The Fighting Fourth, No. 4 Commando at War 1940–45*, Sutton Publishing, Stroud, 2003.

Gilchrist, Donald, *Castle Commando*, Oliver and Boyd, Edinburgh and London, 1960.

Ford, Ken, *D-Day Commando*, Sutton Publishing, Stroud, 2005.

——, *Battle Zone Normandy – Sword Beach*, Sutton Publishing, Stroud, 2004.

Harvey, A.D., *Arnhem*, Cassell & Co, London, 2001.

Hobbs, Brian, 'British Commandos in the Field 1942–45', *Military Illustrated Past and Present*, Nos 26 and 30, July and November 1990.

Howarth, David, *Dawn of D-Day*, The Companion Book Club, London, 1959.

Isby, David, *The German Army on D-Day, Fighting the Invasion*, Greenhill Books, London, 2004.

Jego, Laurent, 'Le 1er Bataillon de Fusiliers-Marins Commandos', *Militaria*, No. 107, 1990.

Johnson, Garry and Dunphie, Christopher, *Brightly Shone the Dawn*, Frederick Warne, London, 1980.

Kieffer, Commandant, *Les Berets Verts Francais du 6 Jun 1944*, France-Empire, 1994.

Ladd, James, *Commando and Rangers*, Book Club Associates, 1978.

Le Penven, Eric, *Commando Kieffer, Free French Commando No. 10 & No. 4 Commando*, Heimdal, Bayeaux, 2006.

Lucas, James and Cooper, Matthew, *Panzer Grenadiers*, Book Club Associates, 1977.

Masters, Peter, *Striking Back, A Jewish Commando's War against the Nazis*, Presidio Press, Novato, 1997.

Mills-Roberts, Derek, *Clash by Night, A Commando Chronicle*, William Kimber, London, 1956.

Mrazek, James D., *The Glider War*, Robert Hale, London, 1975.

Mollo, Andrew, *The Armed Forces of World War II: Uniforms, Insignia and Organisation*, BCA, 1981.

Monsion, Tadwsz, *Commando*, Figaro Press Ltd, 1975.

Moulton, Major General J.L, *The Battle for Antwerp*, Ian Allen Ltd, Shepperton, 1978.

Norris, John, 'How We Fought', *Military Illustrated Past and Present*, No. 95, April, 1996.

North, John, *North West Europe 1944–5*, HMSO, London, 1977.

Rees, Goronwy, *A Bundle of Sensations*, Chatto and Windus, London, 1960.

Ryan, Cornelius Ryan, *A Bridge Too Far*, Simon & Schuster, New York, 1974.

Thompson, Major General Julian, *The Royal Marines, From Sea Soldiers to a Special Force*, Sidgwick & Jackson, London, 2000.

——, *Ready for Anything, the Parachute Regiment at War*, Fontana, London, 1989.

Trew, Simon, *Battle Zone Normandy – Gold Beach*, Sutton Publishing, Stroud, 2004.

Sadler, Ian, 'The British Battle Jerkin', *Military Illustrated Past and Present*, Nos 27 and 29, August and October, 1990.

Saunders, Hilary St George, *The Green Beret*, Four Square, 1959.

Sugarman, Martin, *No. 3 (Jewish) Troop, No. 10 Commando*, www.Jewish Virtual Library, 2004.

Tanter, Joel, *Caen: Une Ville Trop Loin*, Charles Corlet, 1990.

——, *D.Day en Normandie*, Charles Corlet, 1994.

——, *La Bataille de Normandie*, Charles Corlet, 1999.

Thomas, Nigel, *Foreign Volunteers of the Allied Forces 1939–45*, Osprey Men-at-Arms 238, 1991.

War Office, *Notes from Theatres of War No 11. Destruction of a German Battery by No. 4 Commando during the Dieppe Raid*, February 1993.

Contents of Imperial War Museum 65/75/1-3 – ICB Dear (10 Cdo)

HQ No. 10 (Inter-Allied) Commando
War Diary No. 10 (IA) Commando – WO 218/40.
HQ No. 10 (Inter-Allied) Commando.
No. 10 (IA) Commando's Role in the Walcheren Operation – DEFE 2/977.
Report on No. 10 (IA) Commando Detachment Overseas dated 29 Dec 1943 – WO 212/56

The French Troops
Pre D-Day Raids by 1 and 8 Troops, 10 (IA) Cdo.
Report of 1st Mate Fusilier Roger Caron – Op Hardtack 11.
Report of Quartermaster 2nd Class Fusilier Albert Meunier – Op Hardtack 11.
'First Days in France of the 1st Marine Commando Fusilier Battalion' – Commander H. Faure.
Testimony of Lieutenant Colonel Dawson.
The Operations of Schouwen by the 1st Battalion of FM Commandos (Dec 1944 to March 1945).
Operation Overlord – An Account of the Part Taken by No. 1 Special Service Brigade.

2 (Dutch) Troop
The History and Uniforms of No. 2 (Dutch) Troop of No. 10 Inter-Allied Commando; Armamentia, Boesma, Wybo.
No. 2 (Dutch) Troop 10 (Inter-Allied) Commando during Operation Market Garden September 1944, Boesma, Wybo.

205

Testimonies of Rudi Blatt, Herman de Leeuw, Willem de Liefde, Willem de Waard, Herman Cornelius Gobetz, Hubertus Gubbels, Chris Helleman, Tom Italiaander, Willem Kniff, V.G. Kokhuis, Hikolas Jacobus de Koning, K. Kruit, Jan Linzel, Klaas Lutweiler, Jan Mulder, G.P. Ubbels, Martien van Barnveld, I.J.E. van Dulleman, W.G. Van Gelderen, Jan Van Woerden, Johannes van der Bergh, J.P.H. van der Meer and Willem van der Weer.

www.arnhemarchive – Colonel Hilaro Barlow, Captain Jacobus Groenewoud and Lieutenant Harvey Allan Todd.

3 (British) Troop
Naturalisation, 3 Troop, 10 Commando dated 2 May 1956 QT 878/44
No. 3 Troop, No. 10 Commando – Brief History – DEFE 2/977.
Testimonies of Andrew Carsons and Brian Grant.

4 (Belgian) Troop
Report on Operation Romford – WO 218/8.
Operation Romford – WO 218/88.
Testimony of Carlos Seeger.

5 (Norwegian) Troop
Summary of the Activities of No. 5 Troop, No. 10 (IA) Commando – DEFE 2/977.

6 (Polish) Troop
6 Troop – No. 10 (Inter-Allied) Commando.

7 (Yugoslavian) Troop
Move of No. 7 Troop dated 15 Feb 44 – WO 218/88.

Index

208

209

211